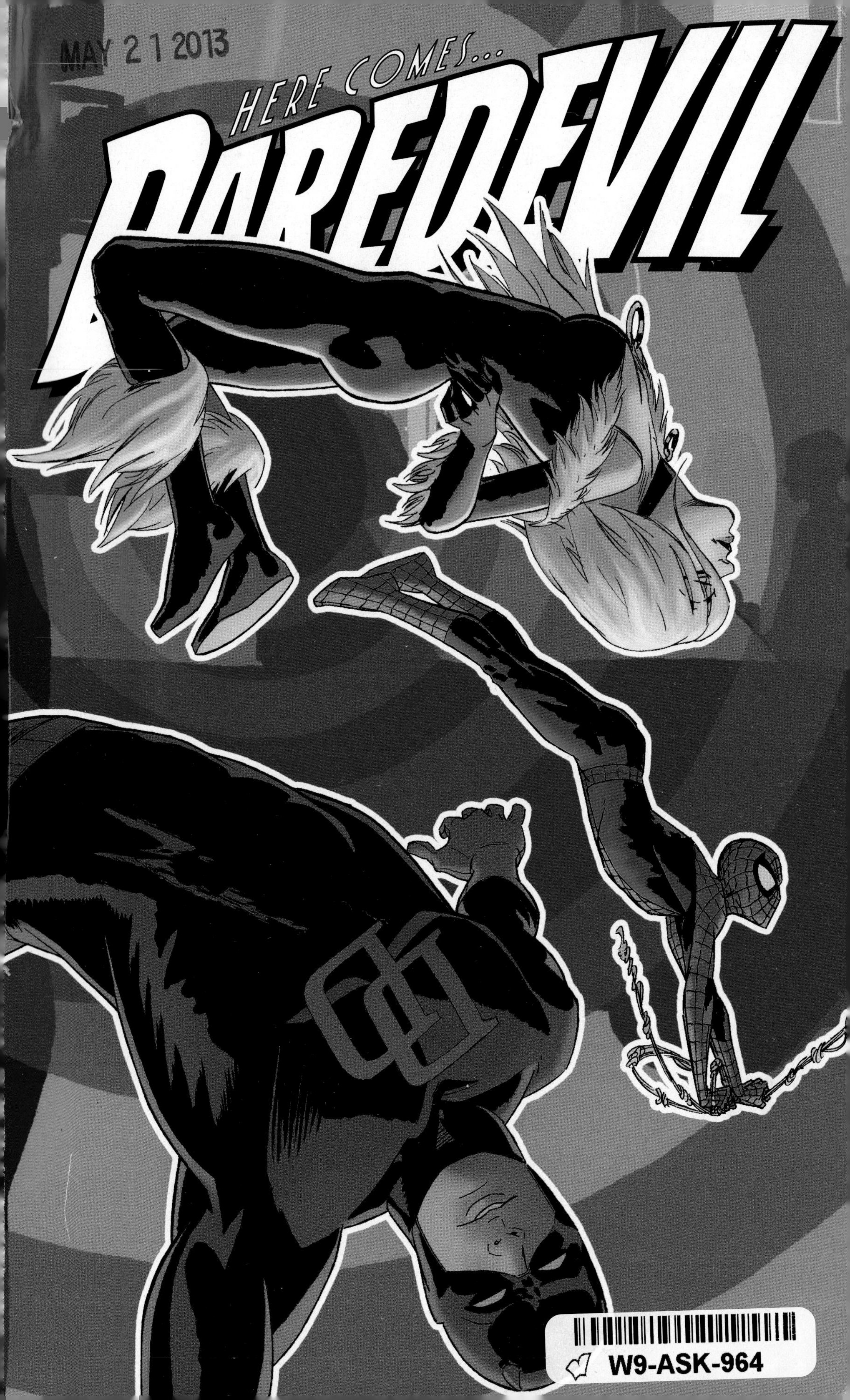
HERE COMES...
DAREDEVIL

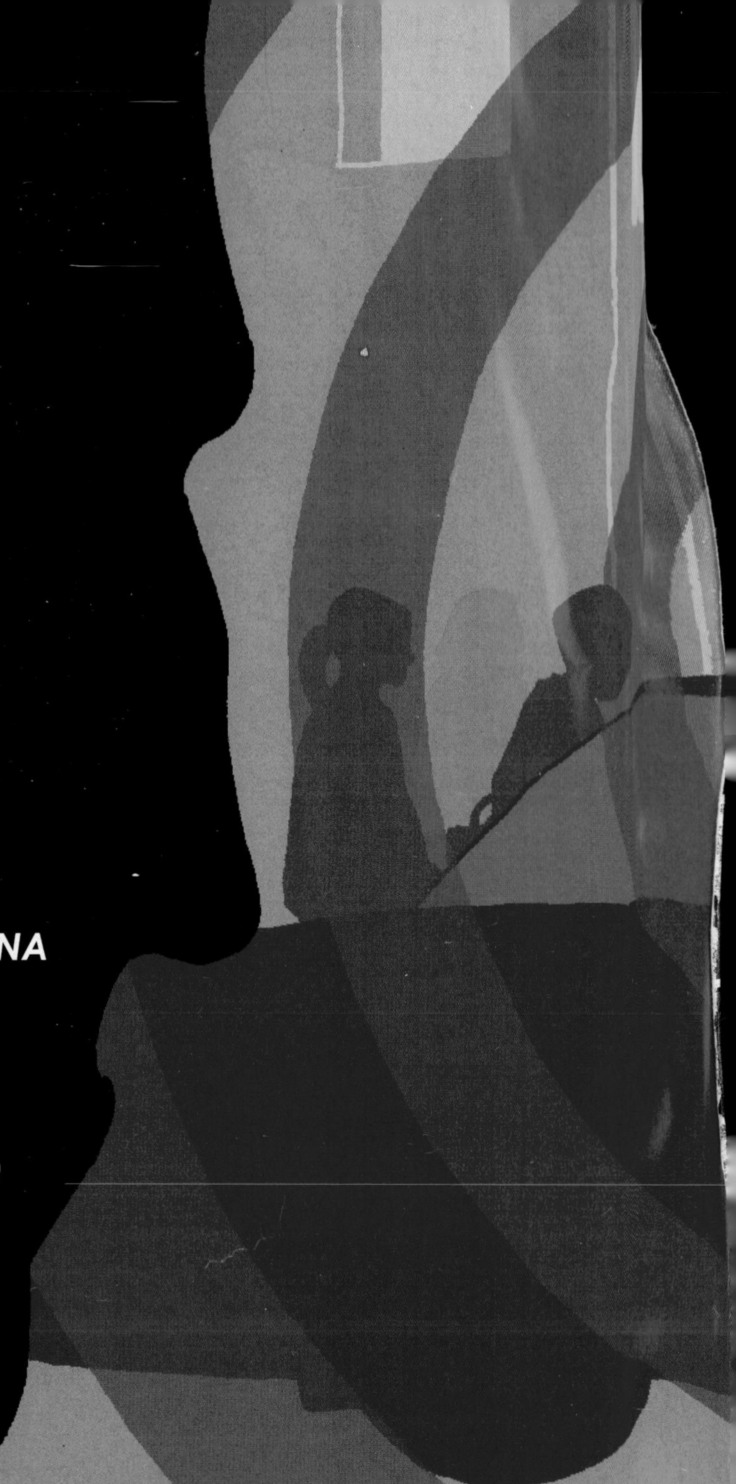

WRITER
MARK WAID

DAREDEVIL #7, 9 & #10

PENCILER
PAOLO RIVERA

INKER
JOE RIVERA

AMAZING SPIDER-MAN #677

ARTIST
EMMA RIOS

DAREDEVIL #8

ARTIST
KANO

DAREDEVIL #10.1

ARTIST
KHOI PHAM

COLOR ARTIST
JAVIER RODRIGUEZ

LETTERER
VC'S JOE CARAMAGNA

COVER ARTISTS
PAOLO RIVERA
(DAREDEVIL #7-10)
HUMBERTO RAMOS
& EDGAR DELGADO
(AMAZING SPIDER-MAN #677)
MARCOS MARTIN
(DAREDEVIL #10.1)

ASSISTANT EDITOR
ELLIE PYLE

EDITOR
STEPHEN WACKER

COLLECTION EDITOR & DESIGN **CORY LEVINE** • ASSISTANT EDITORS **ALEX STARBUCK** & **NELSON RIBEIRO**
EDITORS, SPECIAL PROJECTS **JENNIFER GRÜNWALD** & **MARK D. BEAZLEY**
SENIOR EDITOR, SPECIAL PROJECTS **JEFF YOUNGQUIST** • SENIOR VICE PRESIDENT OF SALES **DAVID GABRIEL**
SVP OF BRAND PLANNING & COMMUNICATIONS **MICHAEL PASCIULLO**

EDITOR IN CHIEF **AXEL ALONSO** • CHIEF CREATIVE OFFICER **JOE QUESADA**
PUBLISHER **DAN BUCKLEY** • EXECUTIVE PRODUCER **ALAN FINE**

DAREDEVIL BY MARK WAID VOL. 2. Contains material originally published in magazine form as DAREDEVIL #7-10 and #10.1, and AMAZING SPIDER-MAN #677. First printing 2012. Hardcover ISBN# 978-0-7851-5239-2. Softcover ISBN# 978-0-7851-5240-8. Published by MARVEL WORLDWIDE, INC., a subsidiary of MARVEL ENTERTAINMENT, LLC. OFFICE OF PUBLICATION: 135 West 50th Street, New York, NY 10020. Hardcover: $19.99 per copy in the U.S. and $21.99 in Canada (GST #R127032852). Softcover: $15.99 per copy in the U.S. and $17.99 in Canada (GST #R127032852). Canadian Agreement #40668537. **Printed in the U.S.A.** ALAN FINE, EVP - Office of the President, Marvel Worldwide, Inc. and EVP & CMO Marvel Characters B.V.; DAN BUCKLEY, Publisher & President - Print, Animation & Digital Divisions; JOE QUESADA, Chief Creative Officer; TOM BREVOORT, SVP of Publishing; DAVID BOGART, SVP of Operations & Procurement, Publishing; RUWAN JAYATILLEKE, SVP & Associate Publisher, Publishing; C.B. CEBULSKI, SVP of Creator & Content Development; DAVID GABRIEL, SVP of Publishing Sales & Circulation; MICHAEL PASCIULLO, SVP of Brand Planning & Communications; JIM O'KEEFE, VP of Operations & Logistics; DAN CARR, Executive Director of Publishing Technology; SUSAN CRESPI, Editorial Operations Manager; ALEX MORALES, Publishing Operations Manager; STAN LEE, Chairman Emeritus. For information regarding advertising in Marvel Comics or on Marvel.com, please contact John Dokes, SVP Integrated Sales and Marketing, at jdokes@marvel.com. For Marvel subscription inquiries, please call 800-217-9158. **Manufactured between 4/30/2012 and 5/28/2012 (hardcover), and 4/30/2012 and 11/26/2012 (softcover), by R.R. DONNELLEY, INC., SALEM, VA, USA.**

0 9 8 7 6 5 4 3 2 1

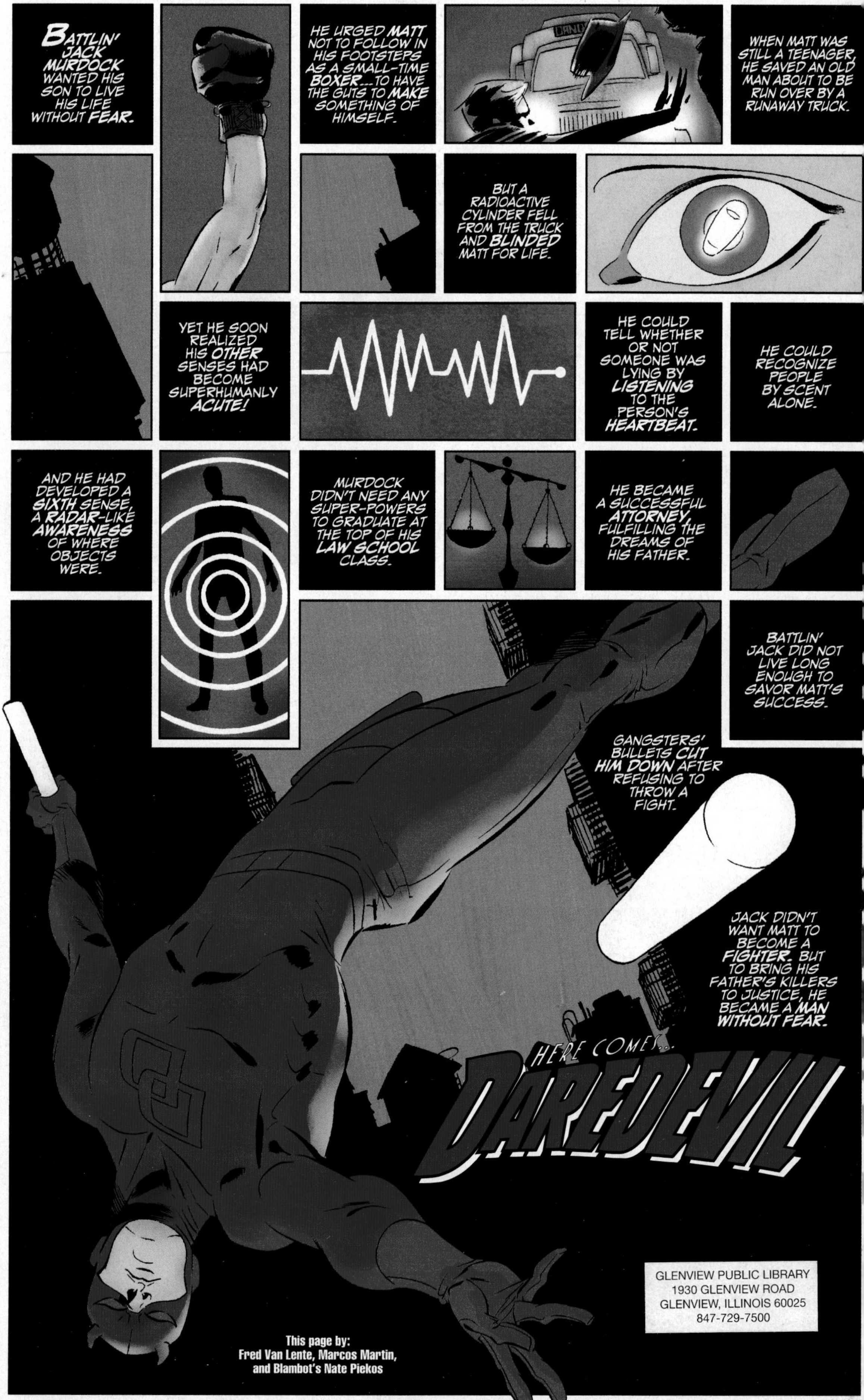
BATTLIN' JACK MURDOCK WANTED HIS SON TO LIVE HIS LIFE WITHOUT FEAR.
HE URGED MATT NOT TO FOLLOW IN HIS FOOTSTEPS AS A SMALL-TIME BOXER... TO HAVE THE GUTS TO MAKE SOMETHING OF HIMSELF.
WHEN MATT WAS STILL A TEENAGER, HE SAVED AN OLD MAN ABOUT TO BE RUN OVER BY A RUNAWAY TRUCK.
BUT A RADIOACTIVE CYLINDER FELL FROM THE TRUCK AND BLINDED MATT FOR LIFE.
YET HE SOON REALIZED HIS OTHER SENSES HAD BECOME SUPERHUMANLY ACUTE!
HE COULD TELL WHETHER OR NOT SOMEONE WAS LYING BY LISTENING TO THE PERSON'S HEARTBEAT.
HE COULD RECOGNIZE PEOPLE BY SCENT ALONE.
AND HE HAD DEVELOPED A SIXTH SENSE, A RADAR-LIKE AWARENESS OF WHERE OBJECTS WERE.
MURDOCK DIDN'T NEED ANY SUPER-POWERS TO GRADUATE AT THE TOP OF HIS LAW SCHOOL CLASS.
HE BECAME A SUCCESSFUL ATTORNEY, FULFILLING THE DREAMS OF HIS FATHER.
BATTLIN' JACK DID NOT LIVE LONG ENOUGH TO SAVOR MATT'S SUCCESS.
GANGSTERS' BULLETS CUT HIM DOWN AFTER REFUSING TO THROW A FIGHT.
JACK DIDN'T WANT MATT TO BECOME A FIGHTER. BUT TO BRING HIS FATHER'S KILLERS TO JUSTICE, HE BECAME A MAN WITHOUT FEAR.
HERE COMES...
DAREDEVIL!
This page by:
Fred Van Lente, Marcos Martin,
and Blambot's Nate Piekos

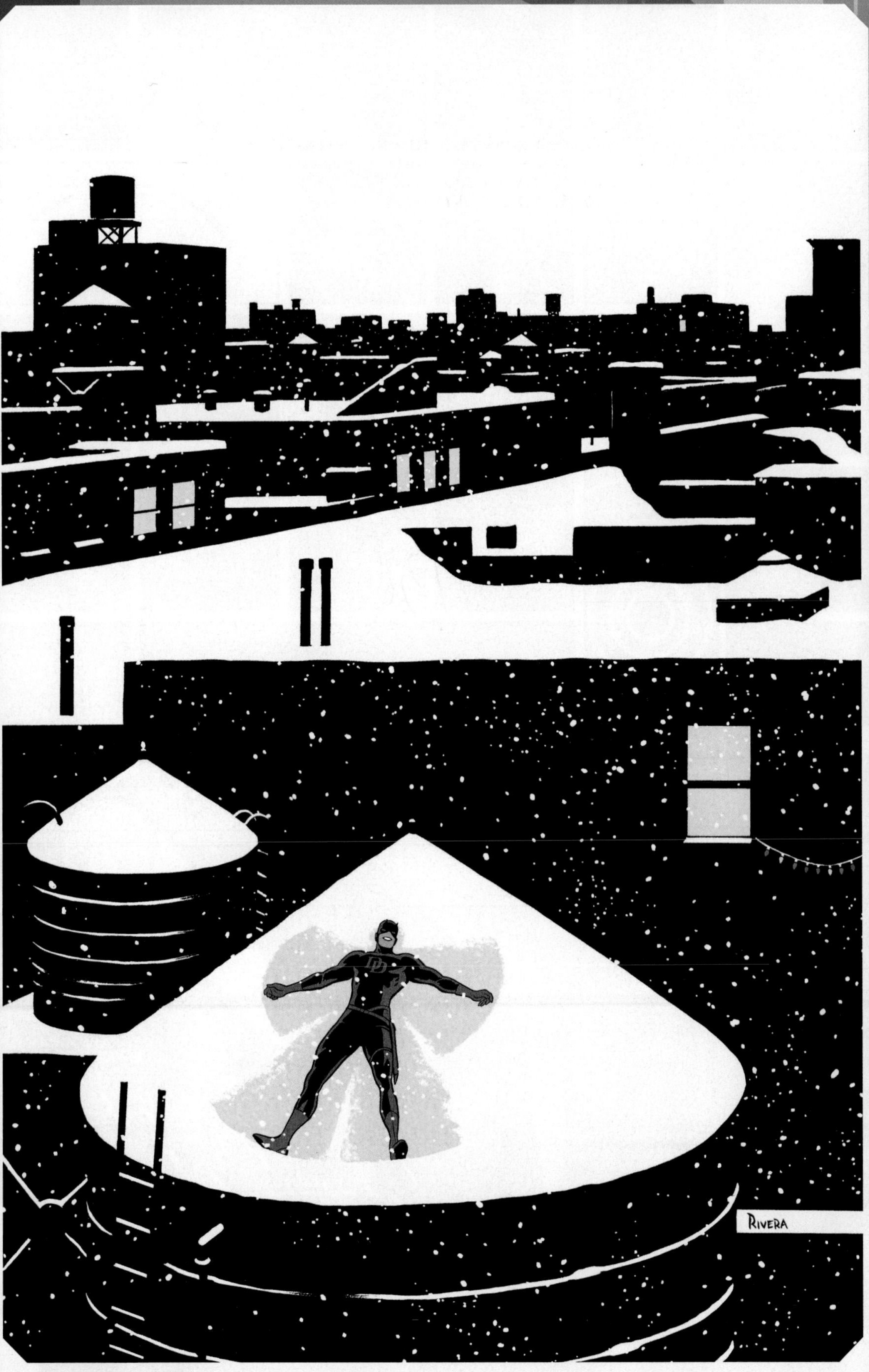
RIVERA

SEVEN

FINAL ☆☆☆☆

DAILY BUGLE®

NEW YORK'S FINEST DAILY NEWSPAPER

SINCE 1897 ☆☆☆☆
$1.00 (in NYC)
$1.50 (outside city)

INSIDE: SKI LODGE MASSACRE BLOODIES HUDSON RIVER VALLEY! MARATHON OVERRUN BY MOLOIDS! MAYOR MISSING; MORE MUTANT AVENGERS?

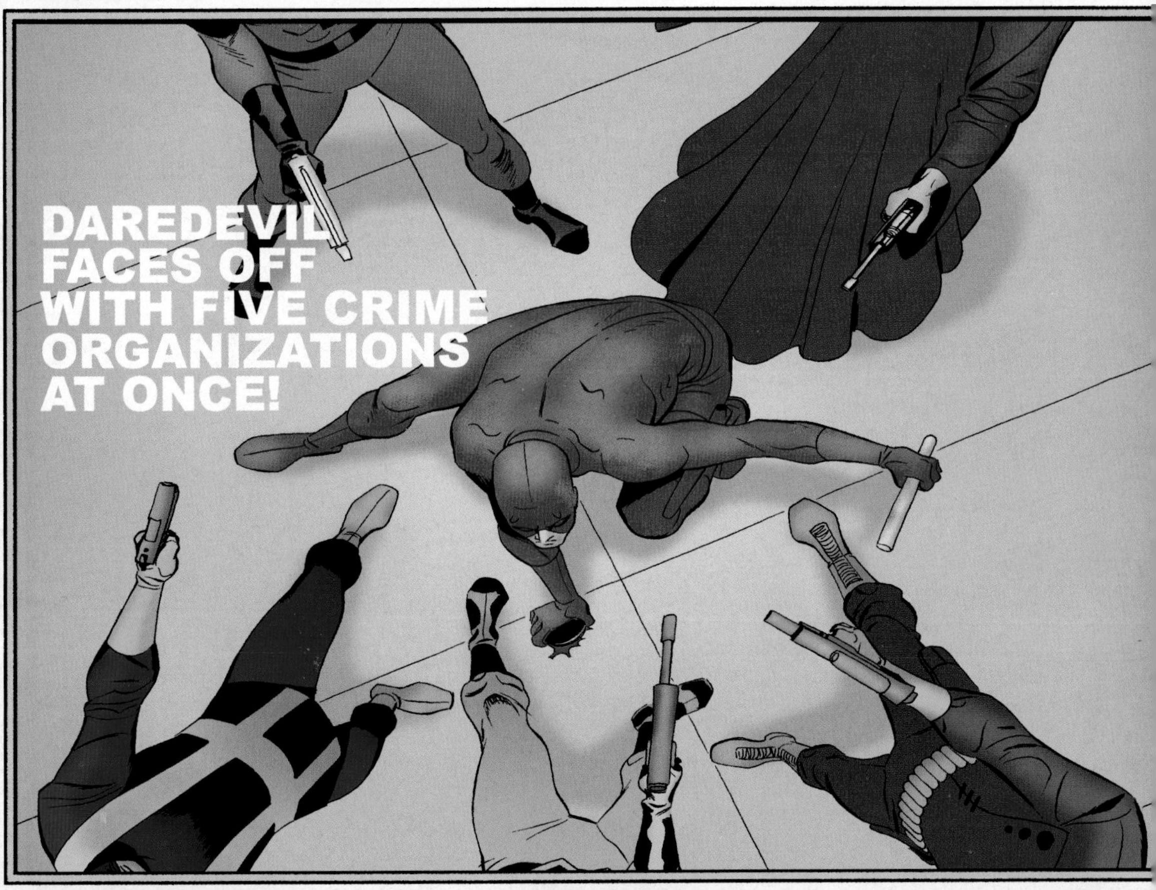
DAREDEVIL FACES OFF WITH FIVE CRIME ORGANIZATIONS AT ONCE!

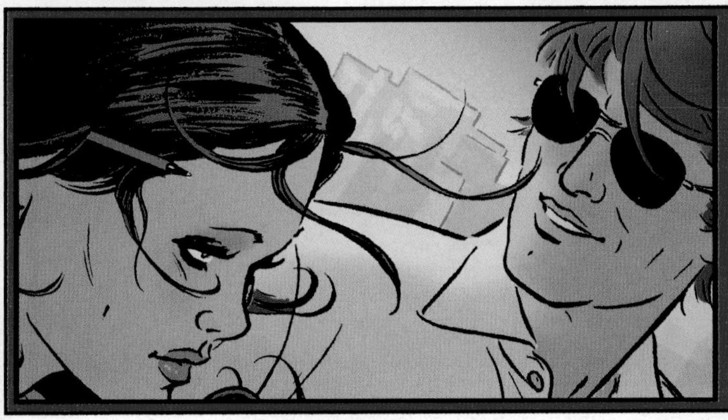

THE MOST WANTED MAN ALIVE

DAREDEVIL WAS SPOTTED WALKING AWAY FROM A CONFRONTATION WITH A.I.M., HYDRA, AGENCE BYZANTIUM, THE SECRET EMPIRE AND BLACK SPECTRE. WHAT COULD HE HAVE THAT WOULD CAUSE ALL OF THOSE GROUPS TO JOIN FORCES FOR HIS DESTRUCTION? AND WHAT WILL IT MEAN FOR MATT MURDOCK, THE BLIND LAWYER WHO KEEPS CLAIMING HE'S NOT DAREDEVIL?

(PICTURED HERE WITH A.D.A. KIRSTEN MCDUFFIE)

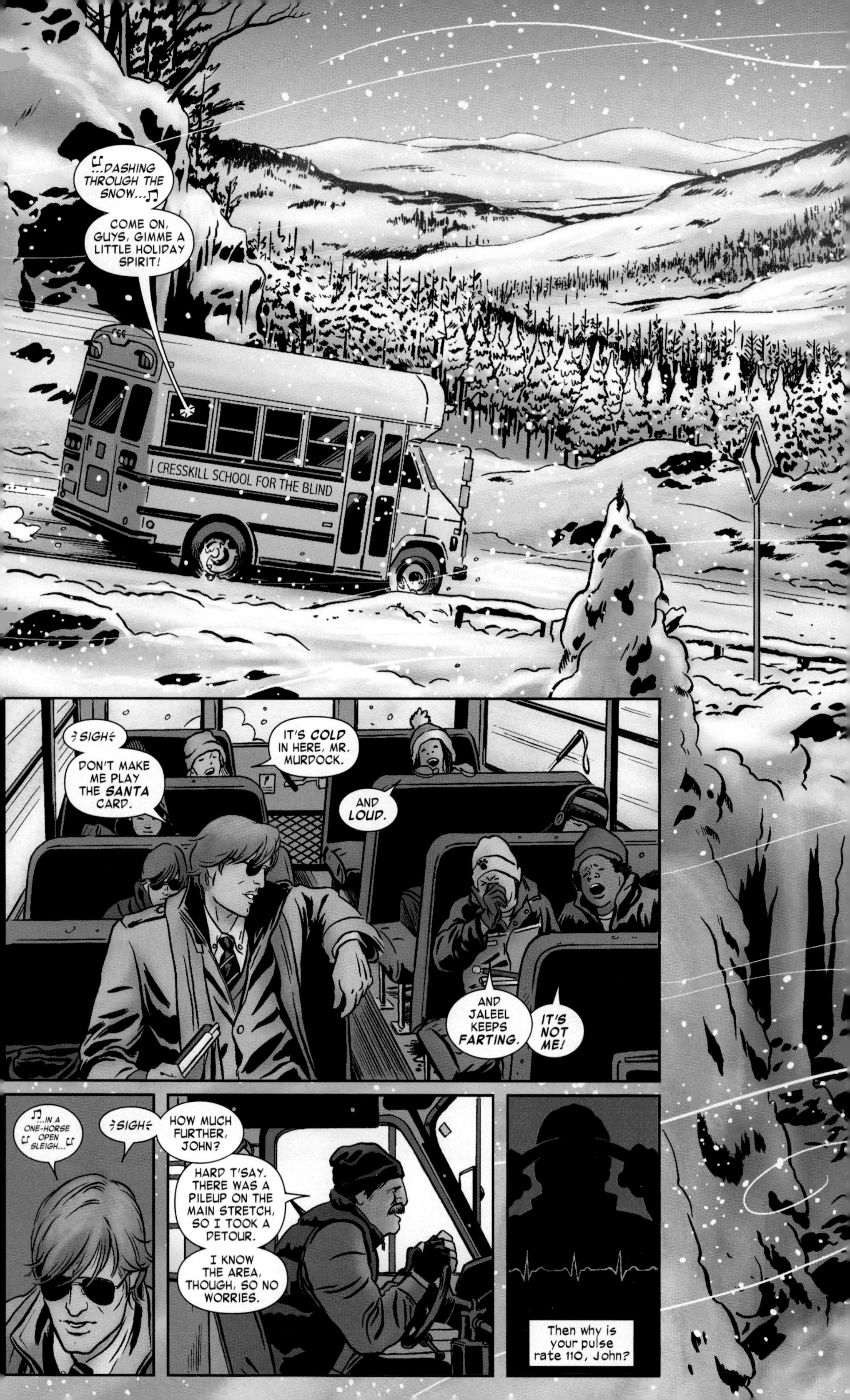
♫...DASHING THROUGH THE SNOW...♫
COME ON, GUYS, GIMME A LITTLE HOLIDAY SPIRIT!
CRESSKILL SCHOOL FOR THE BLIND
SIGH
DON'T MAKE ME PLAY THE SANTA CARD.
IT'S COLD IN HERE, MR. MURDOCK.
AND LOUD.
AND JALEEL KEEPS FARTING.
IT'S NOT ME!
♫...IN A ONE-HORSE OPEN SLEIGH...♫
SIGH
HOW MUCH FURTHER, JOHN?
HARD T'SAY. THERE WAS A PILEUP ON THE MAIN STRETCH, SO I TOOK A DETOUR.
I KNOW THE AREA, THOUGH, SO NO WORRIES.
Then why is your pulse rate 110, John?

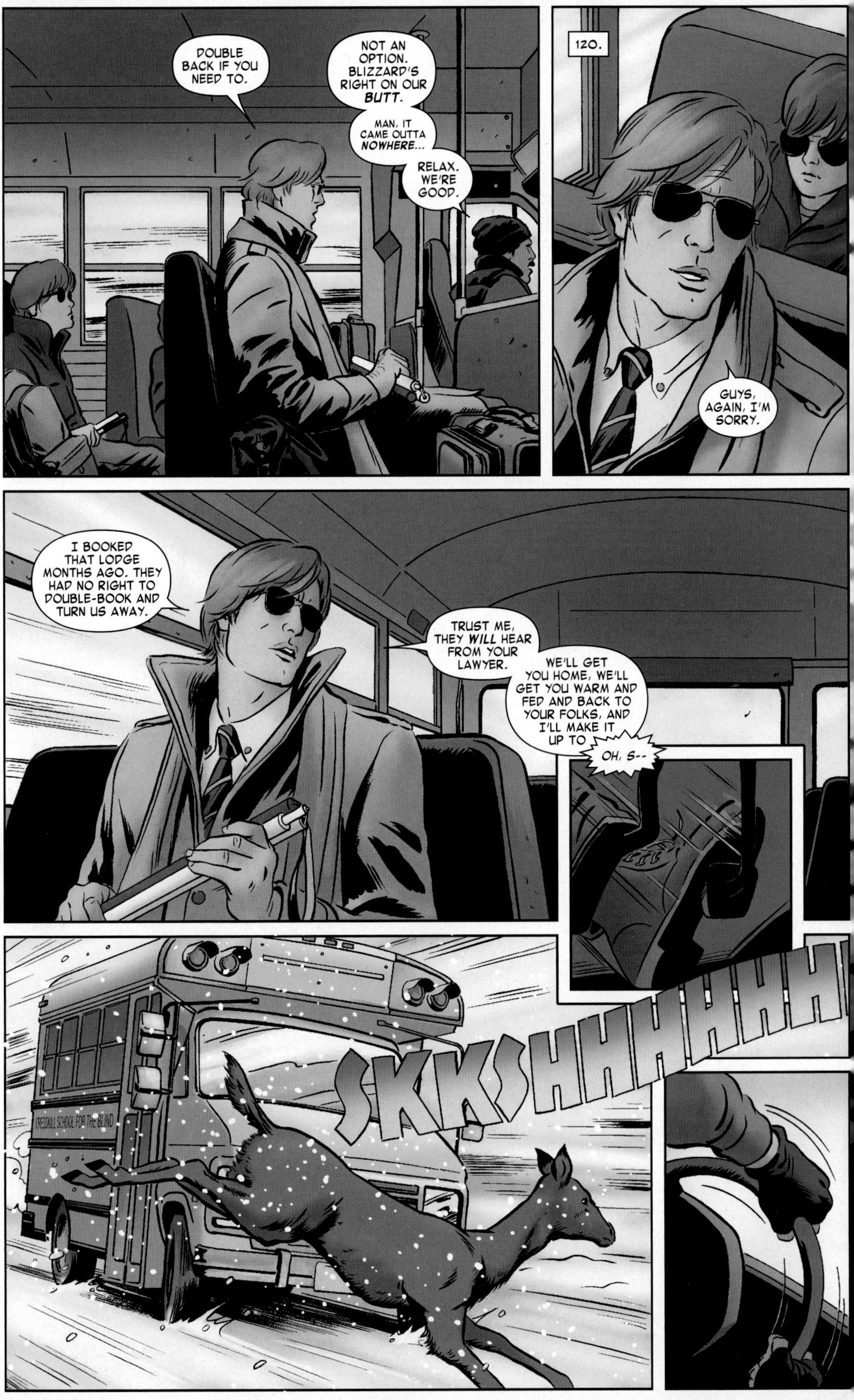
DOUBLE BACK IF YOU NEED TO.
NOT AN OPTION. BLIZZARD'S RIGHT ON OUR BUTT.
MAN, IT CAME OUTTA NOWHERE...
RELAX. WE'RE GOOD.
120.
GUYS, AGAIN, I'M SORRY.
I BOOKED THAT LODGE MONTHS AGO. THEY HAD NO RIGHT TO DOUBLE-BOOK AND TURN US AWAY.
TRUST ME, THEY WILL HEAR FROM YOUR LAWYER.
WE'LL GET YOU HOME, WE'LL GET YOU WARM AND FED AND BACK TO YOUR FOLKS, AND I'LL MAKE IT UP TO
OH, S--
CRESSKILL SCHOOL FOR THE BLIND
SKKSHHHHHHHH

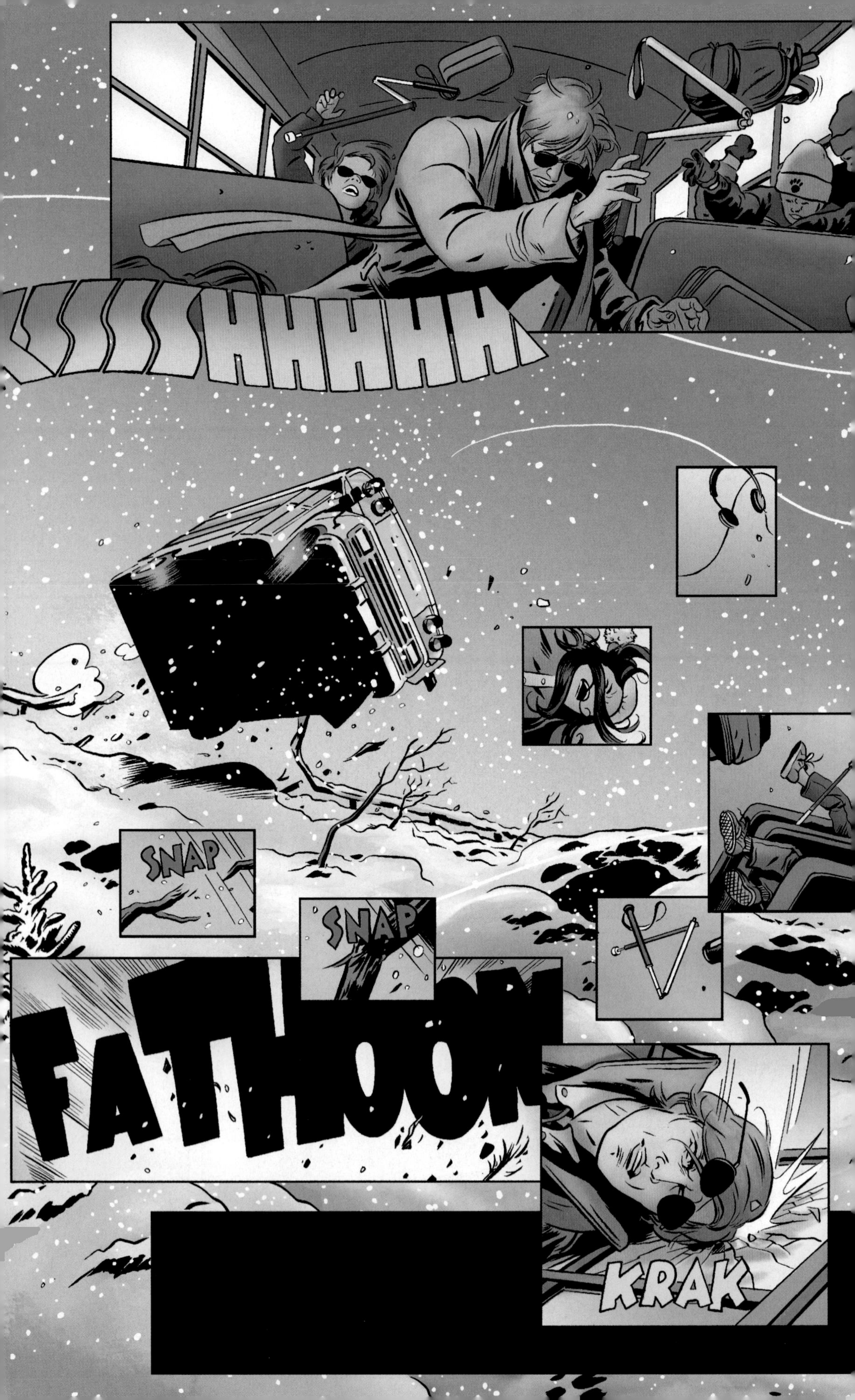

SSSSHHHHH
SNAP
SNAP
FATHOOM
KRAK

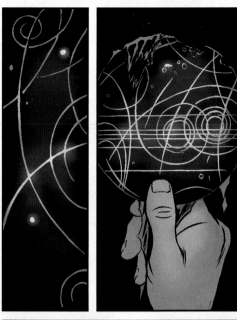

MATT? WE'RE WAITING ON YOU.

WHATCHA GOT THERE?

NOTHING, FOGGY. REMNANT OF A CASE. TRYING TO FIGURE OUT EXACTLY WHAT TO DO WITH IT.

MUST BE A BIG DECISION. YOU LOOK MISERABLE. LIKE THE OLD M--

PRETTY WOMEN OUT THERE, BUDDY. LET'S ROLL.

"LIKE THE OLD MATT"? LIKE THE TORTURED, GUILT-RIDDEN, SELF-DESTRUCTIVE PUNCHING BAG?

...

LIKE THE FRIEND AND PARTNER I KNOW BEST.

YEAH?

I HATE THAT GUY.

LET'S GO.

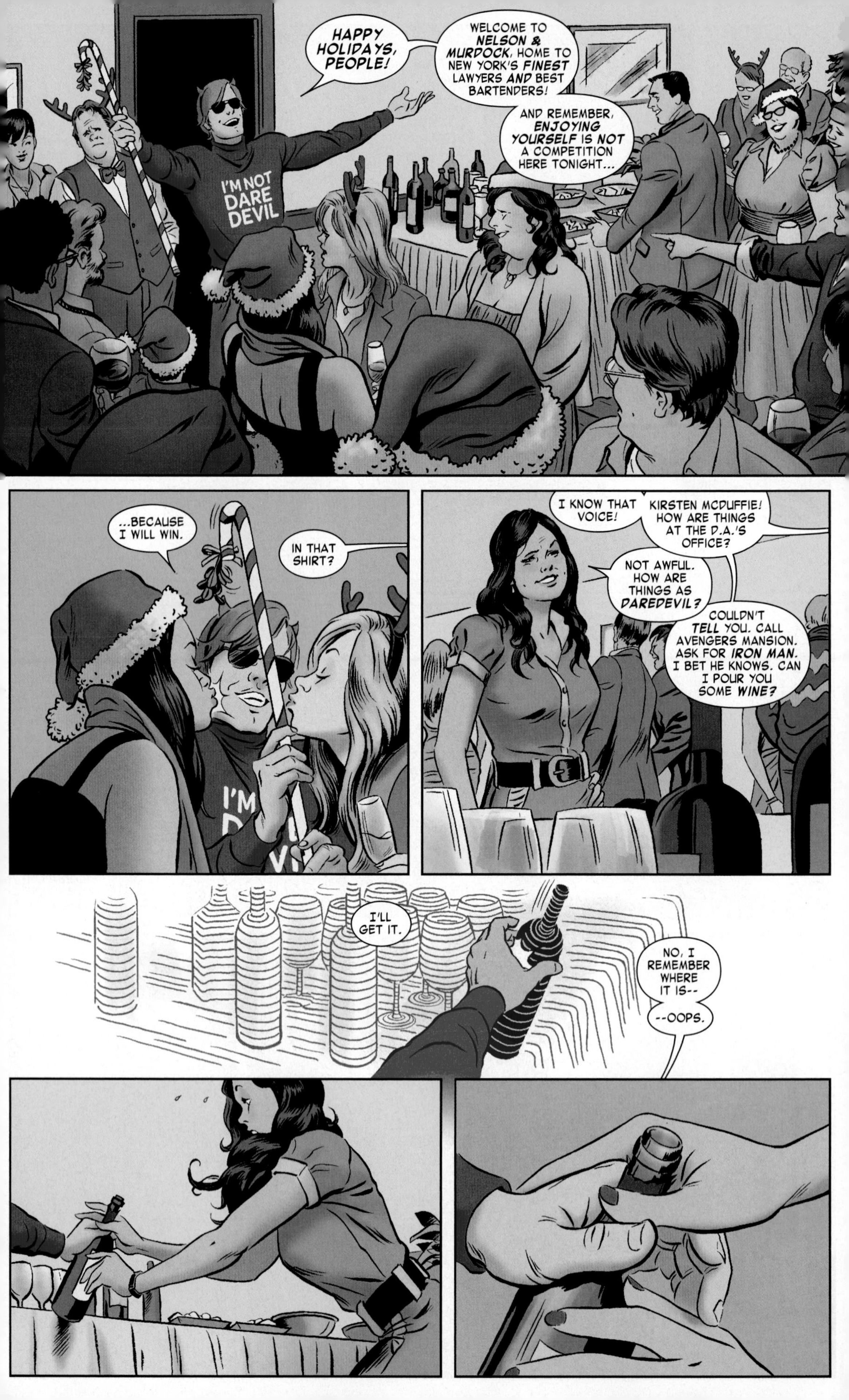
HAPPY HOLIDAYS, PEOPLE!
WELCOME TO NELSON & MURDOCK, HOME TO NEW YORK'S FINEST LAWYERS AND BEST BARTENDERS!
AND REMEMBER, ENJOYING YOURSELF IS NOT A COMPETITION HERE TONIGHT...
I'M NOT DARE DEVIL
...BECAUSE I WILL WIN.
IN THAT SHIRT?
I KNOW THAT VOICE!
KIRSTEN MCDUFFIE! HOW ARE THINGS AT THE D.A.'S OFFICE?
NOT AWFUL. HOW ARE THINGS AS DAREDEVIL?
COULDN'T TELL YOU. CALL AVENGERS MANSION. ASK FOR IRON MAN. I BET HE KNOWS. CAN I POUR YOU SOME WINE?
I'LL GET IT.
NO, I REMEMBER WHERE IT IS--
--OOPS.

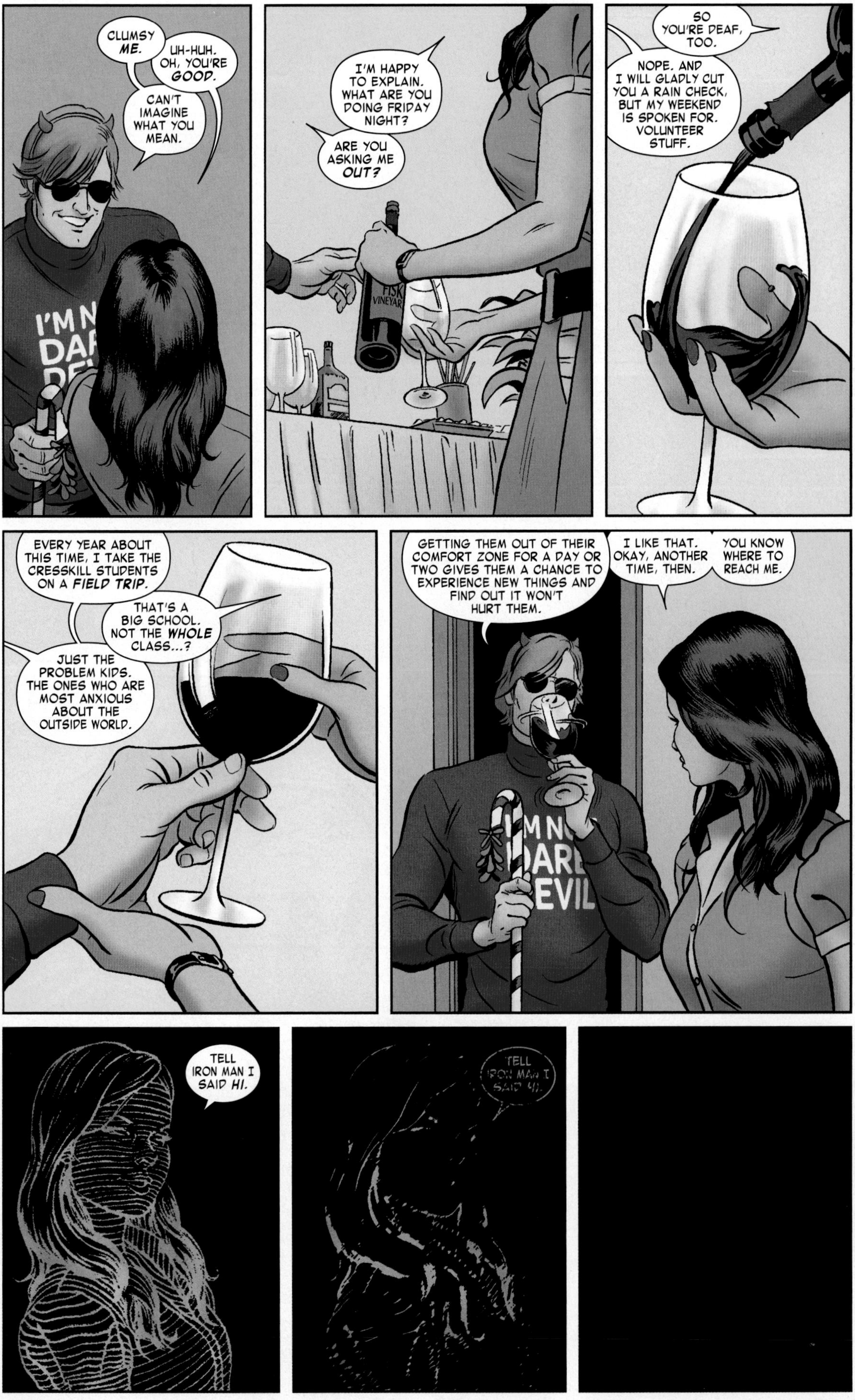
CLUMSY ME.
UH-HUH. OH, YOU'RE GOOD.
CAN'T IMAGINE WHAT YOU MEAN.
I'M HAPPY TO EXPLAIN. WHAT ARE YOU DOING FRIDAY NIGHT?
ARE YOU ASKING ME OUT?
FISK VINEYAR
SO YOU'RE DEAF, TOO.
NOPE. AND I WILL GLADLY CUT YOU A RAIN CHECK, BUT MY WEEKEND IS SPOKEN FOR. VOLUNTEER STUFF.
EVERY YEAR ABOUT THIS TIME, I TAKE THE CRESSKILL STUDENTS ON A FIELD TRIP.
THAT'S A BIG SCHOOL. NOT THE WHOLE CLASS...?
JUST THE PROBLEM KIDS. THE ONES WHO ARE MOST ANXIOUS ABOUT THE OUTSIDE WORLD.
GETTING THEM OUT OF THEIR COMFORT ZONE FOR A DAY OR TWO GIVES THEM A CHANCE TO EXPERIENCE NEW THINGS AND FIND OUT IT WON'T HURT THEM.
I LIKE THAT. OKAY, ANOTHER TIME, THEN.
YOU KNOW WHERE TO REACH ME.
TELL IRON MAN I SAID HI.
TELL IRON MAN I SAID HI.

HNNNNNHH--!

What happened? Where am--?

Leg bleeding.

Cold. *Really* cold.

Head pounding.

Filled with the stink of blood and urine.

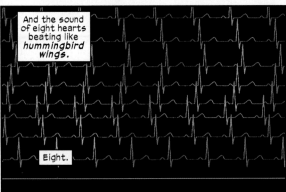

And the sound of eight hearts beating like *hummingbird wings.*

Eight.

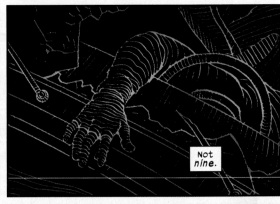

Not *nine.*

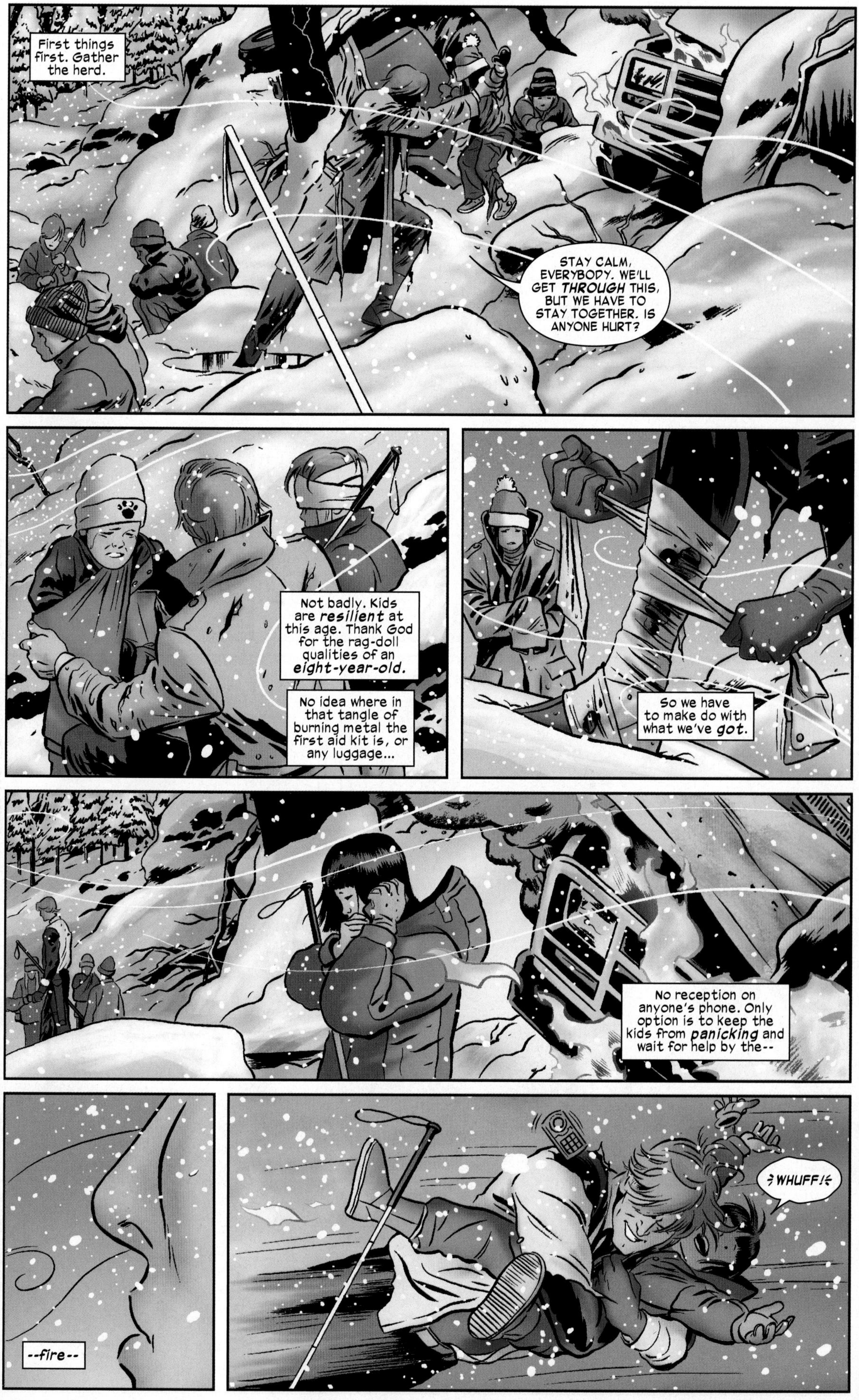

First things first. Gather the herd.
STAY CALM, EVERYBODY. WE'LL GET THROUGH THIS, BUT WE HAVE TO STAY TOGETHER. IS ANYONE HURT?
Not badly. Kids are resilient at this age. Thank God for the rag-doll qualities of an eight-year-old.
No idea where in that tangle of burning metal the first aid kit is, or any luggage...
So we have to make do with what we've got.
No reception on anyone's phone. Only option is to keep the kids from panicking and wait for help by the--
--fire--
WHUFF!

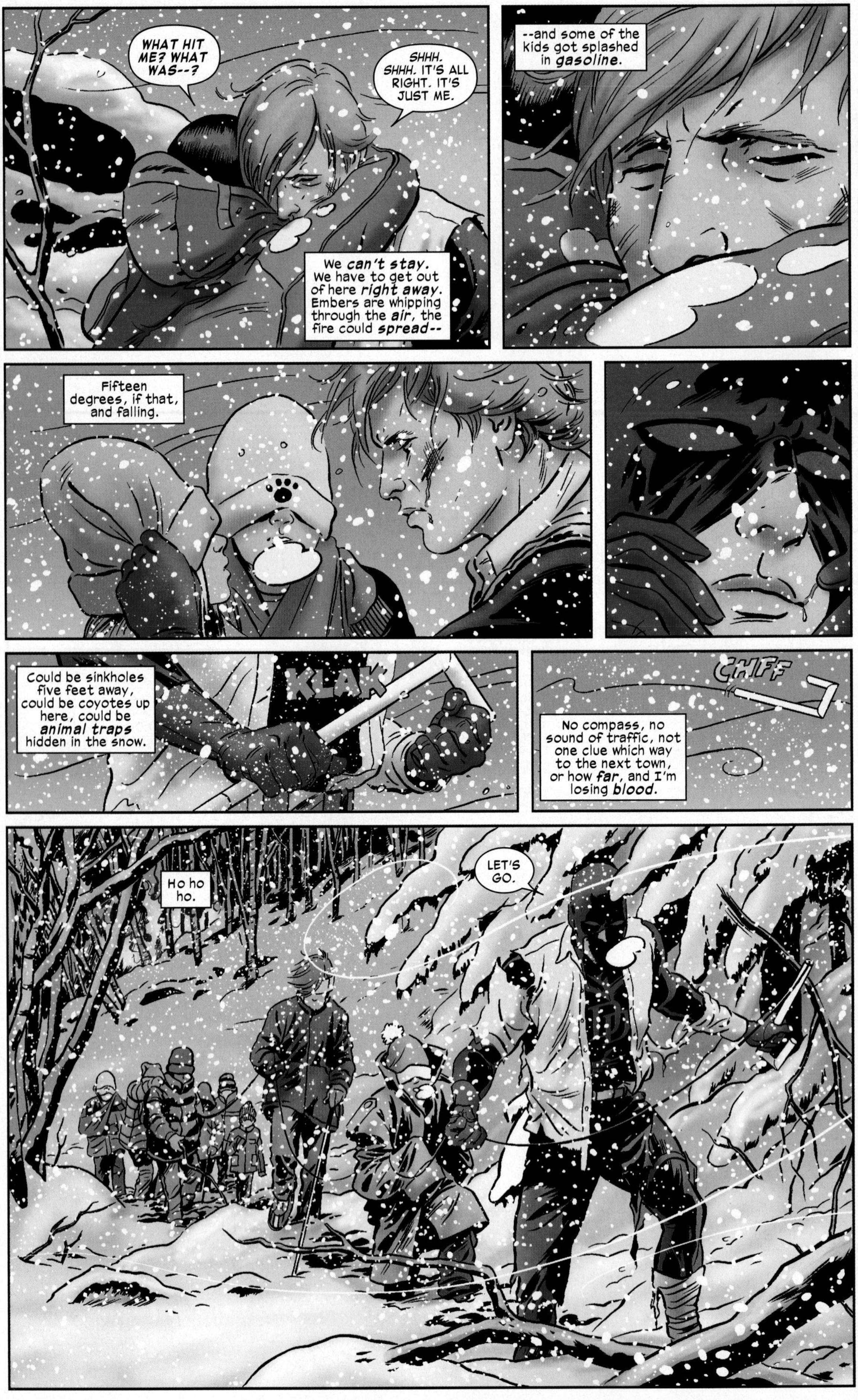
WHAT HIT ME? WHAT WAS--?
SHHH. SHHH. IT'S ALL RIGHT. IT'S JUST ME.
We can't stay. We have to get out of here right away. Embers are whipping through the air, the fire could spread--
--and some of the kids got splashed in gasoline.
Fifteen degrees, if that, and falling.
KLAK
Could be sinkholes five feet away, could be coyotes up here, could be animal traps hidden in the snow.
CHFF
No compass, no sound of traffic, not one clue which way to the next town, or how far, and I'm losing blood.
Ho ho ho.
LET'S GO.

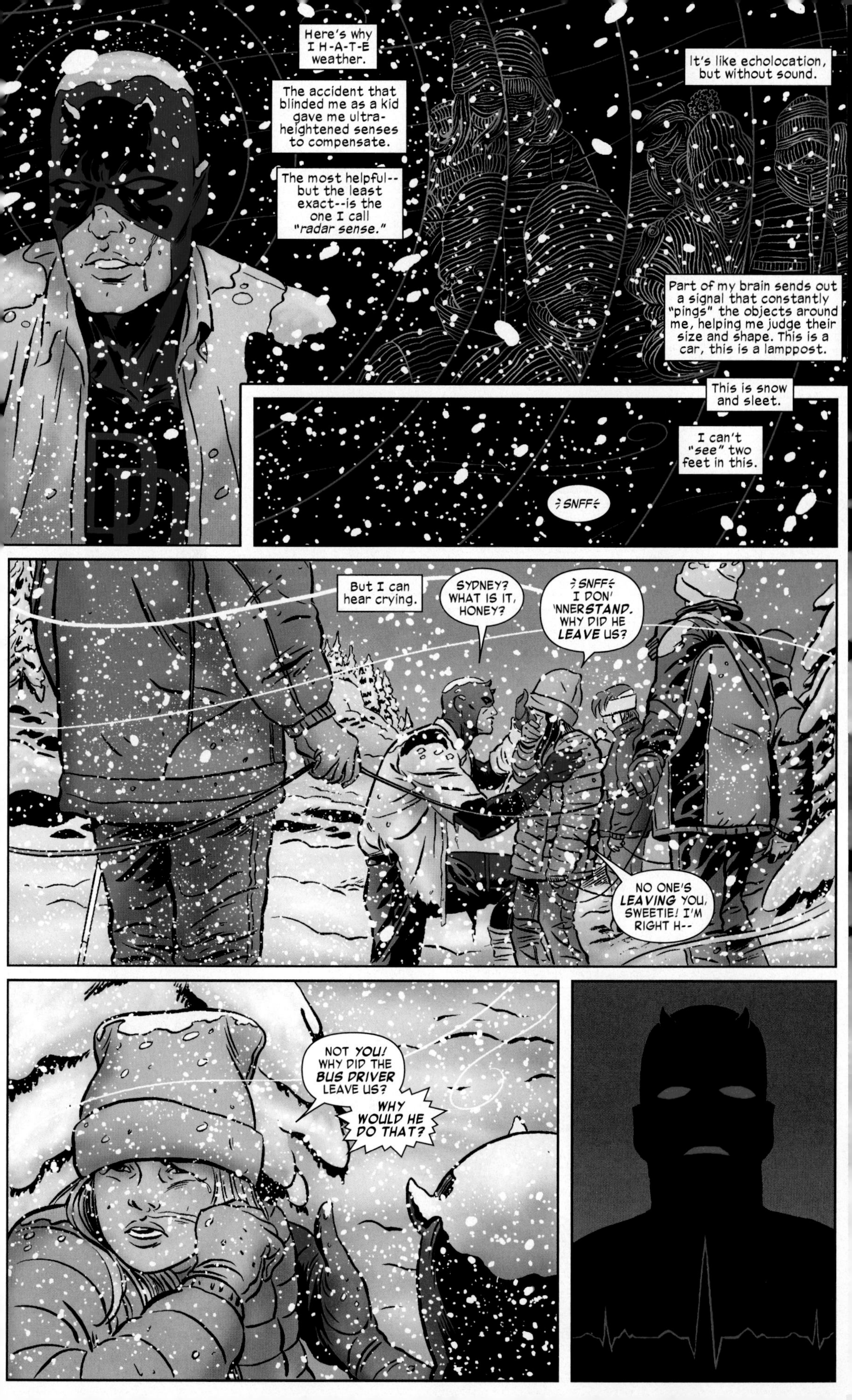
Here's why I H-A-T-E weather.
The accident that blinded me as a kid gave me ultra-heightened senses to compensate.
The most helpful--but the least exact--is the one I call "radar sense."
It's like echolocation, but without sound.
Part of my brain sends out a signal that constantly "pings" the objects around me, helping me judge their size and shape. This is a car, this is a lamppost.
This is snow and sleet.
I can't "see" two feet in this.
SNFF
But I can hear crying.
SYDNEY? WHAT IS IT, HONEY?
SNFF I DON' 'NNERSTAND. WHY DID HE LEAVE US?
NO ONE'S LEAVING YOU, SWEETIE! I'M RIGHT H--
NOT YOU! WHY DID THE BUS DRIVER LEAVE US?
WHY WOULD HE DO THAT?

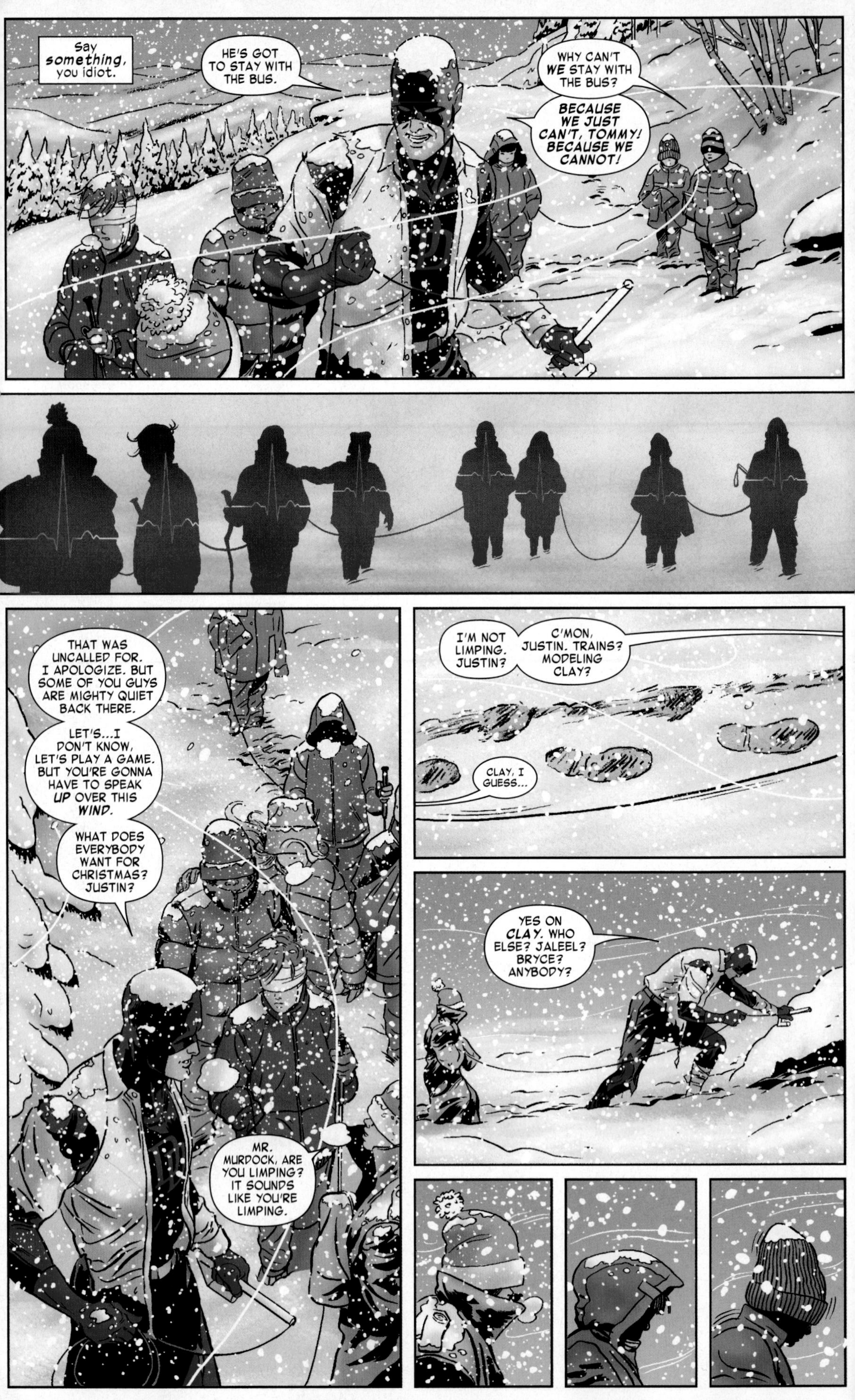
Say something, you idiot.
HE'S GOT TO STAY WITH THE BUS.
WHY CAN'T WE STAY WITH THE BUS?
BECAUSE WE JUST CAN'T, TOMMY! BECAUSE WE CANNOT!
THAT WAS UNCALLED FOR. I APOLOGIZE. BUT SOME OF YOU GUYS ARE MIGHTY QUIET BACK THERE.
LET'S...I DON'T KNOW, LET'S PLAY A GAME. BUT YOU'RE GONNA HAVE TO SPEAK UP OVER THIS WIND.
WHAT DOES EVERYBODY WANT FOR CHRISTMAS? JUSTIN?
MR. MURDOCK, ARE YOU LIMPING? IT SOUNDS LIKE YOU'RE LIMPING.
I'M NOT LIMPING. JUSTIN?
C'MON, JUSTIN. TRAINS? MODELING CLAY?
CLAY, I GUESS...
YES ON CLAY. WHO ELSE? JALEEL? BRYCE? ANYBODY?

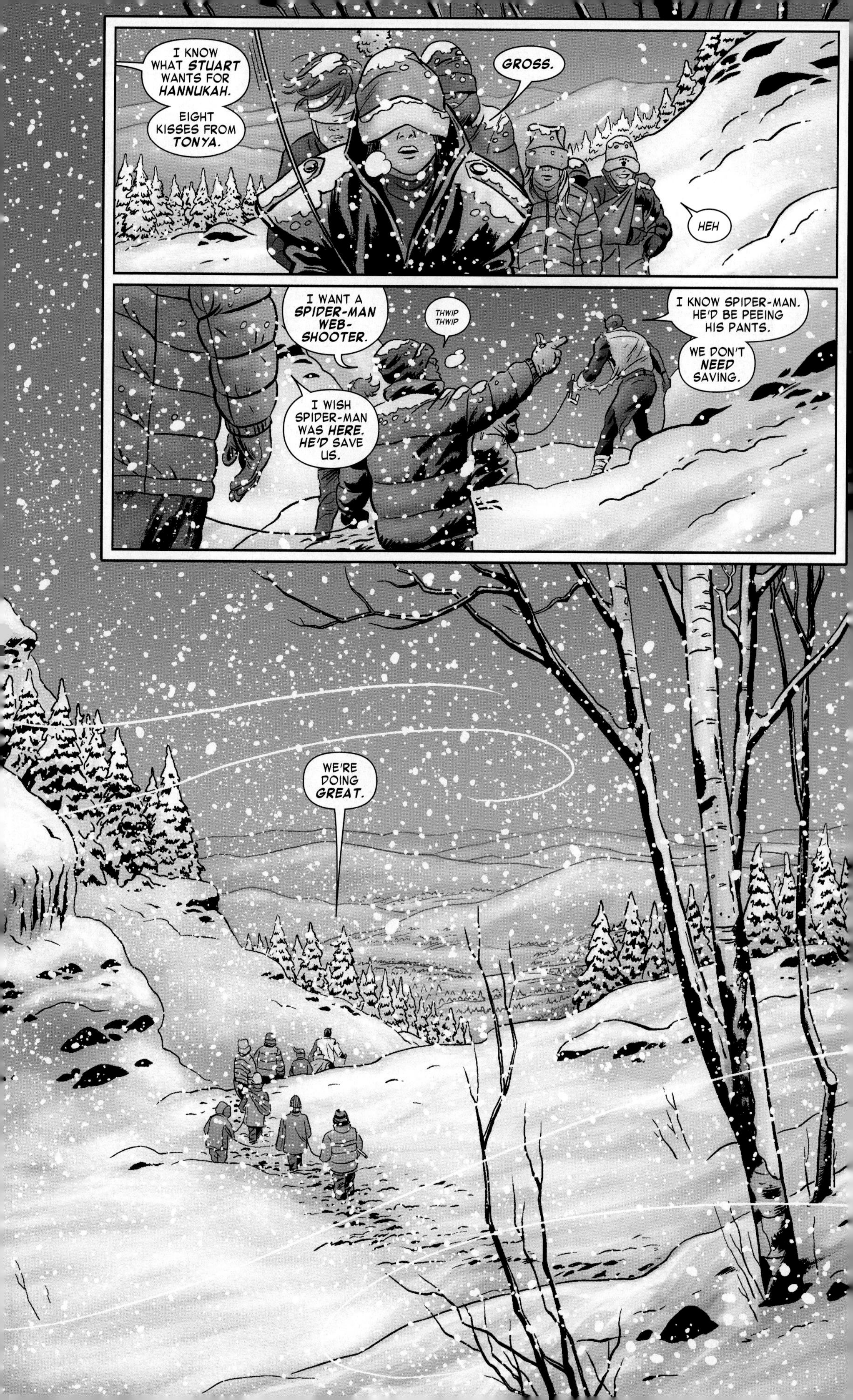

I KNOW WHAT STUART WANTS FOR HANNUKAH.
EIGHT KISSES FROM TONYA.
GROSS.
HEH
I WANT A SPIDER-MAN WEB-SHOOTER.
THWIP THWIP
I WISH SPIDER-MAN WAS HERE. HE'D SAVE US.
I KNOW SPIDER-MAN. HE'D BE PEEING HIS PANTS.
WE DON'T NEED SAVING.
WE'RE DOING GREAT.

Three increasingly lackluster rounds of "*Twelve Days of Christmas*" later, and all it's getting is colder and darker.

It's the Catskills, for God's sake. It's not the Montana wilderness.

This is a gargantuanly stupid way to die.

Either the kids have fallen silent with dread or I can't hear them over the *wind*. Probably both. I can tell I'm still dragging them only because my arm is sore.

I lost the feeling in my hands and feet a while back.

Good thing I've got gloves.

If we've gone three miles, I'd be shocked. For all I know, we're moving in *circles*.

They're just kids. Scared little kids. And if I don't give them more to hang onto soon...

AT EASE, T-TROOPS! NEW P-P-PLAN!

WE'RE G-GONNA PUT TOGETHER A LEAN-TO AND REST UP! EVERYONE BUH-BRING ME WHATEVER BRANCHES THEY CAN FIND CLOSE AT H-HAND!

WE'LL USE THE GUH-GUIDE LINE FOR ROPE! YOU KNOW KNOTS, R-R-RIGHT, JAVI?

HAIL, MARY FULL OF GRACE...

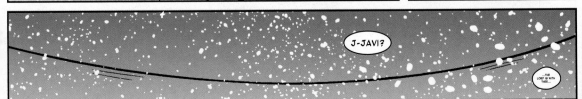

J-JAVI?

THE LORD IS WITH THEE...

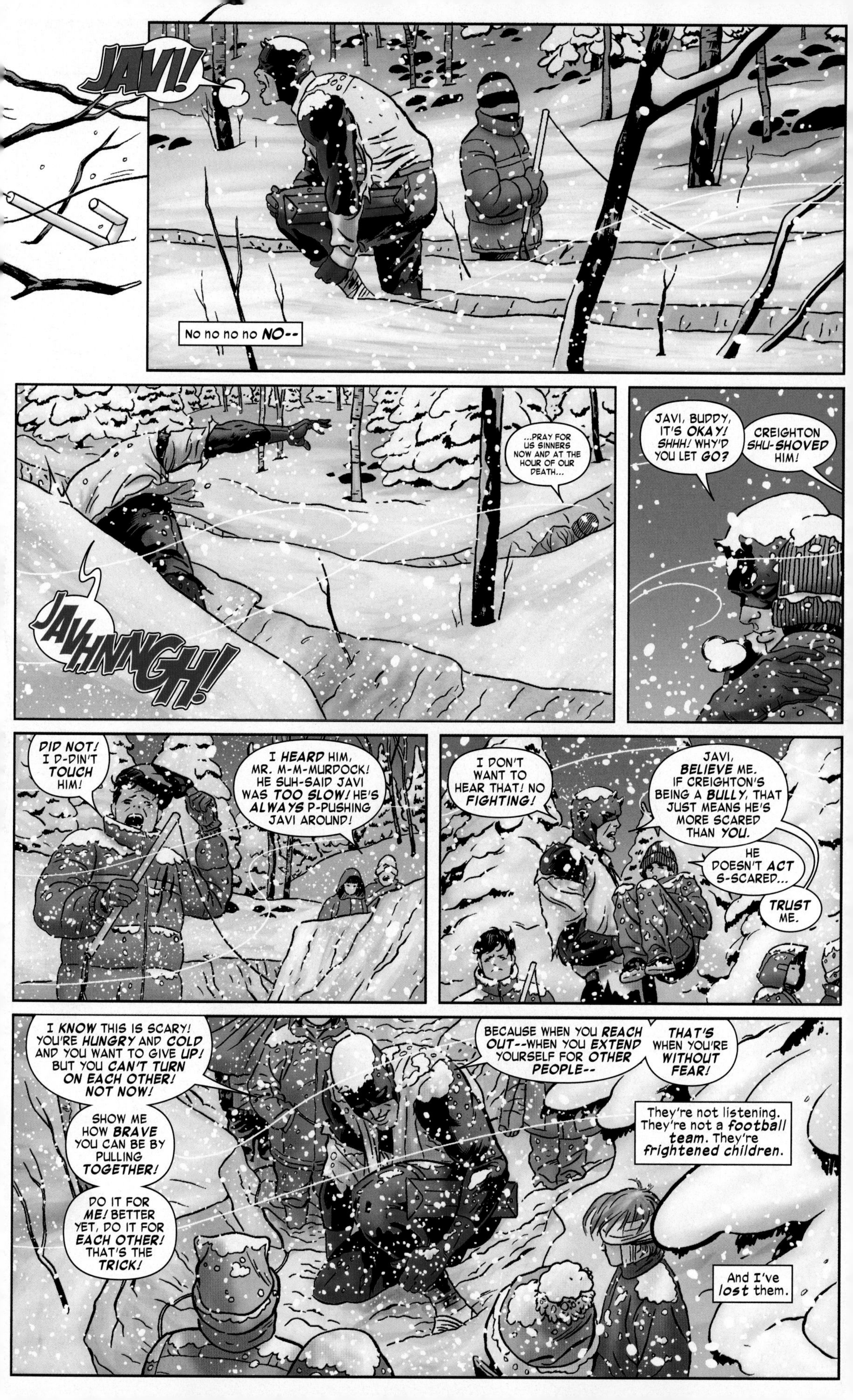
JAVI!
No no no no NO--
...PRAY FOR US SINNERS NOW AND AT THE HOUR OF OUR DEATH...
JAVHNNGH!
JAVI, BUDDY, IT'S OKAY! SHHH! WHY'D YOU LET GO?
CREIGHTON SHU-SHOVED HIM!
DID NOT! I D-DIN'T TOUCH HIM!
I HEARD HIM, MR. M-M-MURDOCK! HE SUH-SAID JAVI WAS TOO SLOW! HE'S ALWAYS P-PUSHING JAVI AROUND!
I DON'T WANT TO HEAR THAT! NO FIGHTING!
JAVI, BELIEVE ME. IF CREIGHTON'S BEING A BULLY, THAT JUST MEANS HE'S MORE SCARED THAN YOU.
HE DOESN'T ACT S-SCARED...
TRUST ME.
I KNOW THIS IS SCARY! YOU'RE HUNGRY AND COLD AND YOU WANT TO GIVE UP! BUT YOU CAN'T TURN ON EACH OTHER! NOT NOW!
SHOW ME HOW BRAVE YOU CAN BE BY PULLING TOGETHER!
DO IT FOR ME! BETTER YET, DO IT FOR EACH OTHER! THAT'S THE TRICK!
BECAUSE WHEN YOU REACH OUT--WHEN YOU EXTEND YOURSELF FOR OTHER PEOPLE--
THAT'S WHEN YOU'RE WITHOUT FEAR!
They're not listening. They're not a football team. They're frightened children.
And I've lost them.

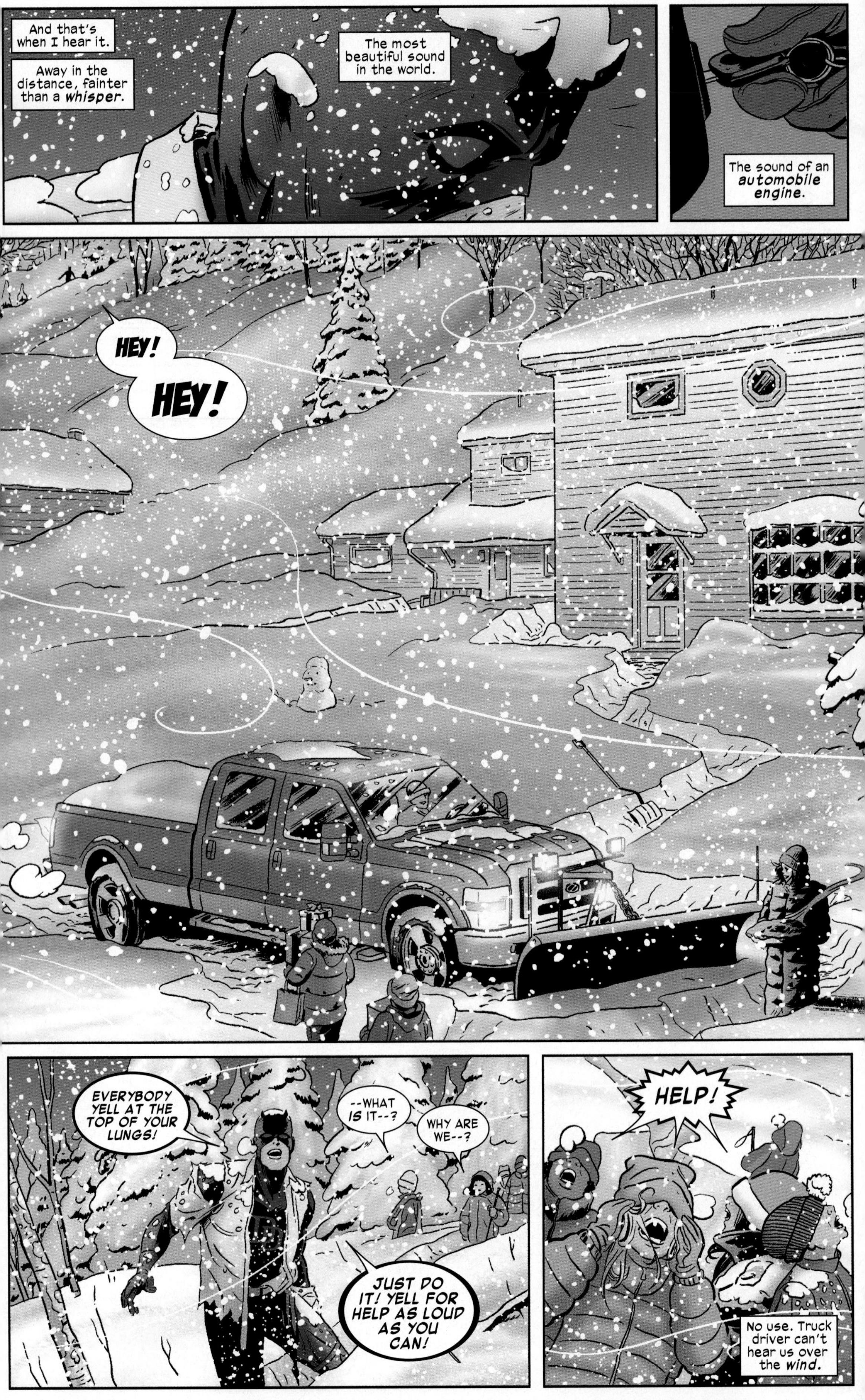
And that's when I hear it.
Away in the distance, fainter than a *whisper*.
The most beautiful sound in the world.
The sound of an *automobile engine*.
HEY!
HEY!
EVERYBODY YELL AT THE TOP OF YOUR LUNGS!
--WHAT *IS* IT--?
WHY ARE WE--?
JUST DO IT! YELL FOR HELP AS LOUD AS YOU CAN!
HELP!
No use. Truck driver can't hear us over the *wind*.

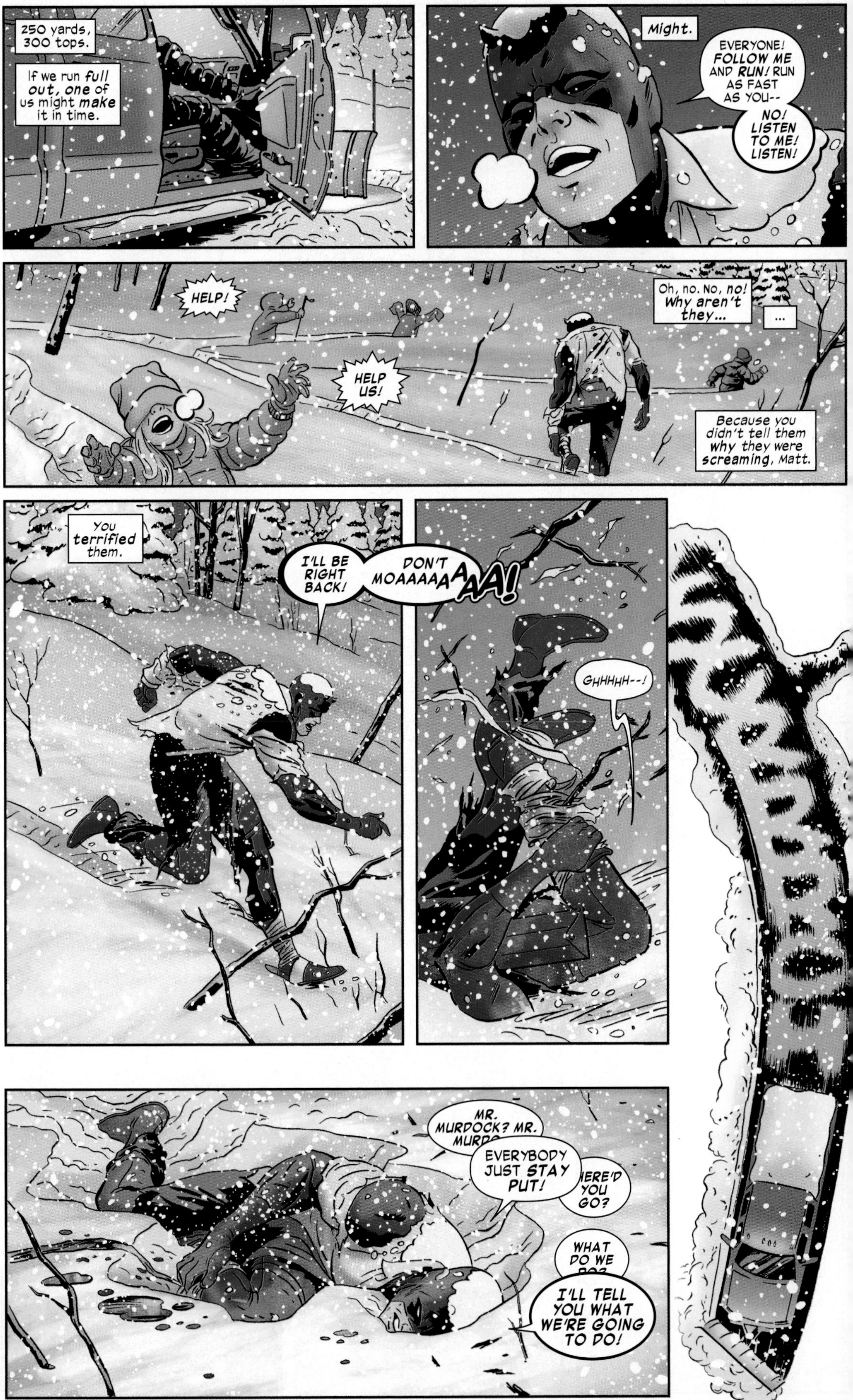

250 yards, 300 tops.
If we run *full out*, *one* of us might *make* it in time.
Might.
EVERYONE! **FOLLOW ME** AND **RUN!** RUN AS FAST AS YOU--
NO! LISTEN TO ME! LISTEN!
HELP!
Oh, no. No, *no!* *Why aren't they...*
...
HELP US!
Because you didn't tell them **why** they were *screaming*, Matt.
You *terrified* them.
I'LL BE RIGHT BACK!
DON'T MOAAAAAAAA!
GHHHHH--!
MR. MURDOCK? MR.
EVERYBODY JUST **STAY** PUT!
ERE'D YOU GO?
WHAT DO WE
I'LL TELL YOU WHAT WE'RE GOING TO DO!

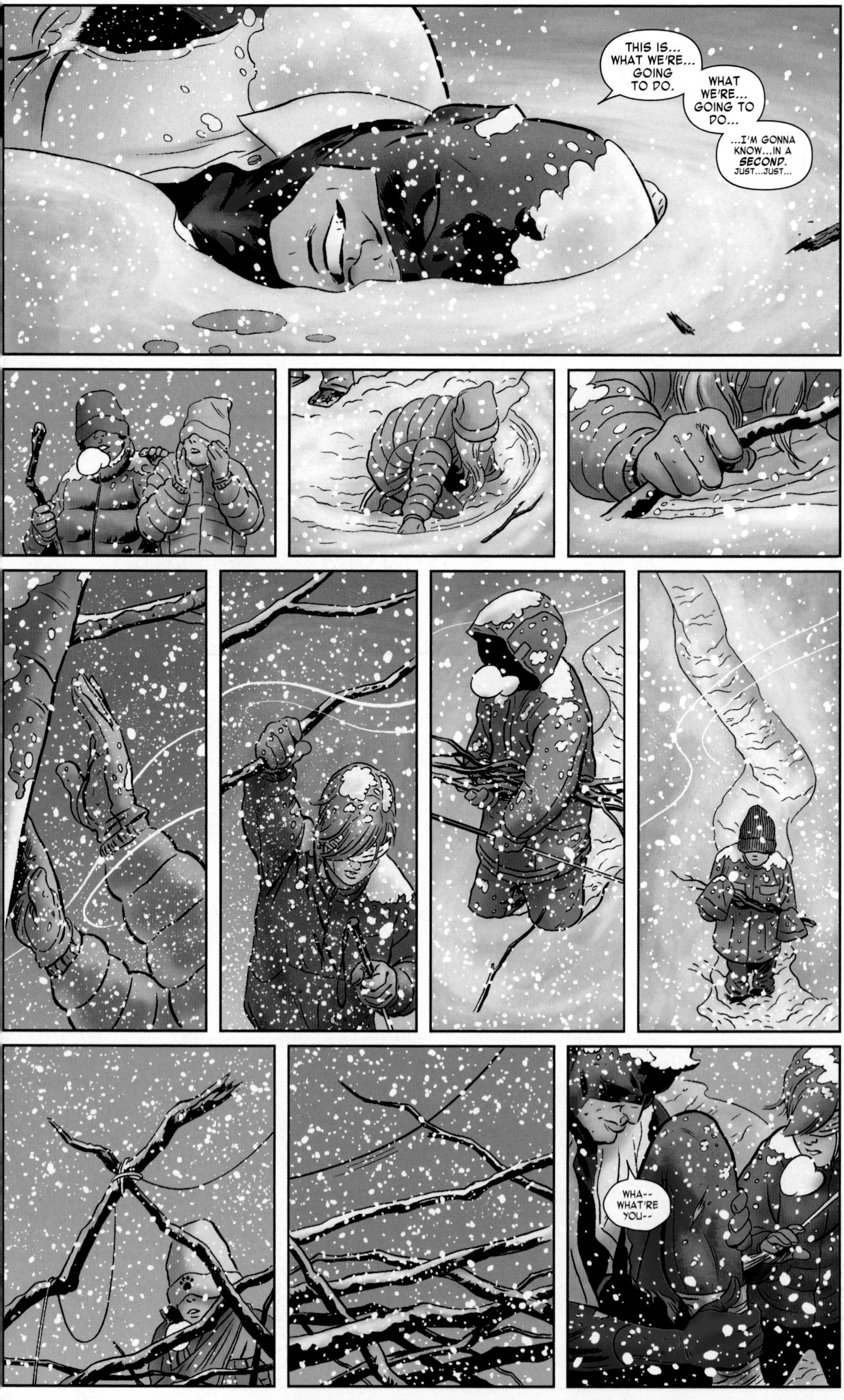
THIS IS... WHAT WE'RE... GOING TO DO.
WHAT WE'RE... GOING TO DO...
...I'M GONNA KNOW...IN A SECOND. JUST...JUST...
WHA-- WHAT'RE YOU--

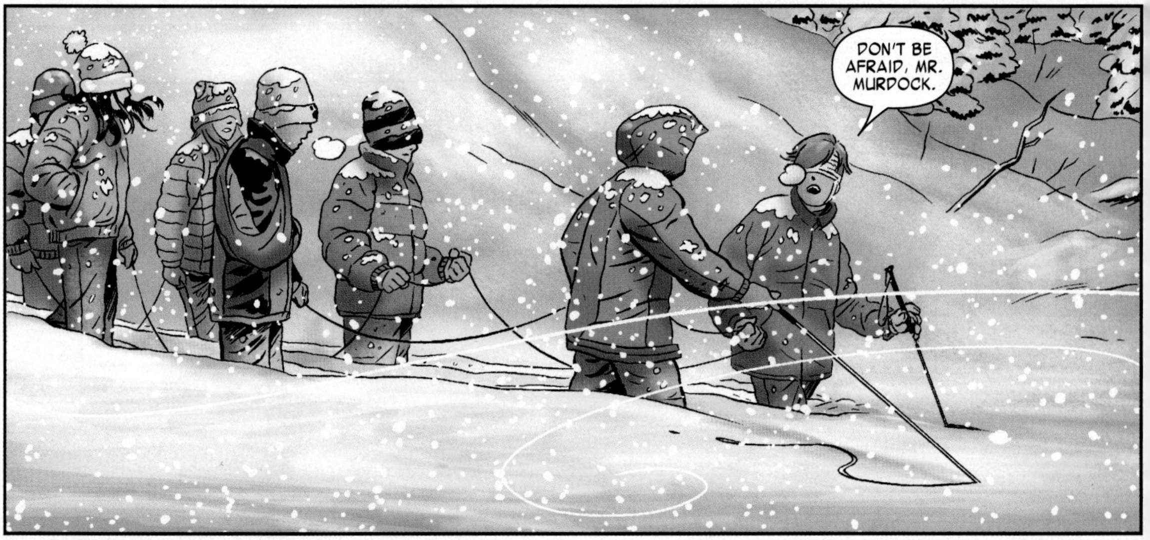
DON'T BE AFRAID, MR. MURDOCK.

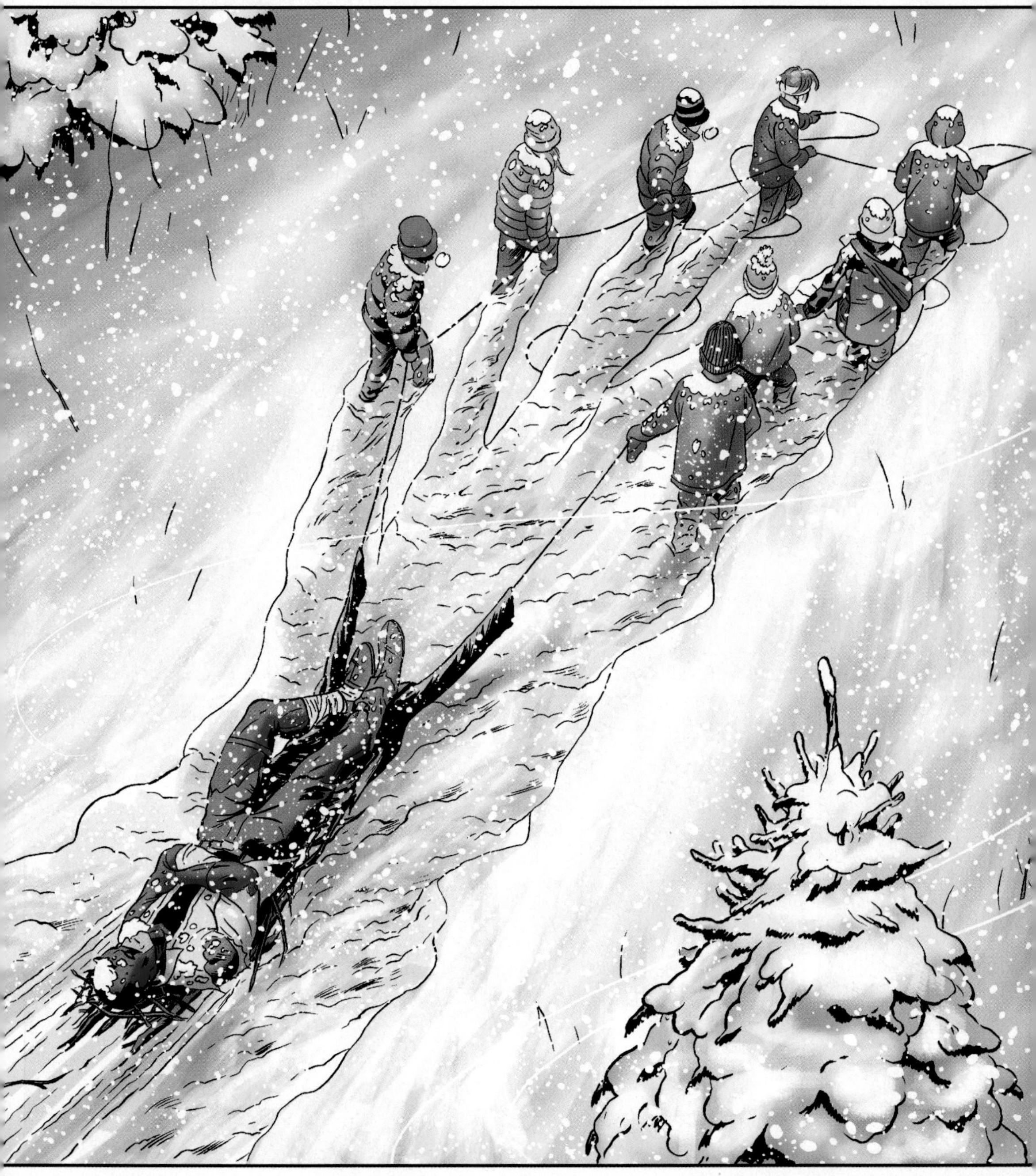

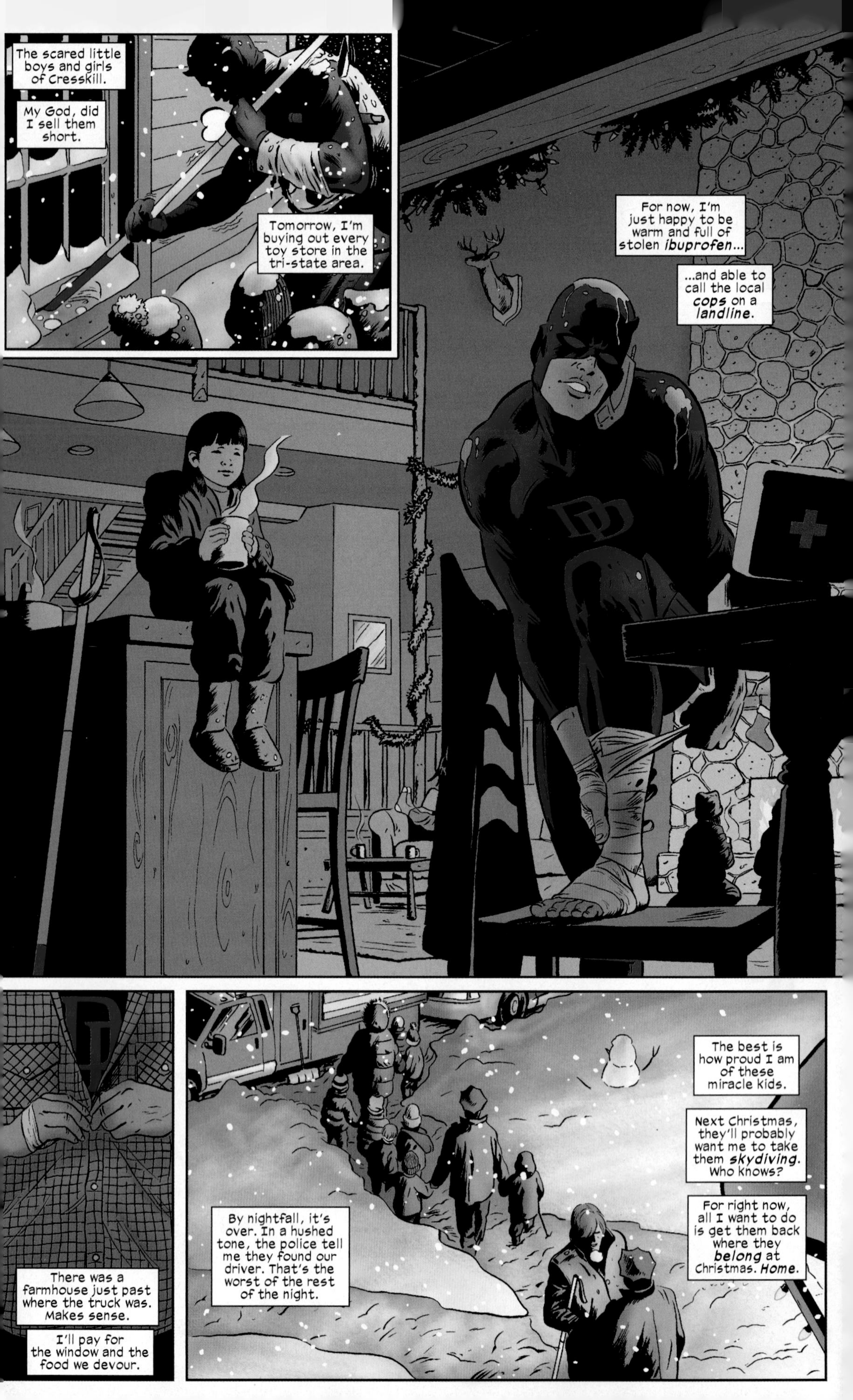
The scared little boys and girls of Cresskill.
My God, did I sell them short.
Tomorrow, I'm buying out every toy store in the tri-state area.
For now, I'm just happy to be warm and full of stolen ibuprofen...
...and able to call the local cops on a landline.
There was a farmhouse just past where the truck was. Makes sense.
I'll pay for the window and the food we devour.
By nightfall, it's over. In a hushed tone, the police tell me they found our driver. That's the worst of the rest of the night.
The best is how proud I am of these miracle kids.
Next Christmas, they'll probably want me to take them skydiving. Who knows?
For right now, all I want to do is get them back where they belong at Christmas. Home.

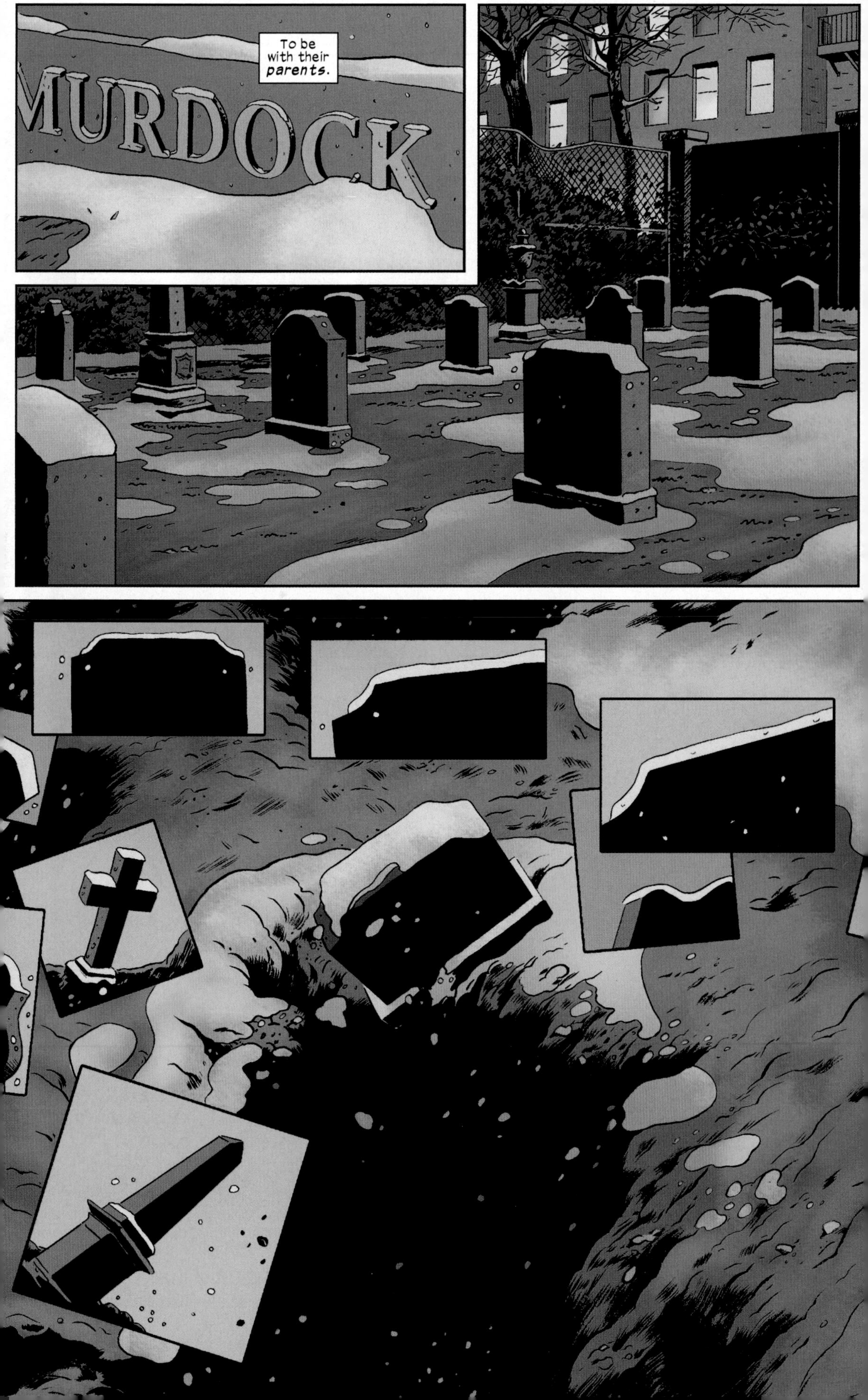
To be with their parents.
MURDOCK

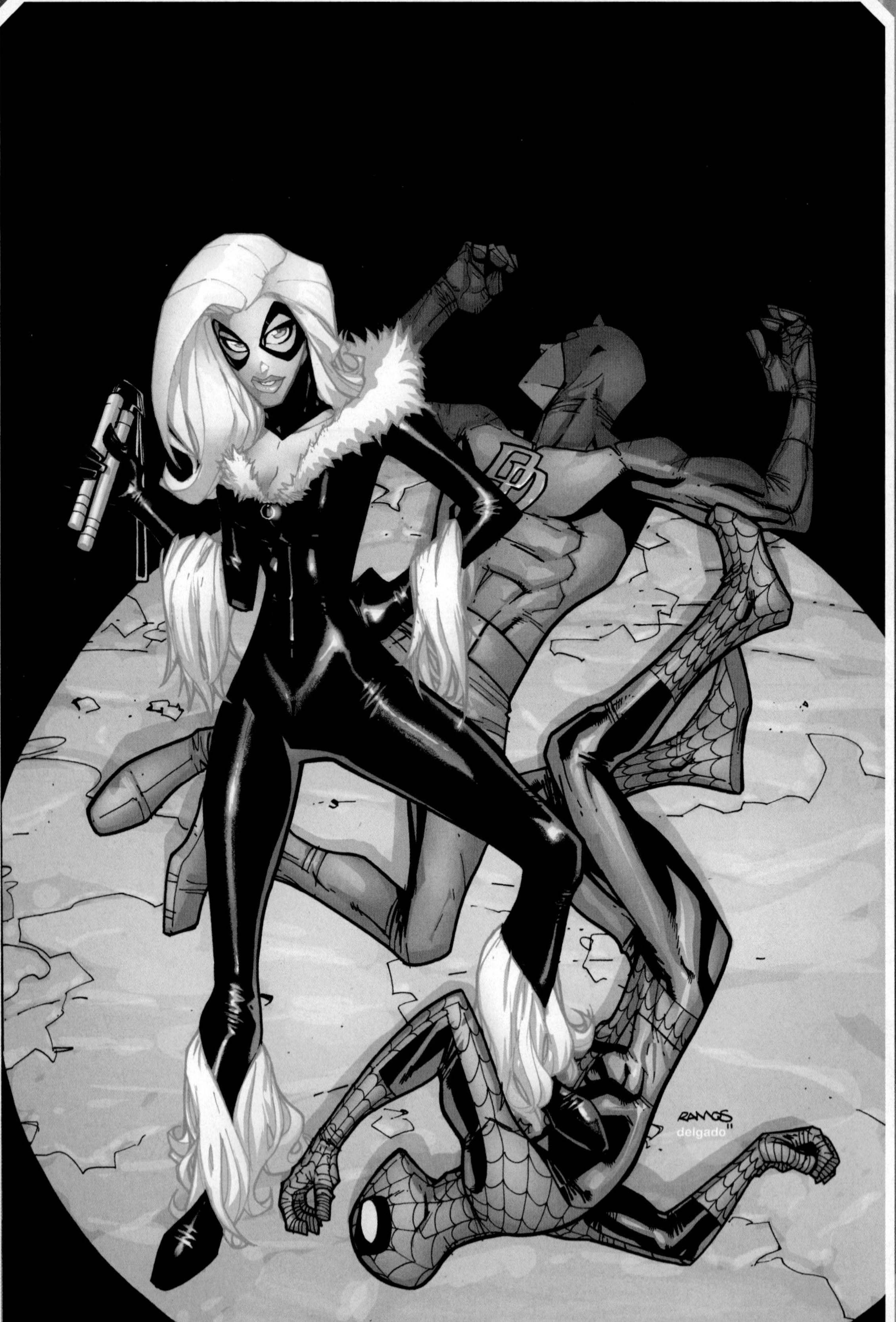
RAMOS '11
delgado

AMAZING SPIDER-MAN #677

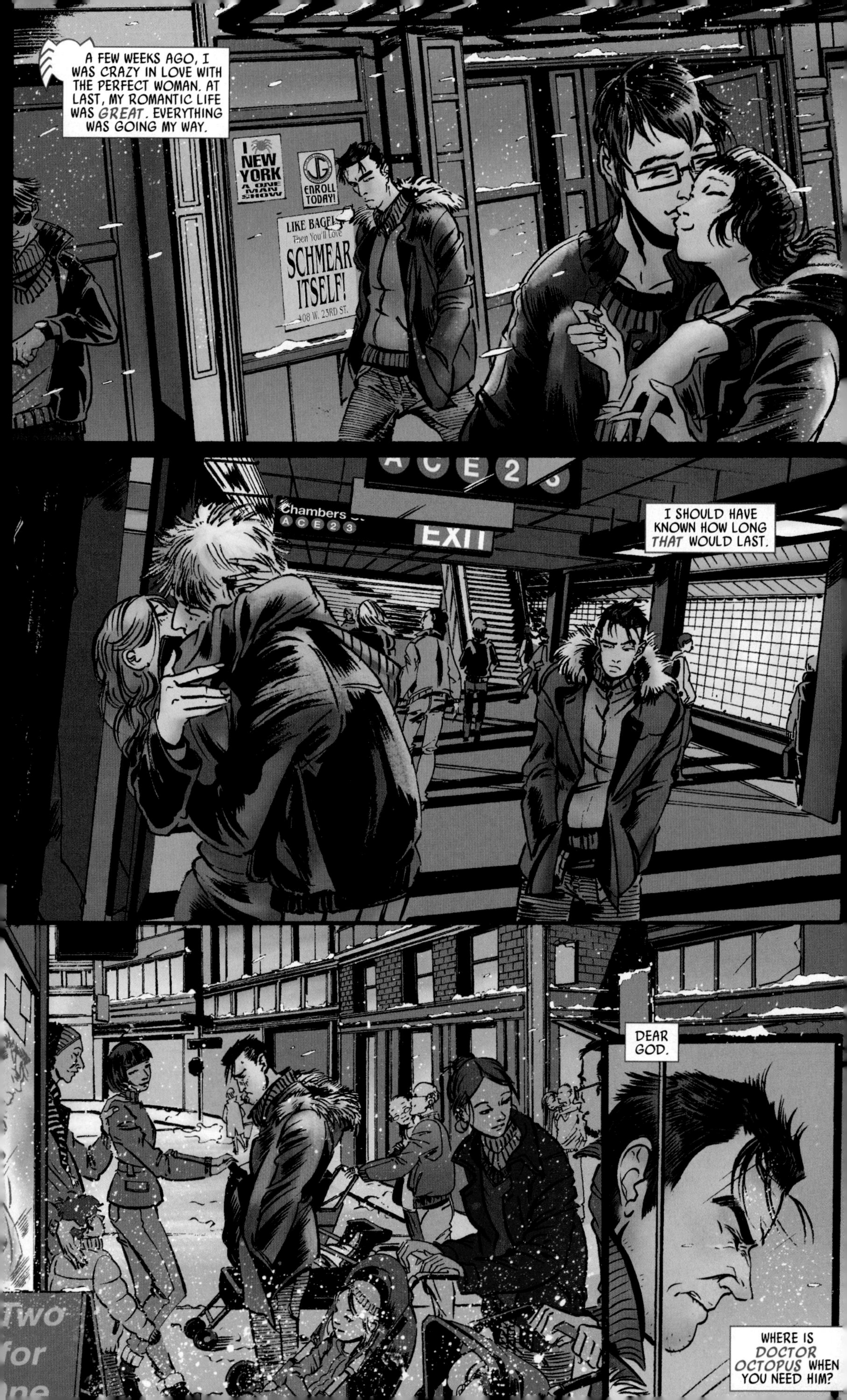
A FEW WEEKS AGO, I WAS CRAZY IN LOVE WITH THE PERFECT WOMAN. AT LAST, MY ROMANTIC LIFE WAS GREAT. EVERYTHING WAS GOING MY WAY.
I NEW YORK A ONE MAN SHOW
ENROLL TODAY!
LIKE BAGELS? Then You'll Love SCHMEAR ITSELF! 408 W. 23RD ST.
Chambers
A C E 2 3
EXIT
I SHOULD HAVE KNOWN HOW LONG THAT WOULD LAST.
DEAR GOD.
WHERE IS DOCTOR OCTOPUS WHEN YOU NEED HIM?

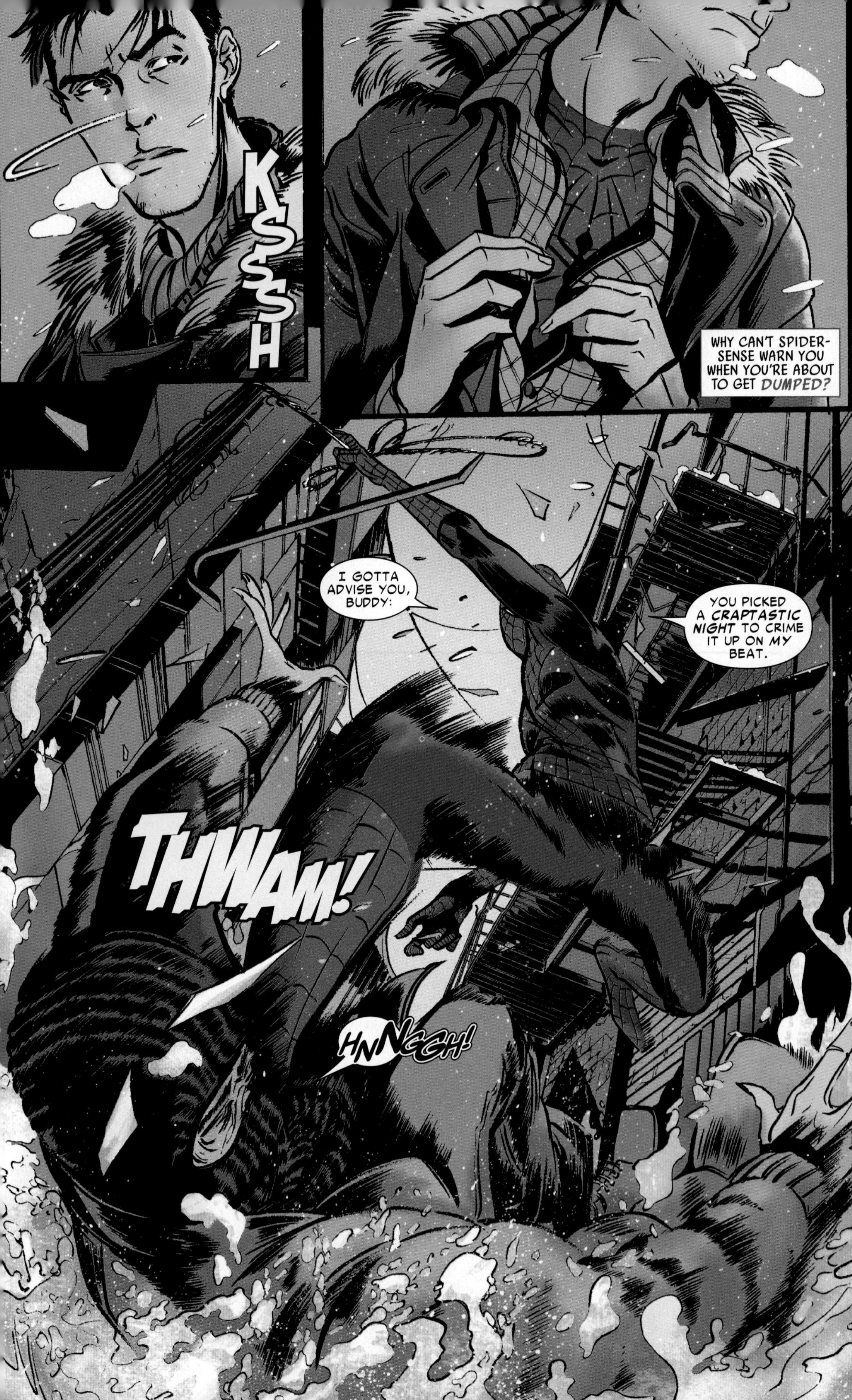
KSSSH
WHY CAN'T SPIDER-SENSE WARN YOU WHEN YOU'RE ABOUT TO GET DUMPED?
I GOTTA ADVISE YOU, BUDDY:
YOU PICKED A CRAPTASTIC NIGHT TO CRIME IT UP ON MY BEAT.
THWAM!
HNNGGH!

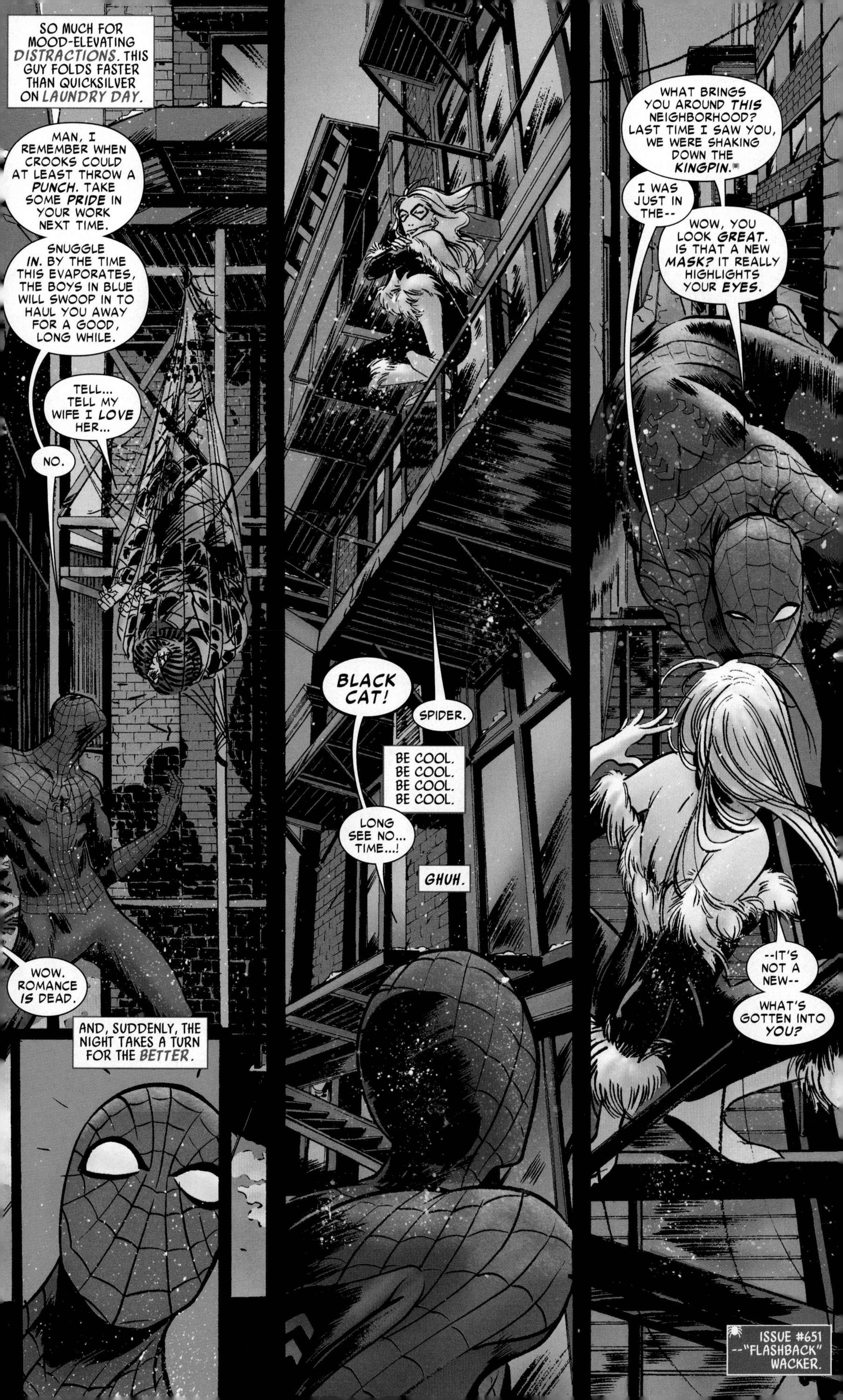
SO MUCH FOR MOOD-ELEVATING DISTRACTIONS. THIS GUY FOLDS FASTER THAN QUICKSILVER ON LAUNDRY DAY.
MAN, I REMEMBER WHEN CROOKS COULD AT LEAST THROW A PUNCH. TAKE SOME PRIDE IN YOUR WORK NEXT TIME.
SNUGGLE IN. BY THE TIME THIS EVAPORATES, THE BOYS IN BLUE WILL SWOOP IN TO HAUL YOU AWAY FOR A GOOD, LONG WHILE.
TELL... TELL MY WIFE I LOVE HER...
NO.
WOW. ROMANCE IS DEAD.
AND, SUDDENLY, THE NIGHT TAKES A TURN FOR THE BETTER.
BLACK CAT!
SPIDER.
BE COOL. BE COOL. BE COOL. BE COOL.
LONG SEE NO... TIME...!
GHUH.
WHAT BRINGS YOU AROUND THIS NEIGHBORHOOD? LAST TIME I SAW YOU, WE WERE SHAKING DOWN THE KINGPIN.
I WAS JUST IN THE--
WOW, YOU LOOK GREAT. IS THAT A NEW MASK? IT REALLY HIGHLIGHTS YOUR EYES.
--IT'S NOT A NEW--
WHAT'S GOTTEN INTO YOU?
ISSUE #651 --"FLASHBACK" WACKER.

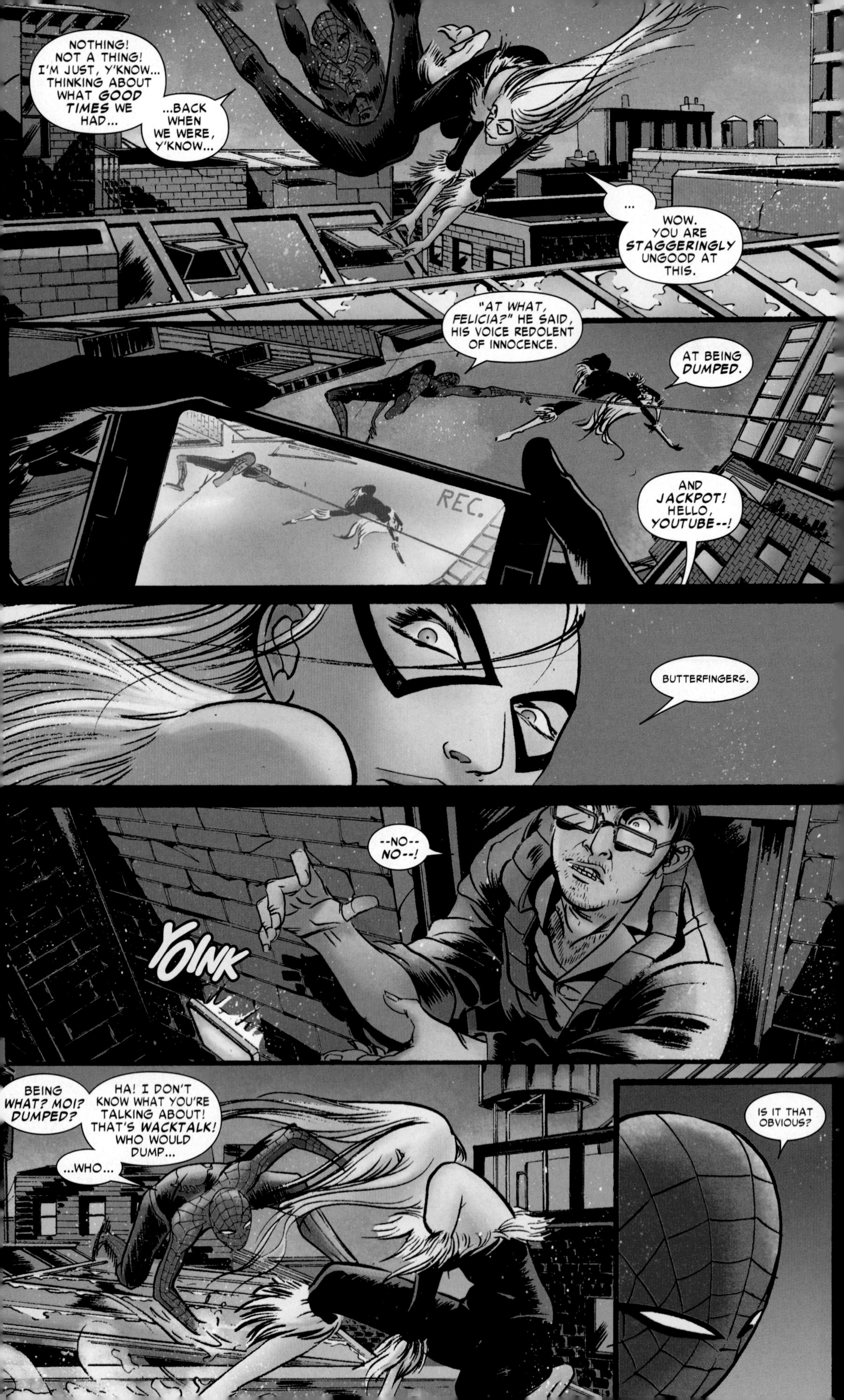
NOTHING! NOT A THING! I'M JUST, Y'KNOW... THINKING ABOUT WHAT GOOD TIMES WE HAD...
...BACK WHEN WE WERE, Y'KNOW...
...
WOW. YOU ARE STAGGERINGLY UNGOOD AT THIS.
"AT WHAT, FELICIA?" HE SAID, HIS VOICE REDOLENT OF INNOCENCE.
AT BEING DUMPED.
REC.
AND JACKPOT! HELLO, YOUTUBE--!
BUTTERFINGERS.
--NO-- NO--!
YOINK
BEING WHAT? MOI? DUMPED?
HA! I DON'T KNOW WHAT YOU'RE TALKING ABOUT! THAT'S WACKTALK! WHO WOULD DUMP...
...WHO...
IS IT THAT OBVIOUS?

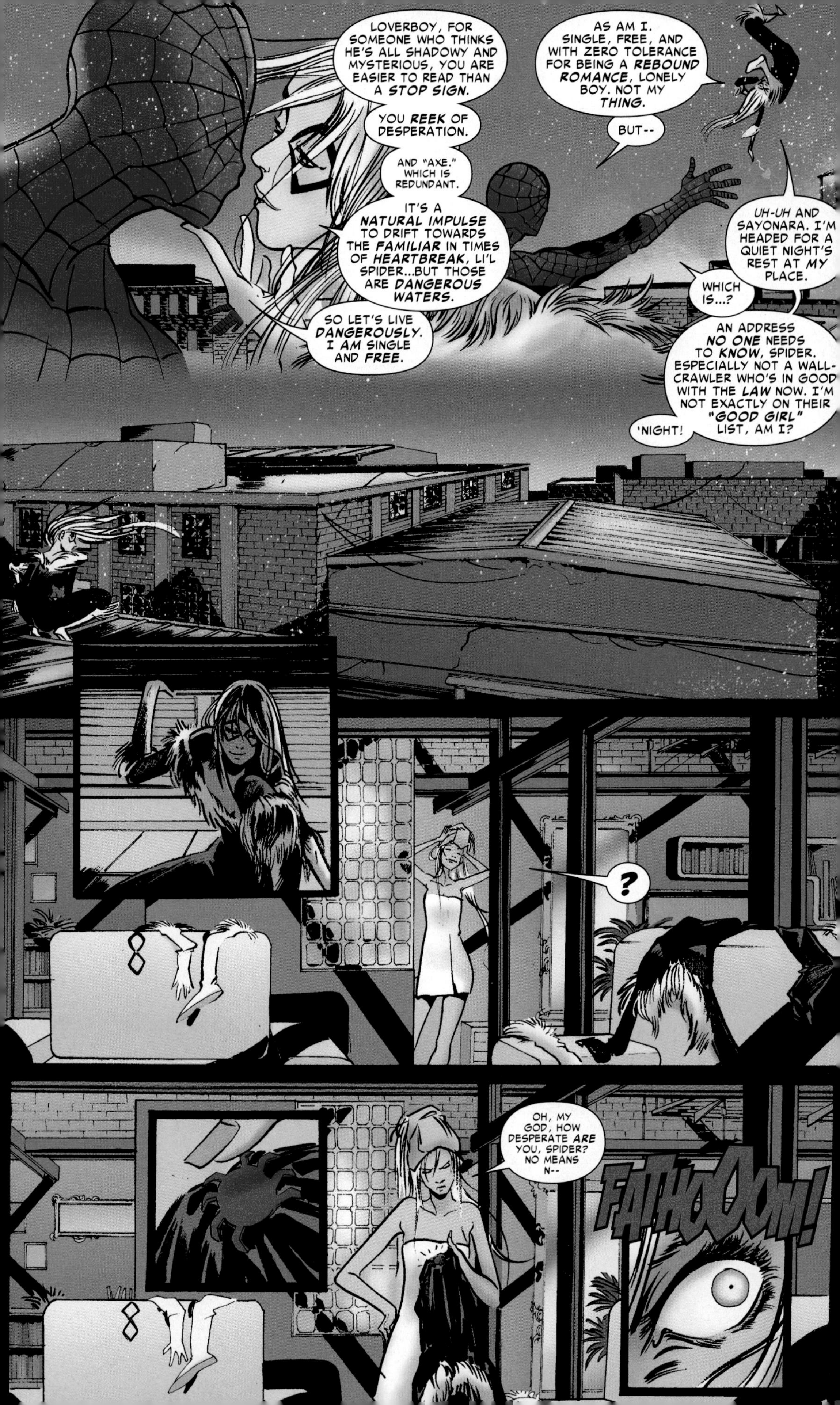

LOVERBOY, FOR SOMEONE WHO THINKS HE'S ALL SHADOWY AND MYSTERIOUS, YOU ARE EASIER TO READ THAN A STOP SIGN.
YOU REEK OF DESPERATION.
AND "AXE." WHICH IS REDUNDANT.
IT'S A NATURAL IMPULSE TO DRIFT TOWARDS THE FAMILIAR IN TIMES OF HEARTBREAK, LI'L SPIDER...BUT THOSE ARE DANGEROUS WATERS.
SO LET'S LIVE DANGEROUSLY. I AM SINGLE AND FREE.
AS AM I. SINGLE, FREE, AND WITH ZERO TOLERANCE FOR BEING A REBOUND ROMANCE, LONELY BOY. NOT MY THING.
BUT--
UH-UH AND SAYONARA. I'M HEADED FOR A QUIET NIGHT'S REST AT MY PLACE.
WHICH IS...?
AN ADDRESS NO ONE NEEDS TO KNOW, SPIDER. ESPECIALLY NOT A WALL-CRAWLER WHO'S IN GOOD WITH THE LAW NOW. I'M NOT EXACTLY ON THEIR "GOOD GIRL" LIST, AM I?
'NIGHT!
?
OH, MY GOD, HOW DESPERATE ARE YOU, SPIDER? NO MEANS N--
FATHOOOM!

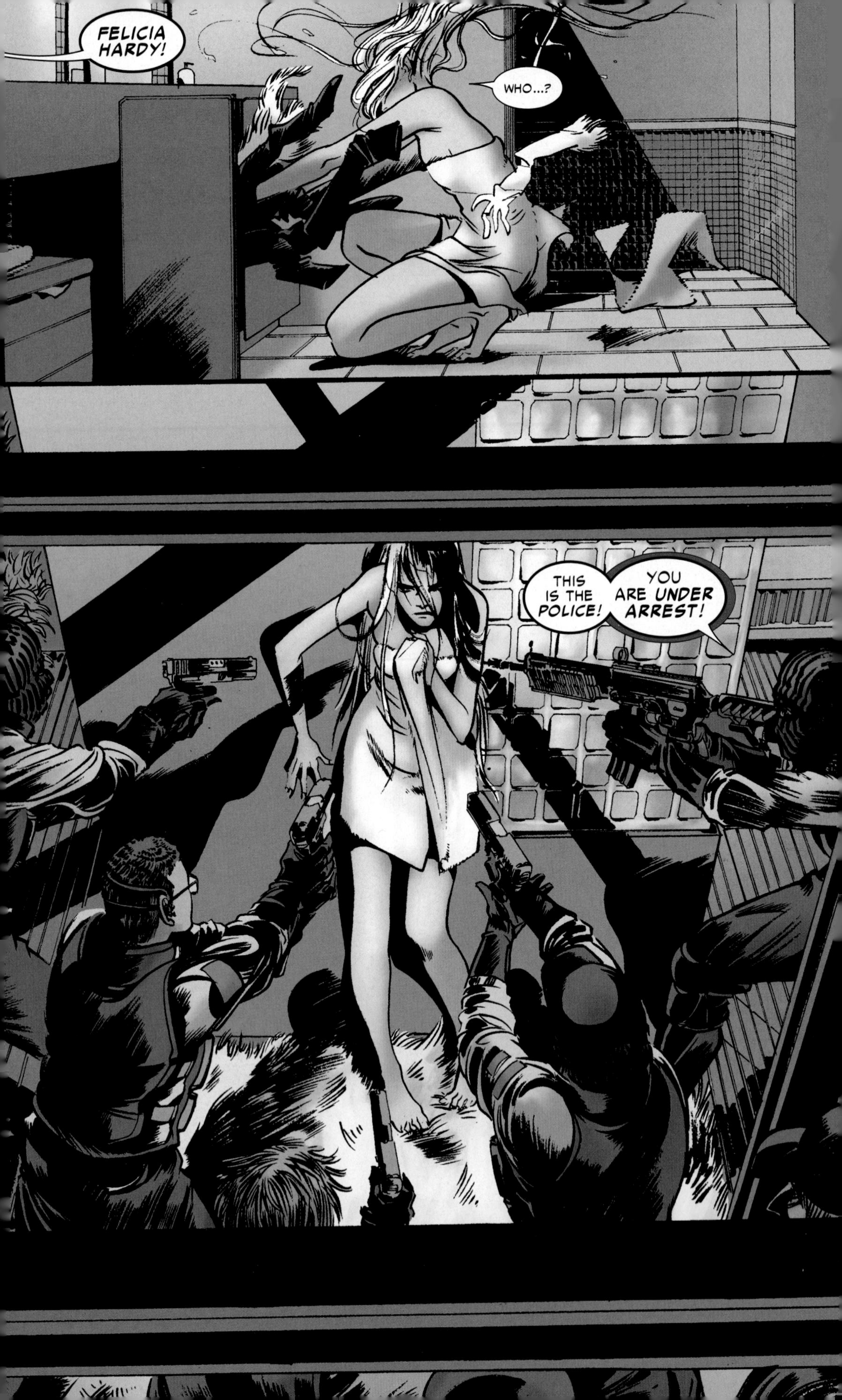
FELICIA HARDY!
WHO...?
THIS IS THE POLICE!
YOU ARE UNDER ARREST!

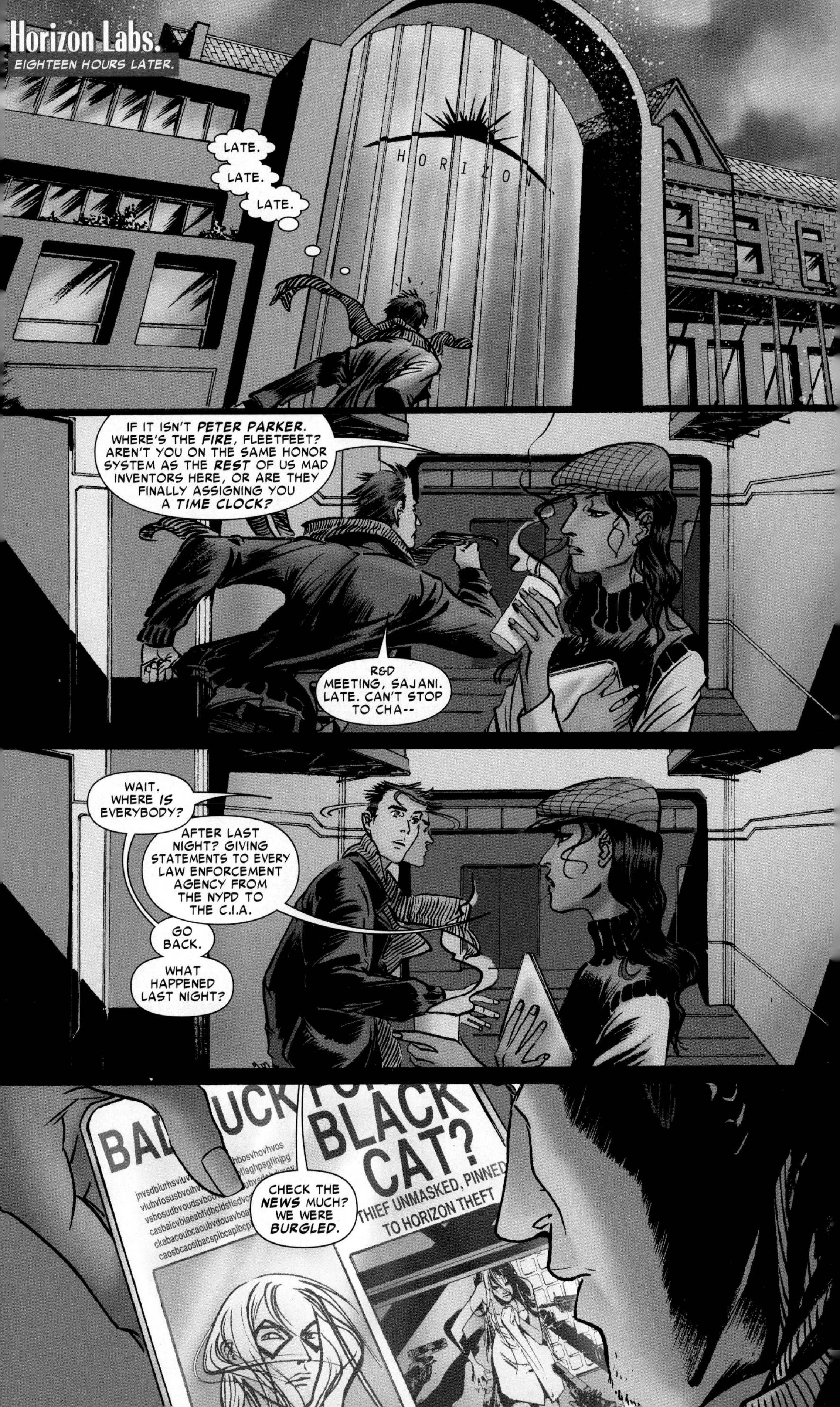

Horizon Labs.
EIGHTEEN HOURS LATER.
HORIZON
LATE.
LATE.
LATE.
IF IT ISN'T PETER PARKER. WHERE'S THE FIRE, FLEETFEET? AREN'T YOU ON THE SAME HONOR SYSTEM AS THE REST OF US MAD INVENTORS HERE, OR ARE THEY FINALLY ASSIGNING YOU A TIME CLOCK?
R&D MEETING, SAJANI. LATE. CAN'T STOP TO CHA--
WAIT. WHERE IS EVERYBODY?
AFTER LAST NIGHT? GIVING STATEMENTS TO EVERY LAW ENFORCEMENT AGENCY FROM THE NYPD TO THE C.I.A.
GO BACK.
WHAT HAPPENED LAST NIGHT?
BLACK CAT?
THIEF UNMASKED, PINNED TO HORIZON THEFT
CHECK THE NEWS MUCH? WE WERE BURGLED.

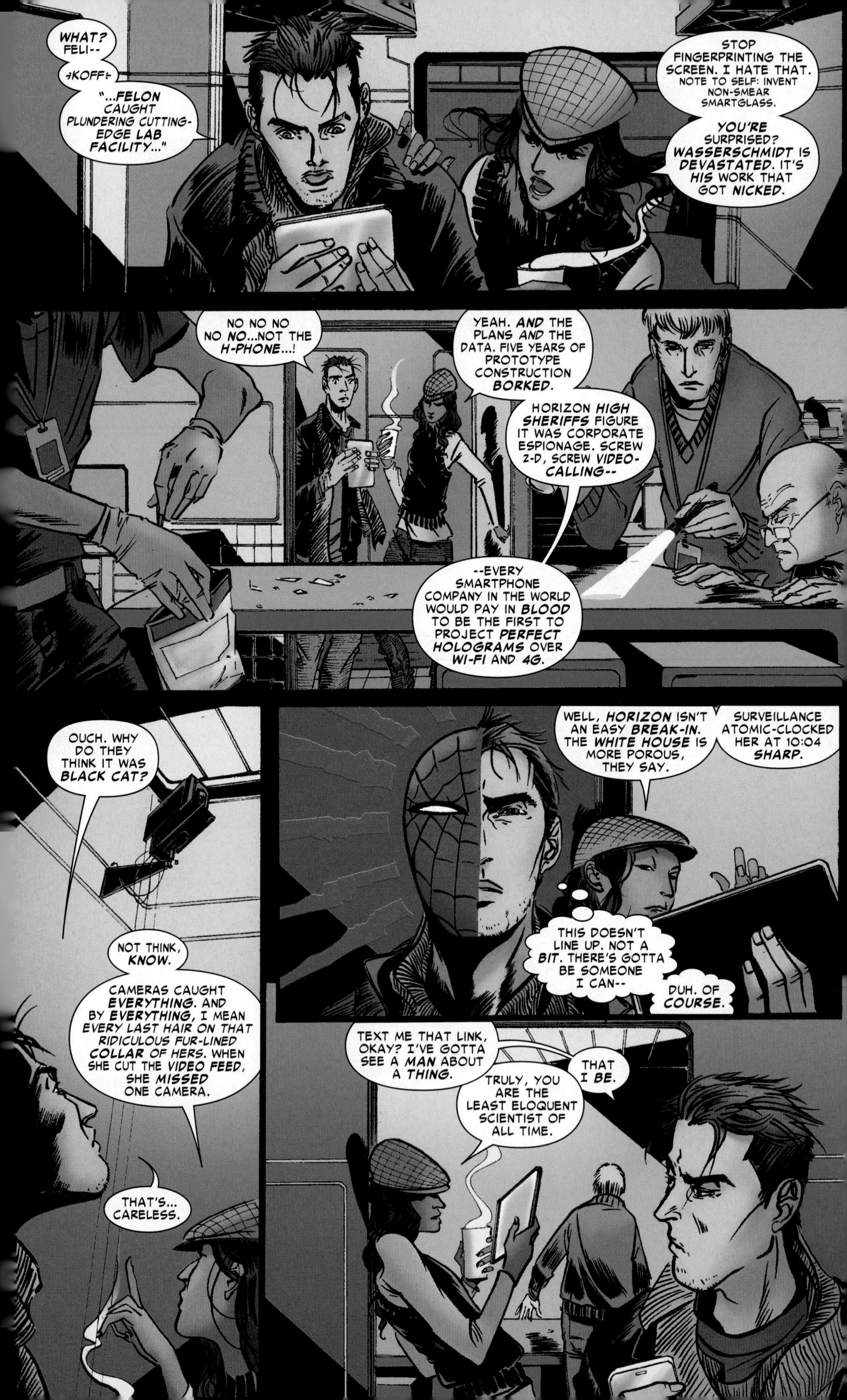
WHAT? FELI--
-KOFF-
"...FELON CAUGHT PLUNDERING CUTTING-EDGE LAB FACILITY..."
STOP FINGERPRINTING THE SCREEN. I HATE THAT. NOTE TO SELF: INVENT NON-SMEAR SMARTGLASS.
YOU'RE SURPRISED? WASSERSCHMIDT IS DEVASTATED. IT'S HIS WORK THAT GOT NICKED.
NO NO NO NO NO...NOT THE H-PHONE...!
YEAH. AND THE PLANS AND THE DATA. FIVE YEARS OF PROTOTYPE CONSTRUCTION BORKED.
HORIZON HIGH SHERIFFS FIGURE IT WAS CORPORATE ESPIONAGE. SCREW 2-D, SCREW VIDEO-CALLING--
--EVERY SMARTPHONE COMPANY IN THE WORLD WOULD PAY IN BLOOD TO BE THE FIRST TO PROJECT PERFECT HOLOGRAMS OVER WI-FI AND 4G.
OUCH. WHY DO THEY THINK IT WAS BLACK CAT?
NOT THINK, KNOW.
CAMERAS CAUGHT EVERYTHING. AND BY EVERYTHING, I MEAN EVERY LAST HAIR ON THAT RIDICULOUS FUR-LINED COLLAR OF HERS. WHEN SHE CUT THE VIDEO FEED, SHE MISSED ONE CAMERA.
THAT'S... CARELESS.
WELL, HORIZON ISN'T AN EASY BREAK-IN. THE WHITE HOUSE IS MORE POROUS, THEY SAY.
SURVEILLANCE ATOMIC-CLOCKED HER AT 10:04 SHARP.
THIS DOESN'T LINE UP. NOT A BIT. THERE'S GOTTA BE SOMEONE I CAN--
DUH. OF COURSE.
TEXT ME THAT LINK, OKAY? I'VE GOTTA SEE A MAN ABOUT A THING.
THAT I BE.
TRULY, YOU ARE THE LEAST ELOQUENT SCIENTIST OF ALL TIME.

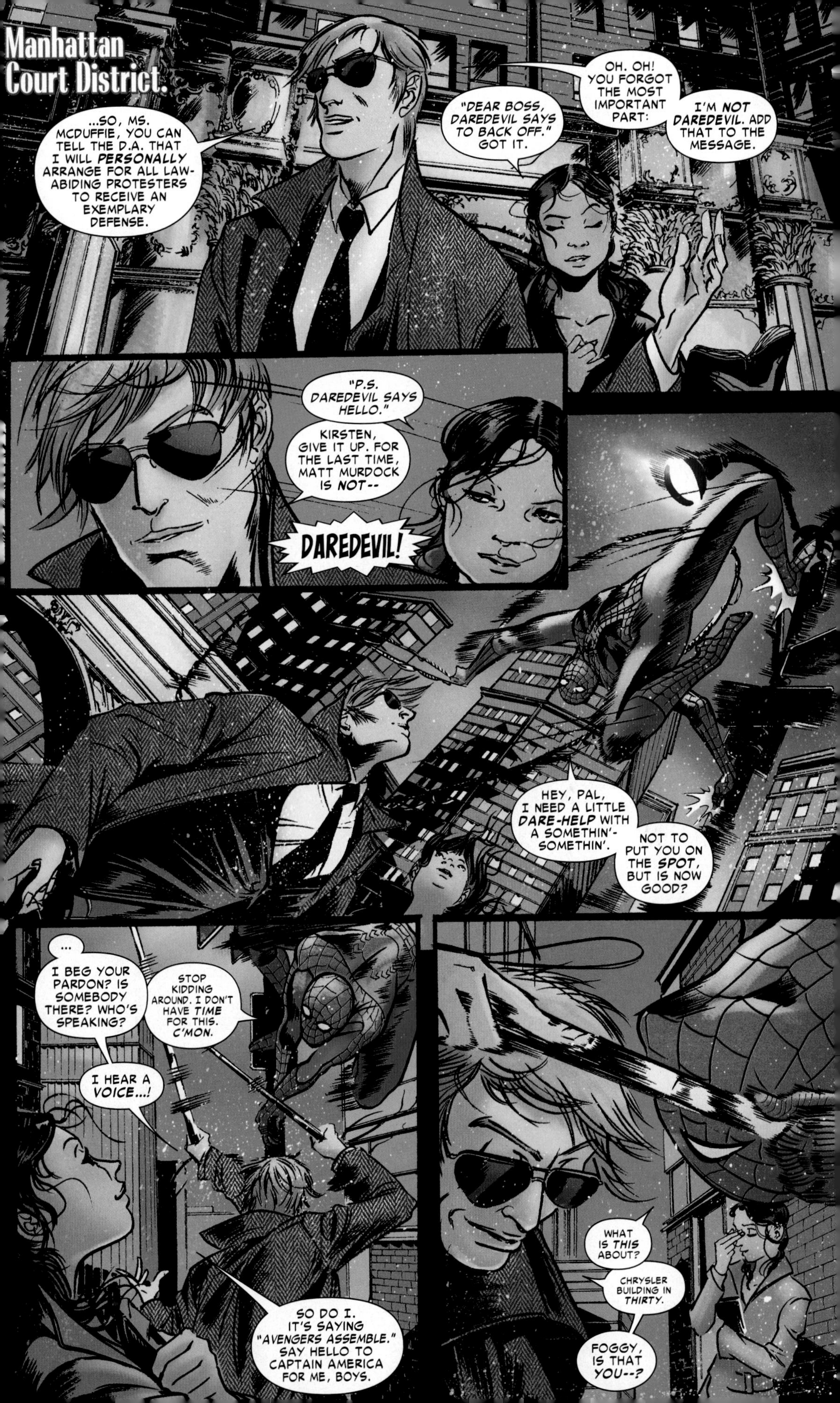
Manhattan Court District.
...SO, MS. MCDUFFIE, YOU CAN TELL THE D.A. THAT I WILL PERSONALLY ARRANGE FOR ALL LAW-ABIDING PROTESTERS TO RECEIVE AN EXEMPLARY DEFENSE.
"DEAR BOSS, DAREDEVIL SAYS TO BACK OFF." GOT IT.
OH. OH! YOU FORGOT THE MOST IMPORTANT PART:
I'M NOT DAREDEVIL. ADD THAT TO THE MESSAGE.
"P.S. DAREDEVIL SAYS HELLO."
KIRSTEN, GIVE IT UP. FOR THE LAST TIME, MATT MURDOCK IS NOT--
DAREDEVIL!
HEY, PAL, I NEED A LITTLE DARE-HELP WITH A SOMETHIN'-SOMETHIN'.
NOT TO PUT YOU ON THE SPOT, BUT IS NOW GOOD?
...
I BEG YOUR PARDON? IS SOMEBODY THERE? WHO'S SPEAKING?
STOP KIDDING AROUND. I DON'T HAVE TIME FOR THIS. C'MON.
I HEAR A VOICE...!
SO DO I. IT'S SAYING "AVENGERS ASSEMBLE." SAY HELLO TO CAPTAIN AMERICA FOR ME, BOYS.
WHAT IS THIS ABOUT?
CHRYSLER BUILDING IN THIRTY.
FOGGY, IS THAT YOU--?

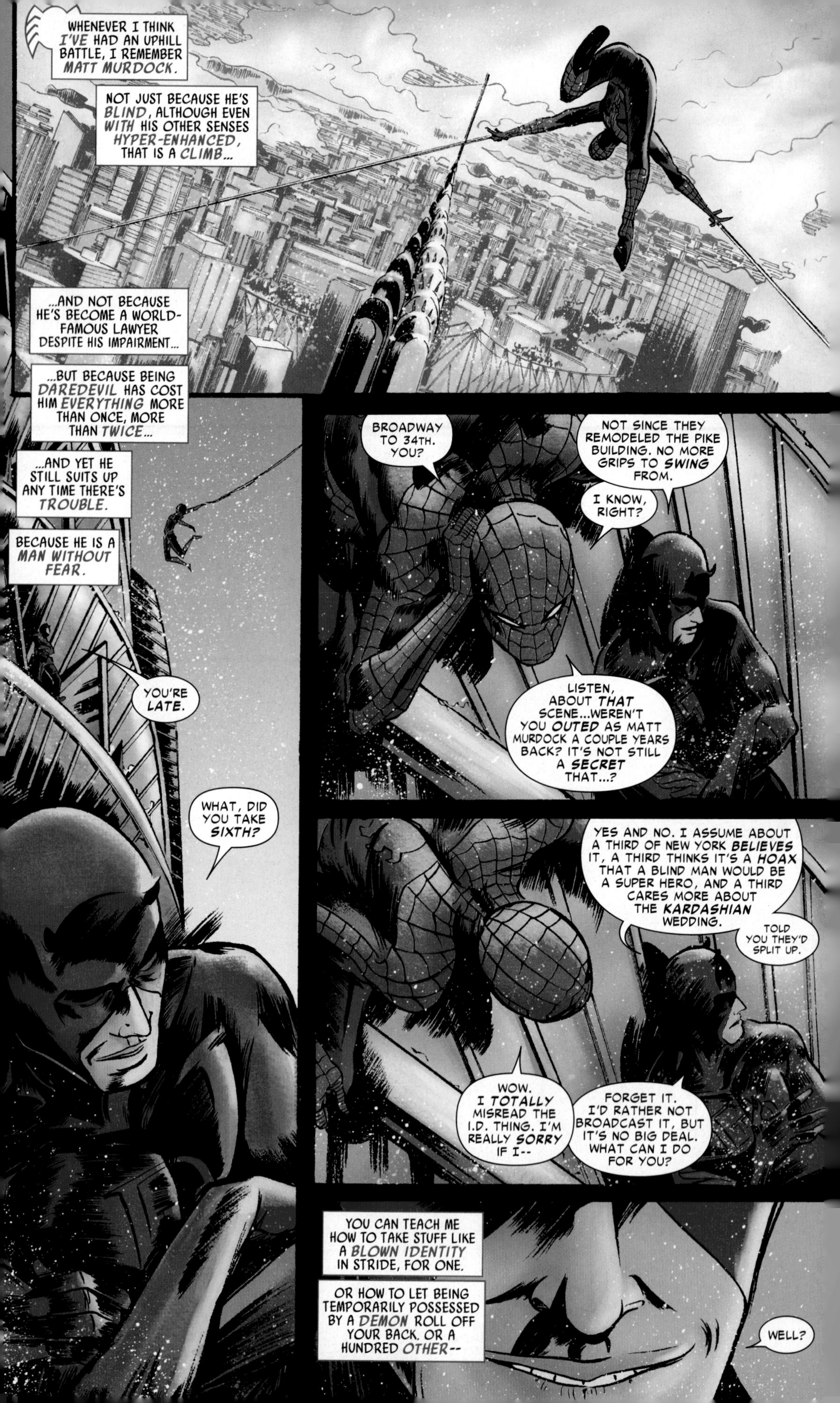

WHENEVER I THINK I'VE HAD AN UPHILL BATTLE, I REMEMBER MATT MURDOCK.
NOT JUST BECAUSE HE'S BLIND, ALTHOUGH EVEN WITH HIS OTHER SENSES HYPER-ENHANCED, THAT IS A CLIMB...
...AND NOT BECAUSE HE'S BECOME A WORLD-FAMOUS LAWYER DESPITE HIS IMPAIRMENT...
...BUT BECAUSE BEING DAREDEVIL HAS COST HIM EVERYTHING MORE THAN ONCE, MORE THAN TWICE...
...AND YET HE STILL SUITS UP ANY TIME THERE'S TROUBLE.
BECAUSE HE IS A MAN WITHOUT FEAR.
YOU'RE LATE.
WHAT, DID YOU TAKE SIXTH?
BROADWAY TO 34TH. YOU?
NOT SINCE THEY REMODELED THE PIKE BUILDING. NO MORE GRIPS TO SWING FROM.
I KNOW, RIGHT?
LISTEN, ABOUT THAT SCENE...WEREN'T YOU OUTED AS MATT MURDOCK A COUPLE YEARS BACK? IT'S NOT STILL A SECRET THAT...?
YES AND NO. I ASSUME ABOUT A THIRD OF NEW YORK BELIEVES IT, A THIRD THINKS IT'S A HOAX THAT A BLIND MAN WOULD BE A SUPER HERO, AND A THIRD CARES MORE ABOUT THE KARDASHIAN WEDDING.
TOLD YOU THEY'D SPLIT UP.
WOW. I TOTALLY MISREAD THE I.D. THING. I'M REALLY SORRY IF I--
FORGET IT. I'D RATHER NOT BROADCAST IT, BUT IT'S NO BIG DEAL. WHAT CAN I DO FOR YOU?
YOU CAN TEACH ME HOW TO TAKE STUFF LIKE A BLOWN IDENTITY IN STRIDE, FOR ONE.
OR HOW TO LET BEING TEMPORARILY POSSESSED BY A DEMON ROLL OFF YOUR BACK. OR A HUNDRED OTHER--
WELL?

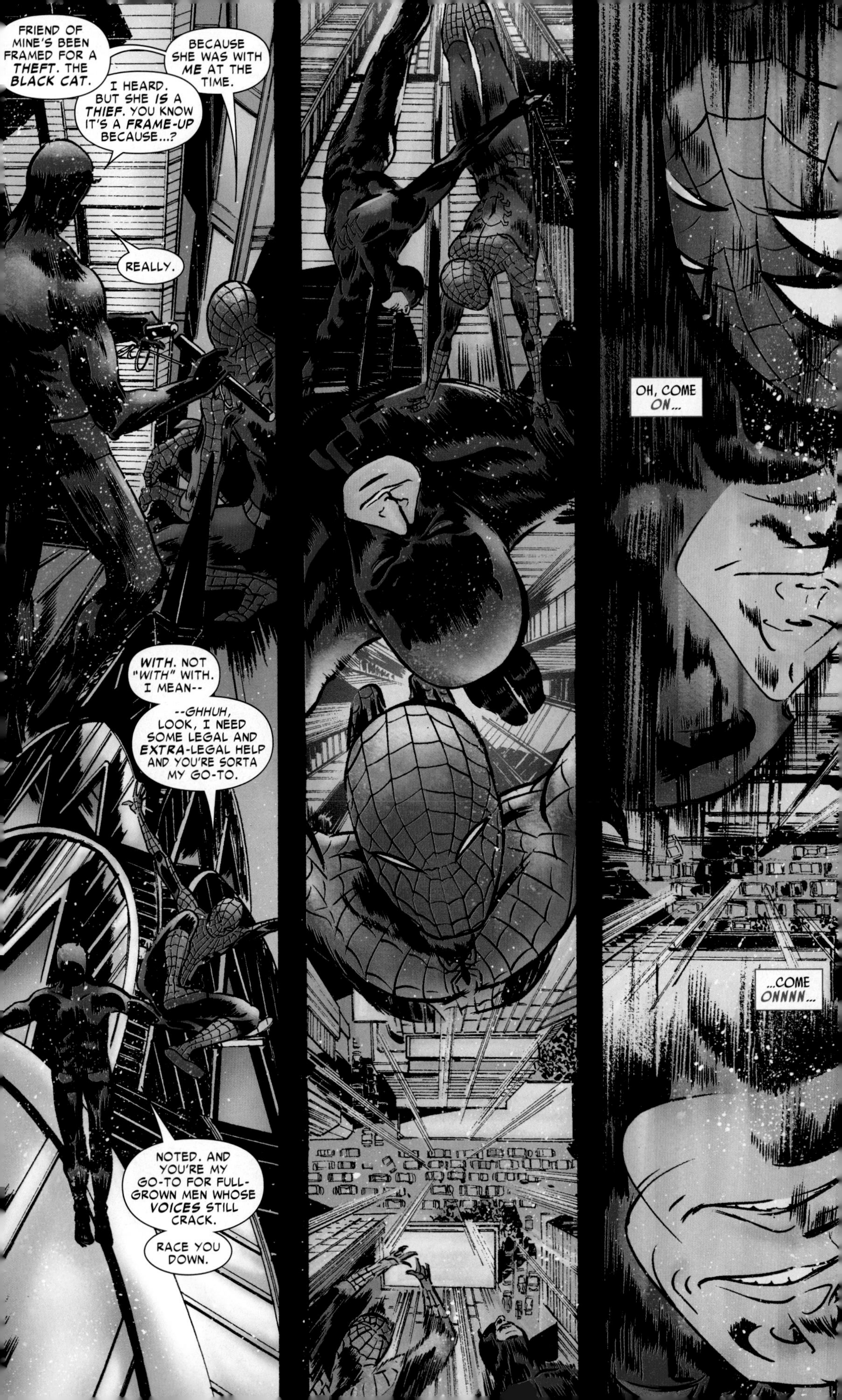
FRIEND OF MINE'S BEEN FRAMED FOR A THEFT. THE BLACK CAT.
I HEARD. BUT SHE IS A THIEF. YOU KNOW IT'S A FRAME-UP BECAUSE...?
BECAUSE SHE WAS WITH ME AT THE TIME.
REALLY.
WITH. NOT "WITH" WITH. I MEAN--
--GHHUH, LOOK, I NEED SOME LEGAL AND EXTRA-LEGAL HELP AND YOU'RE SORTA MY GO-TO.
NOTED. AND YOU'RE MY GO-TO FOR FULL-GROWN MEN WHOSE VOICES STILL CRACK.
RACE YOU DOWN.
OH, COME ON...
...COME ONNNN...

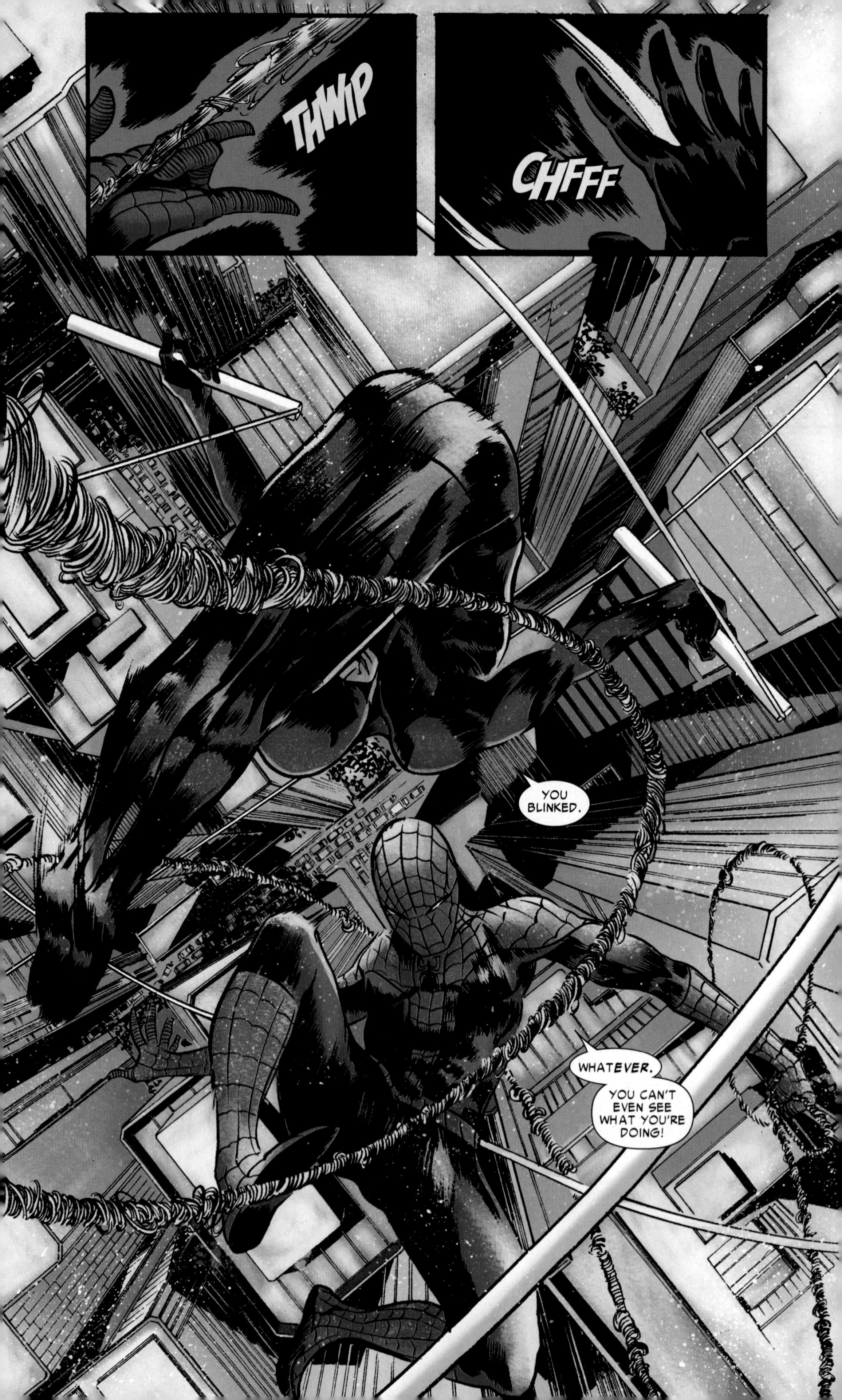
THWIP
CHFFF
YOU BLINKED.
WHATEVER.
YOU CAN'T EVEN SEE WHAT YOU'RE DOING!

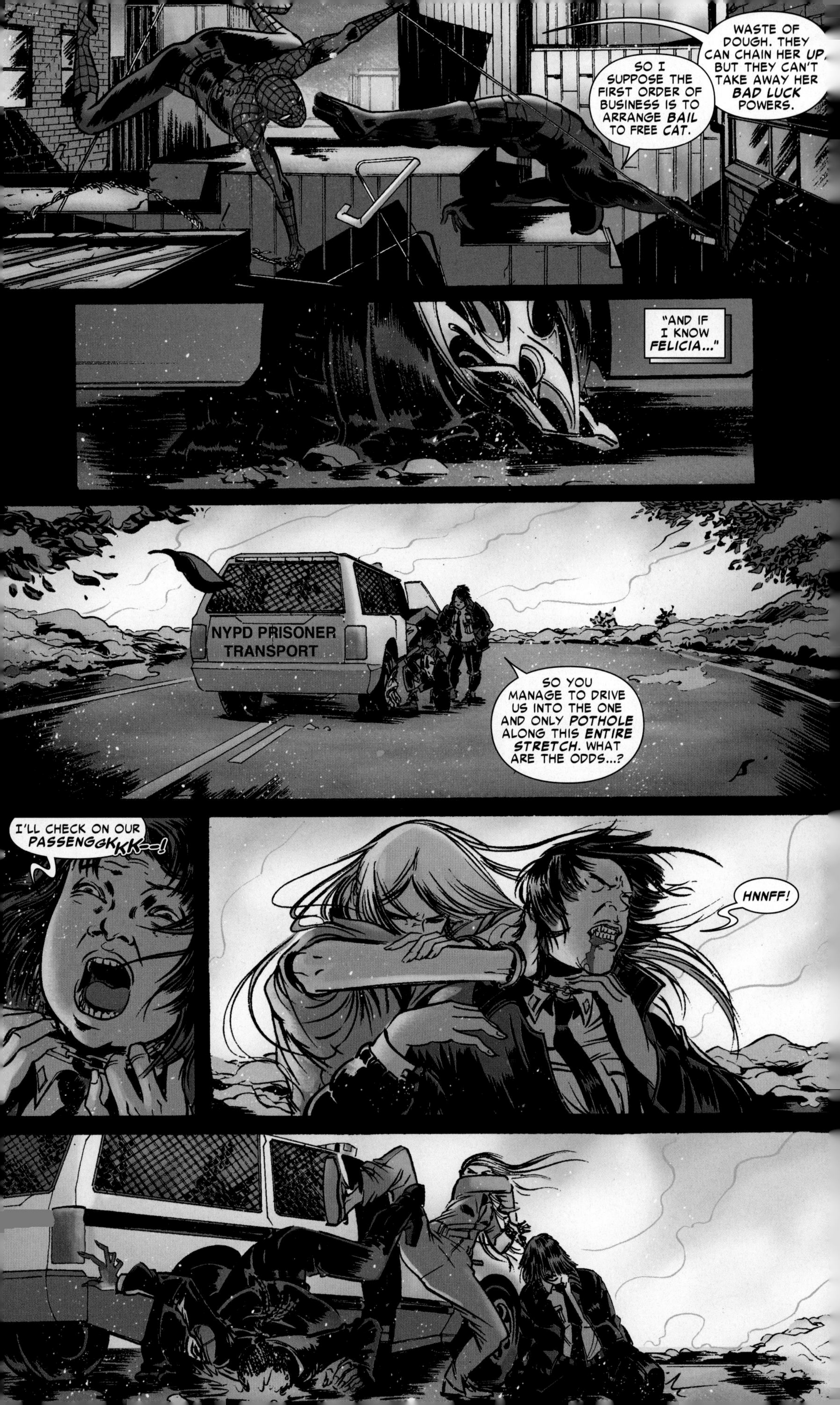
SO I SUPPOSE THE FIRST ORDER OF BUSINESS IS TO ARRANGE BAIL TO FREE CAT.
WASTE OF DOUGH. THEY CAN CHAIN HER UP, BUT THEY CAN'T TAKE AWAY HER BAD LUCK POWERS.
"AND IF I KNOW FELICIA..."
NYPD PRISONER TRANSPORT
SO YOU MANAGE TO DRIVE US INTO THE ONE AND ONLY POTHOLE ALONG THIS ENTIRE STRETCH. WHAT ARE THE ODDS...?
I'LL CHECK ON OUR PASSENGGKKK--!
HNNFF!

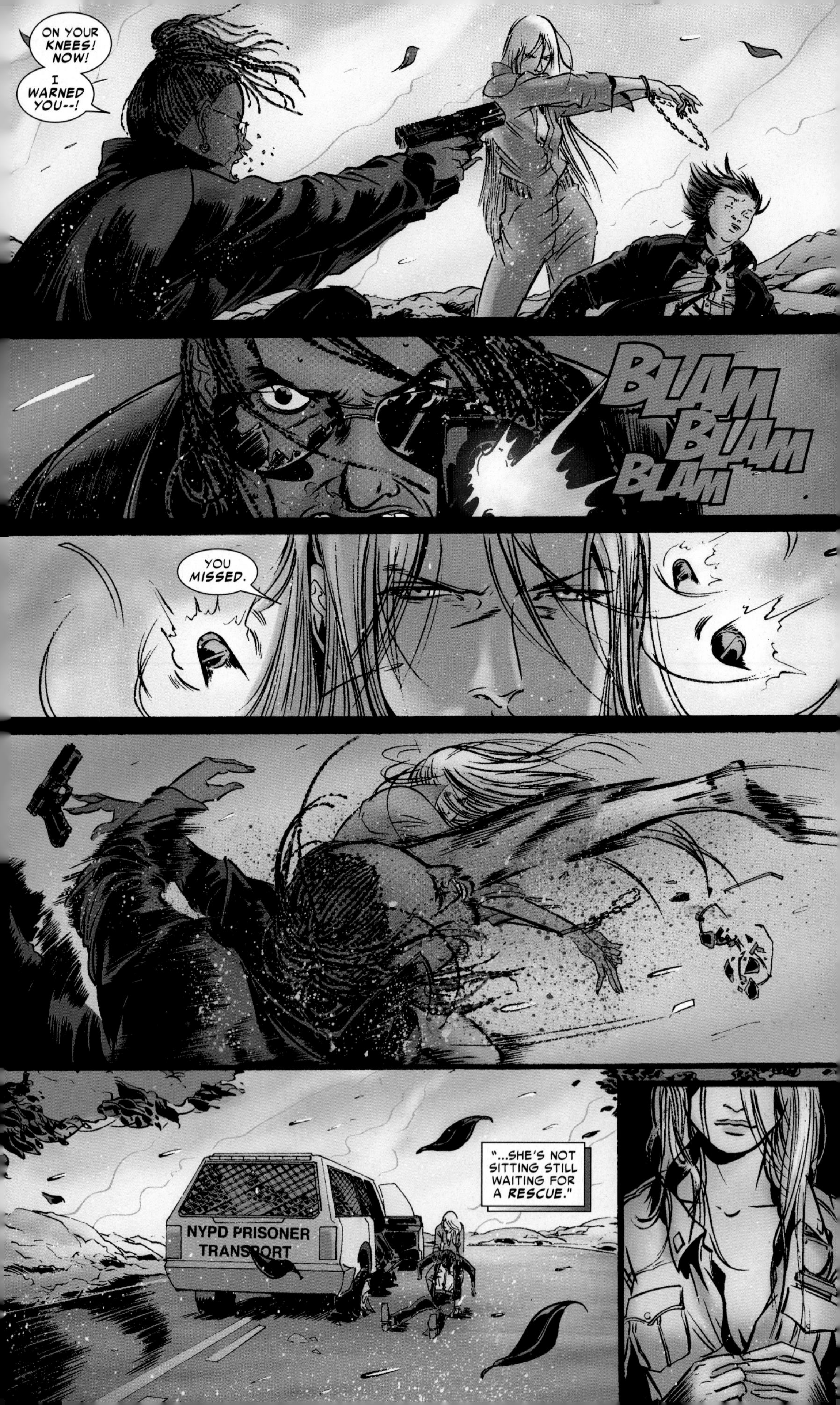
ON YOUR KNEES! NOW!
I WARNED YOU--!
BLAM
BLAM
BLAM
YOU MISSED.
NYPD PRISONER TRANSPORT
"...SHE'S NOT SITTING STILL WAITING FOR A RESCUE."

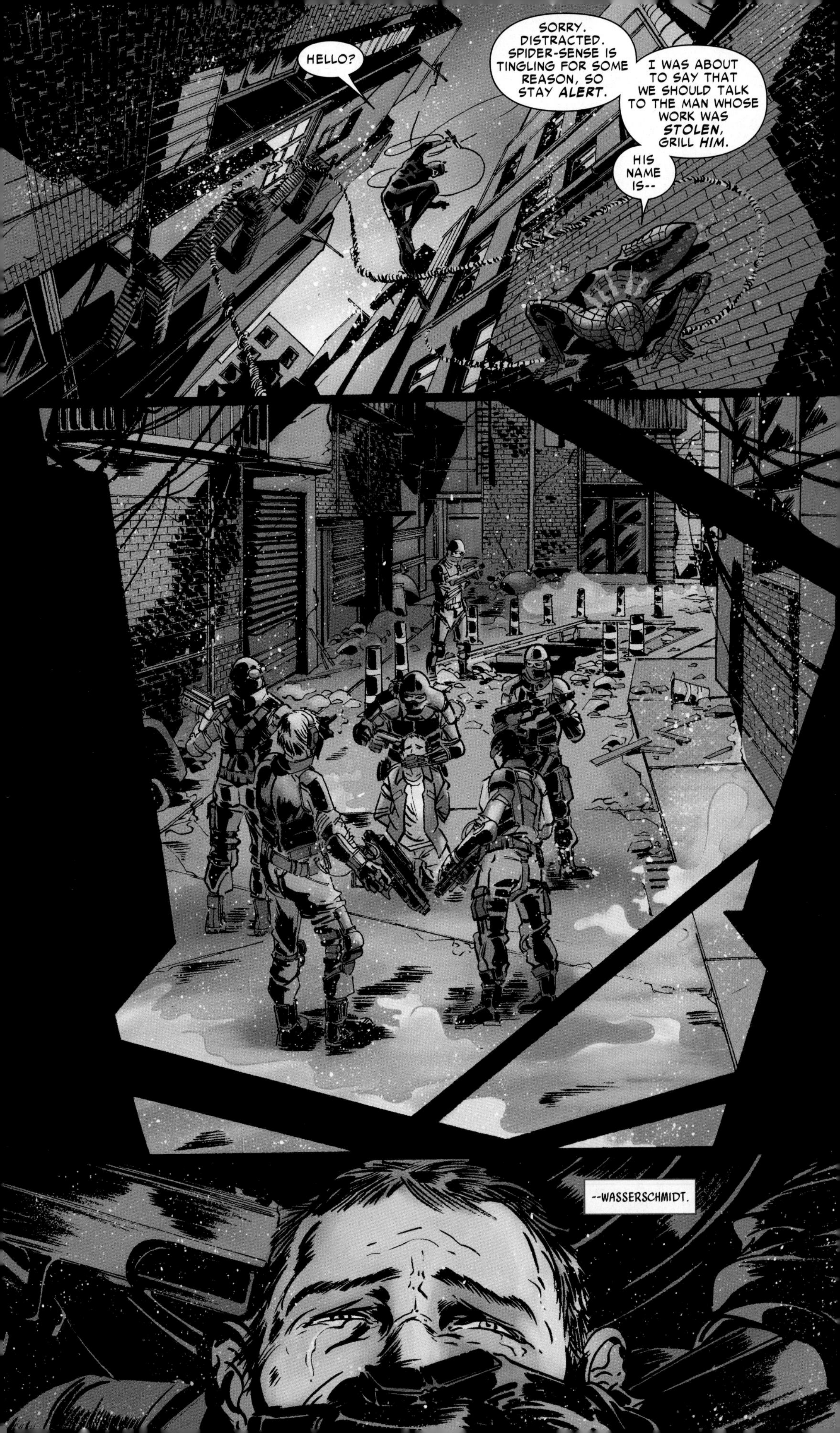
HELLO?
SORRY. DISTRACTED. SPIDER-SENSE IS TINGLING FOR SOME REASON, SO STAY ALERT.
I WAS ABOUT TO SAY THAT WE SHOULD TALK TO THE MAN WHOSE WORK WAS STOLEN, GRILL HIM.
HIS NAME IS--
--WASSERSCHMIDT.

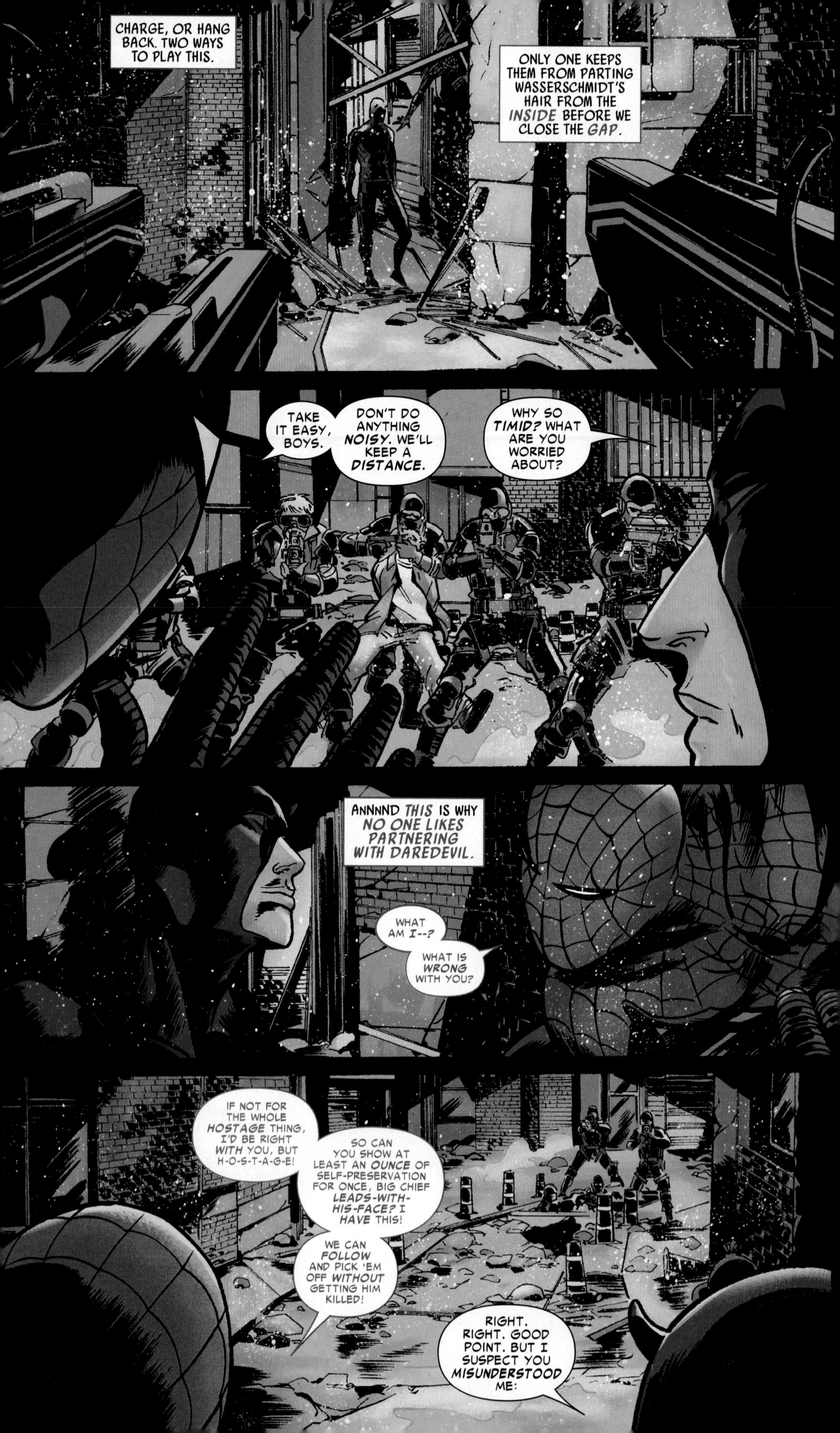
CHARGE, OR HANG BACK. TWO WAYS TO PLAY THIS.
ONLY ONE KEEPS THEM FROM PARTING WASSERSCHMIDT'S HAIR FROM THE INSIDE BEFORE WE CLOSE THE GAP.
TAKE IT EASY, BOYS.
DON'T DO ANYTHING NOISY. WE'LL KEEP A DISTANCE.
WHY SO TIMID? WHAT ARE YOU WORRIED ABOUT?
ANNNND THIS IS WHY NO ONE LIKES PARTNERING WITH DAREDEVIL.
WHAT AM I--?
WHAT IS WRONG WITH YOU?
IF NOT FOR THE WHOLE HOSTAGE THING, I'D BE RIGHT WITH YOU, BUT H-O-S-T-A-G-E!
SO CAN YOU SHOW AT LEAST AN OUNCE OF SELF-PRESERVATION FOR ONCE, BIG CHIEF LEADS-WITH-HIS-FACE? I HAVE THIS!
WE CAN FOLLOW AND PICK 'EM OFF WITHOUT GETTING HIM KILLED!
RIGHT. RIGHT. GOOD POINT. BUT I SUSPECT YOU MISUNDERSTOOD ME:

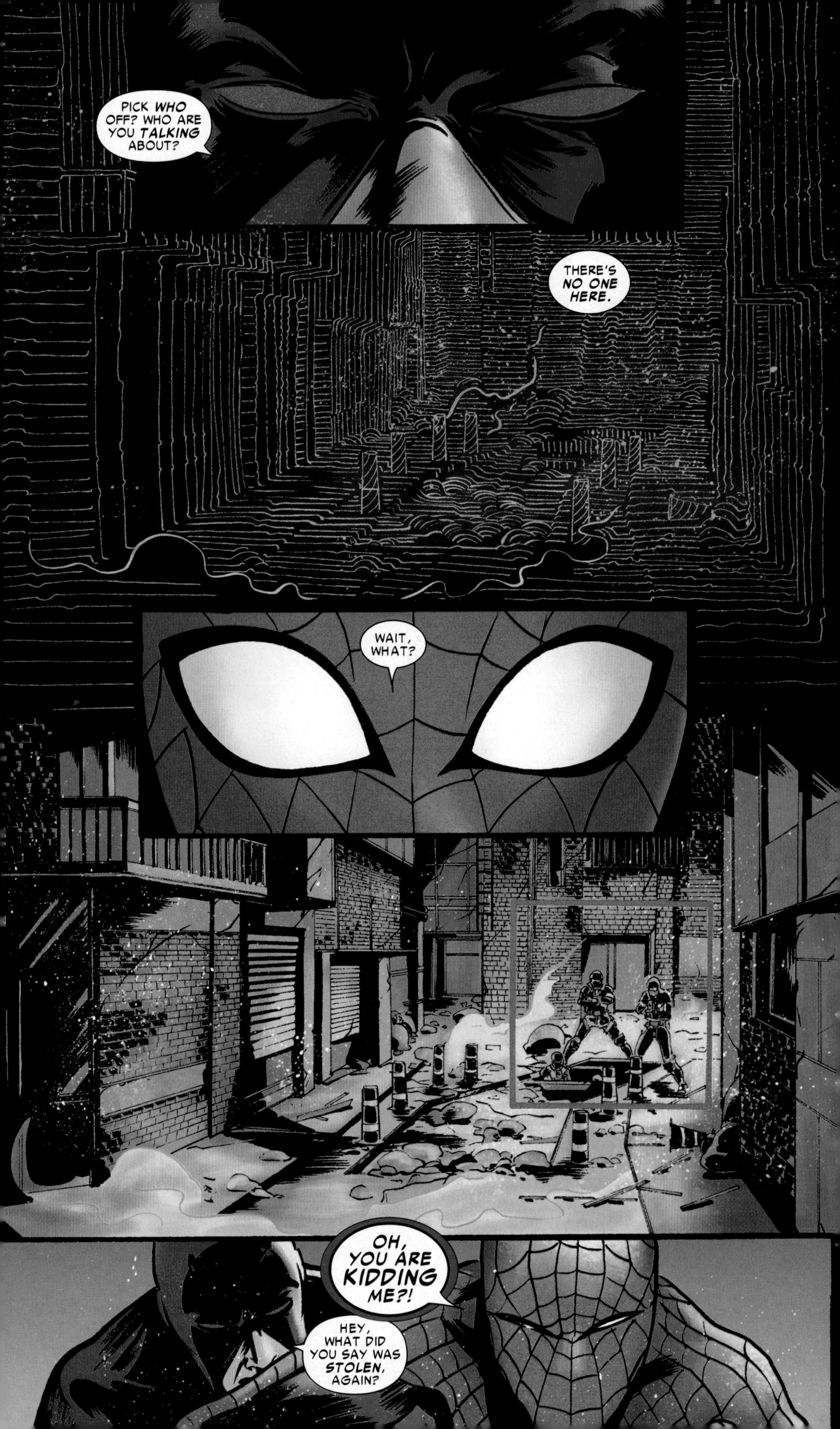
PICK WHO OFF? WHO ARE YOU TALKING ABOUT?
THERE'S NO ONE HERE.
WAIT, WHAT?
OH, YOU ARE KIDDING ME?!
HEY, WHAT DID YOU SAY WAS STOLEN, AGAIN?

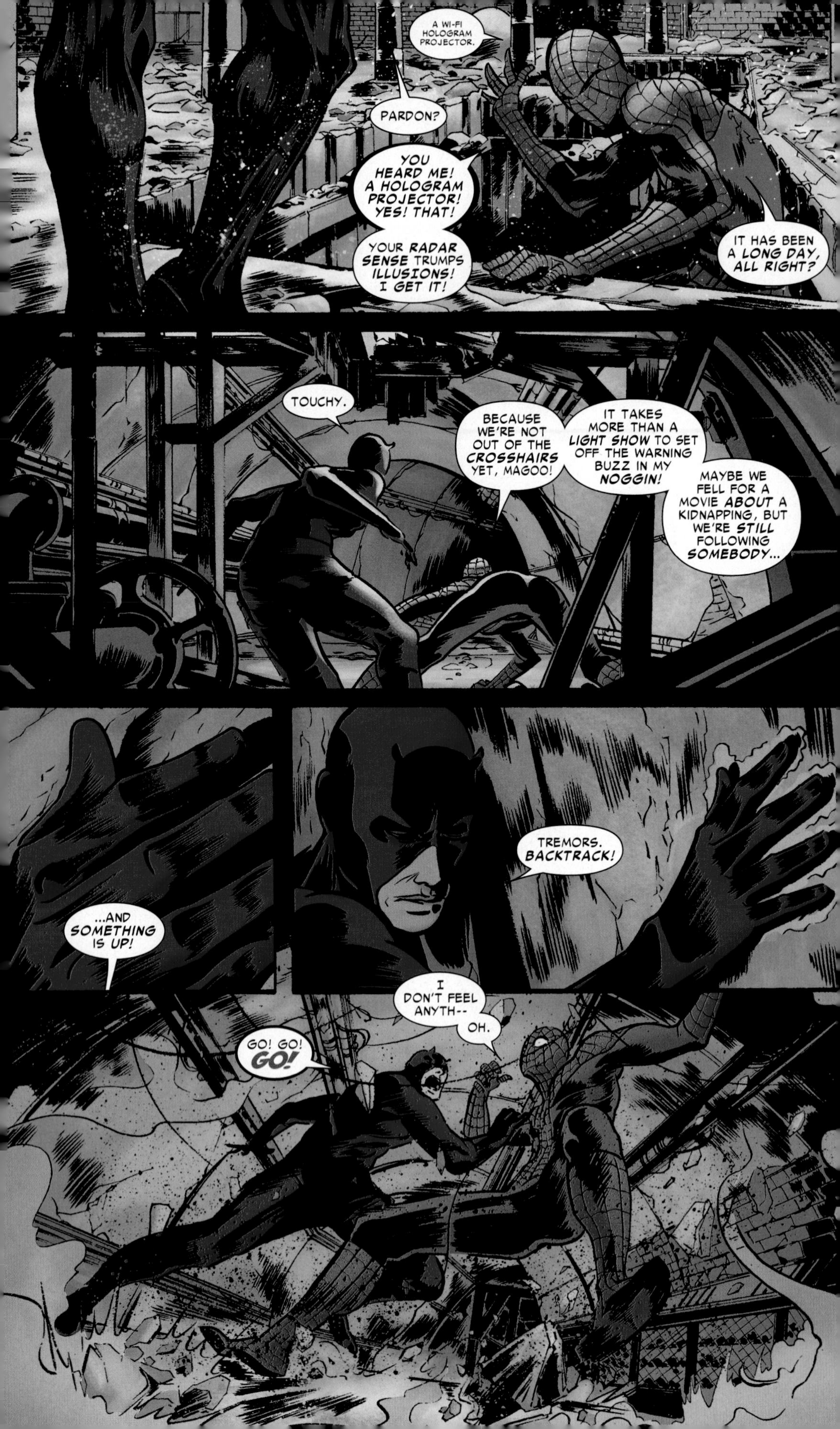

A WI-FI HOLOGRAM PROJECTOR.
PARDON?
YOU HEARD ME! A HOLOGRAM PROJECTOR! YES! THAT!
YOUR RADAR SENSE TRUMPS ILLUSIONS! I GET IT!
IT HAS BEEN A LONG DAY, ALL RIGHT?
TOUCHY.
BECAUSE WE'RE NOT OUT OF THE CROSSHAIRS YET, MAGOO!
IT TAKES MORE THAN A LIGHT SHOW TO SET OFF THE WARNING BUZZ IN MY NOGGIN!
MAYBE WE FELL FOR A MOVIE ABOUT A KIDNAPPING, BUT WE'RE STILL FOLLOWING SOMEBODY...
...AND SOMETHING IS UP!
TREMORS. BACKTRACK!
I DON'T FEEL ANYTH--
OH.
GO! GO! GO!

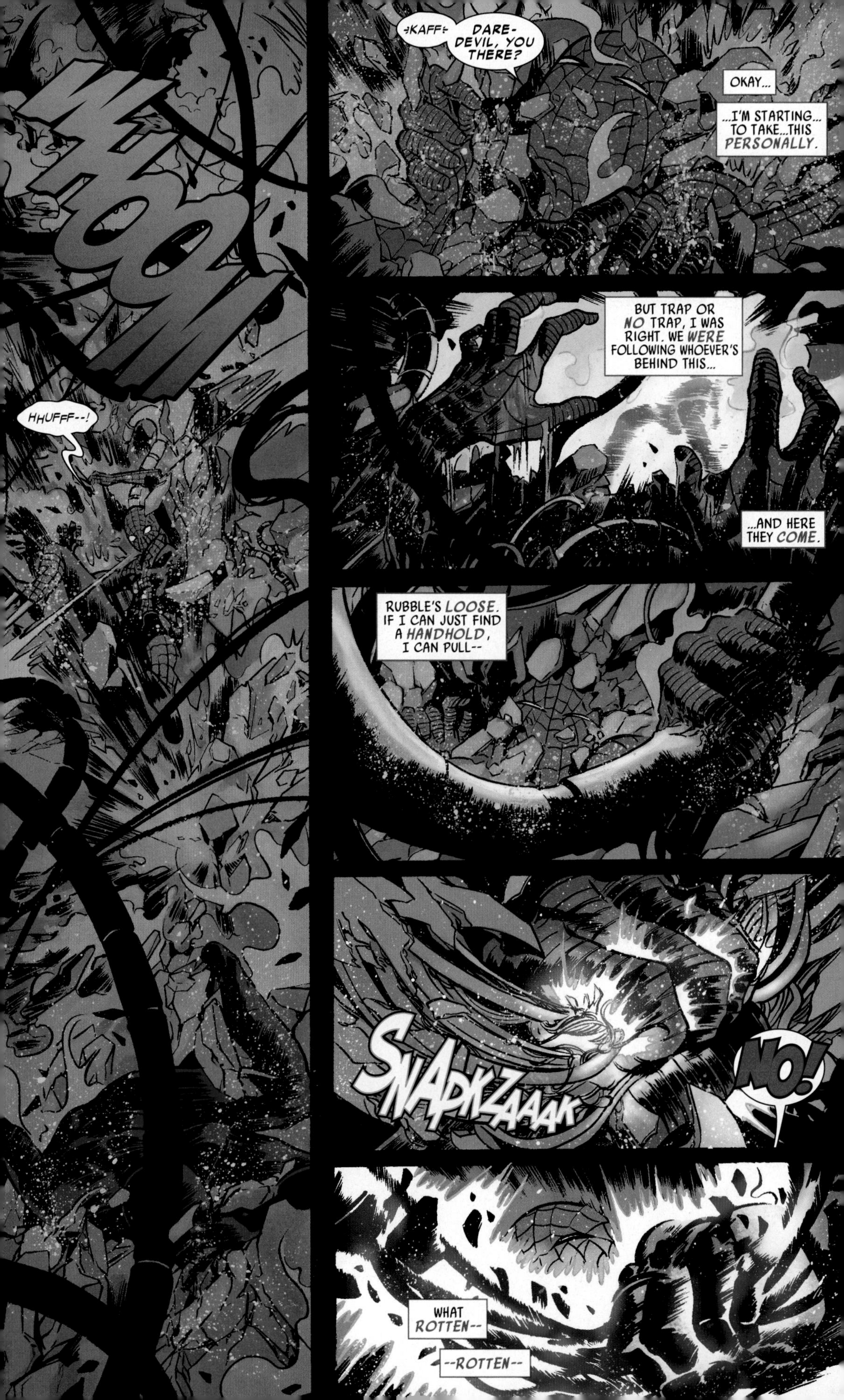
WHOOM
HHUFFF--!
=KAFF= DARE-DEVIL, YOU THERE?
OKAY...
...I'M STARTING... TO TAKE...THIS PERSONALLY.
BUT TRAP OR NO TRAP, I WAS RIGHT. WE WERE FOLLOWING WHOEVER'S BEHIND THIS...
...AND HERE THEY COME.
RUBBLE'S LOOSE. IF I CAN JUST FIND A HANDHOLD, I CAN PULL--
SNAPKZAAAK
NO!
WHAT ROTTEN--
--ROTTEN--

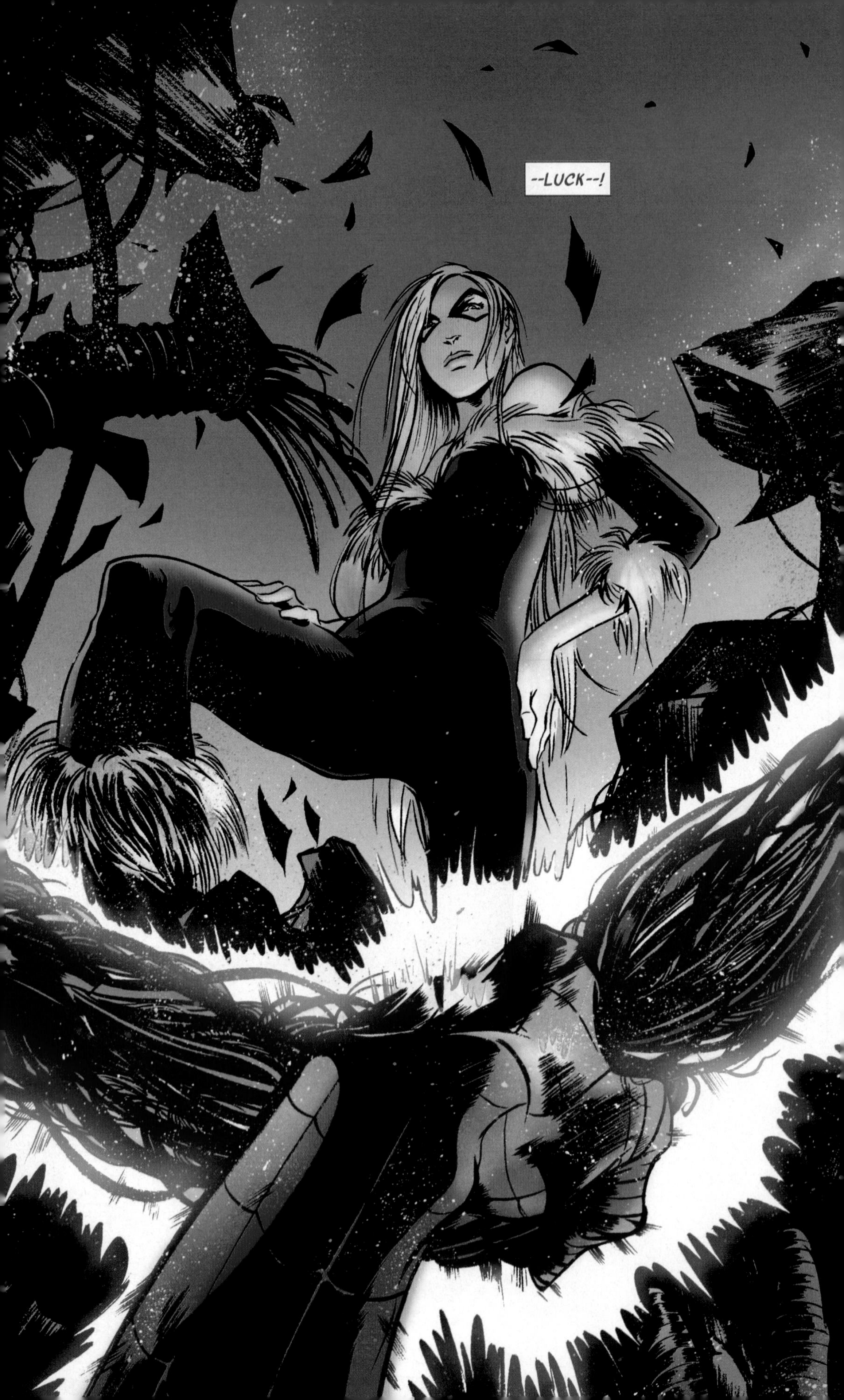
--LUCK--!

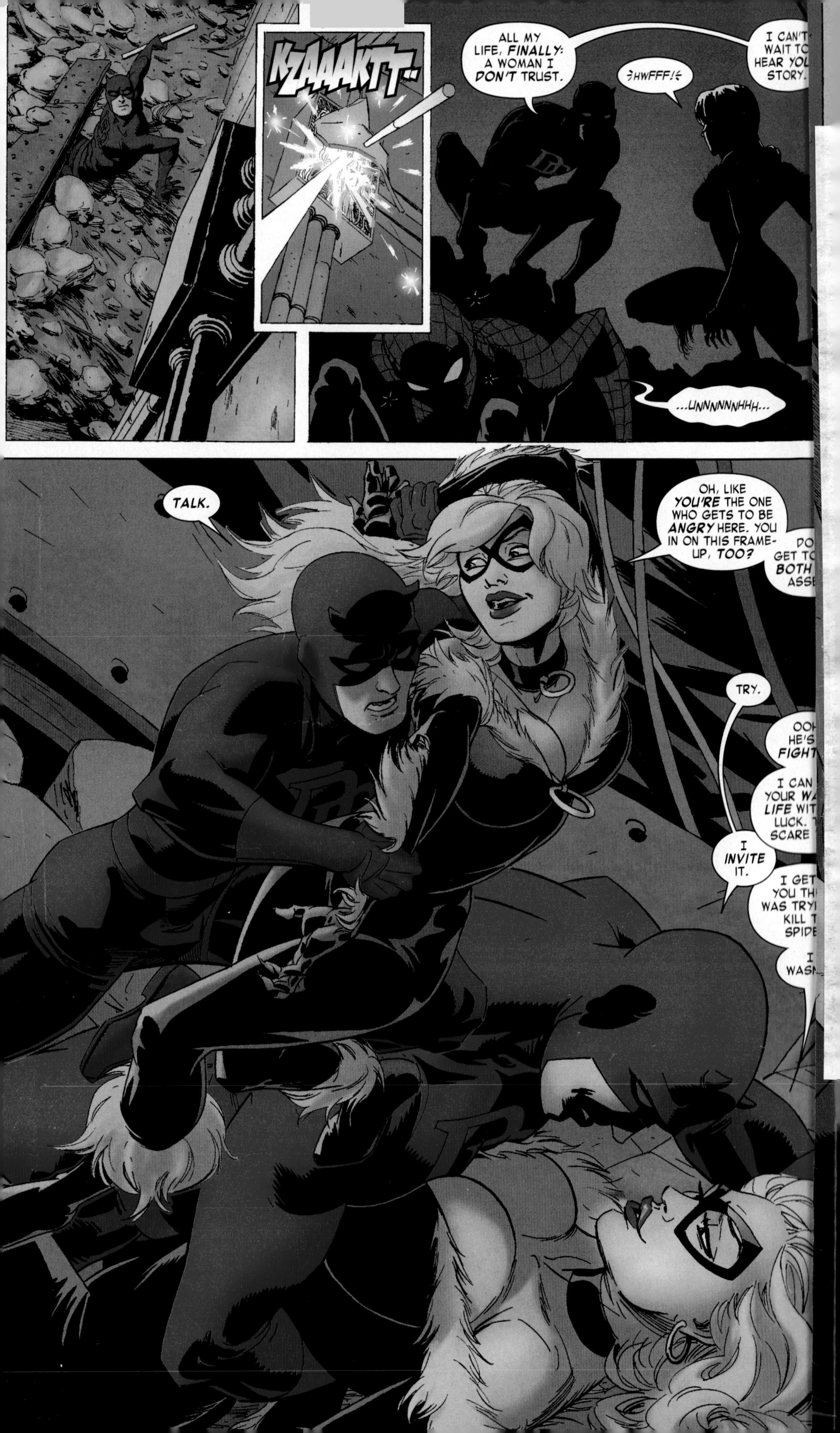
KZAAAKTT-
ALL MY LIFE, FINALLY: A WOMAN I DON'T TRUST.
I CAN'T WAIT TO HEAR YOU STORY.
HWFFF!
...UNNNNNNHHH...
TALK.
OH, LIKE YOU'RE THE ONE WHO GETS TO BE ANGRY HERE. YOU IN ON THIS FRAME-UP, TOO?
DO GET TO BOTH ASSE
TRY.
OOH HE'S FIGHT
I CAN YOUR WA LIFE WIT LUCK. SCARE
I INVITE IT.
I GET YOU TH WAS TRY KILL SPIDE
I WASN

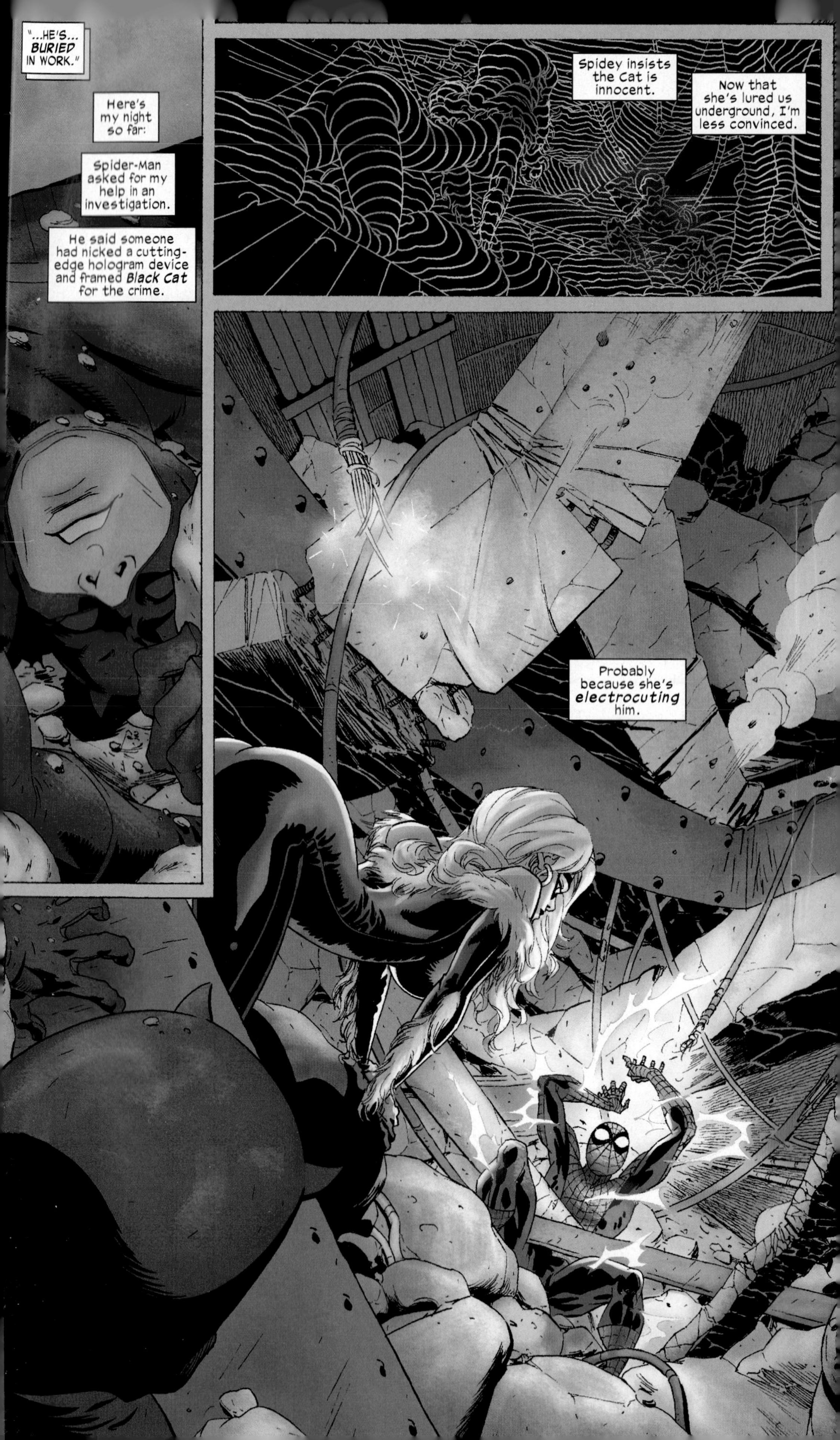
"...HE'S... BURIED IN WORK."
Here's my night so far:
Spider-Man asked for my help in an investigation.
He said someone had nicked a cutting-edge hologram device and framed Black Cat for the crime.
Spidey insists the Cat is innocent.
Now that she's lured us underground, I'm less convinced.
Probably because she's electrocuting him.

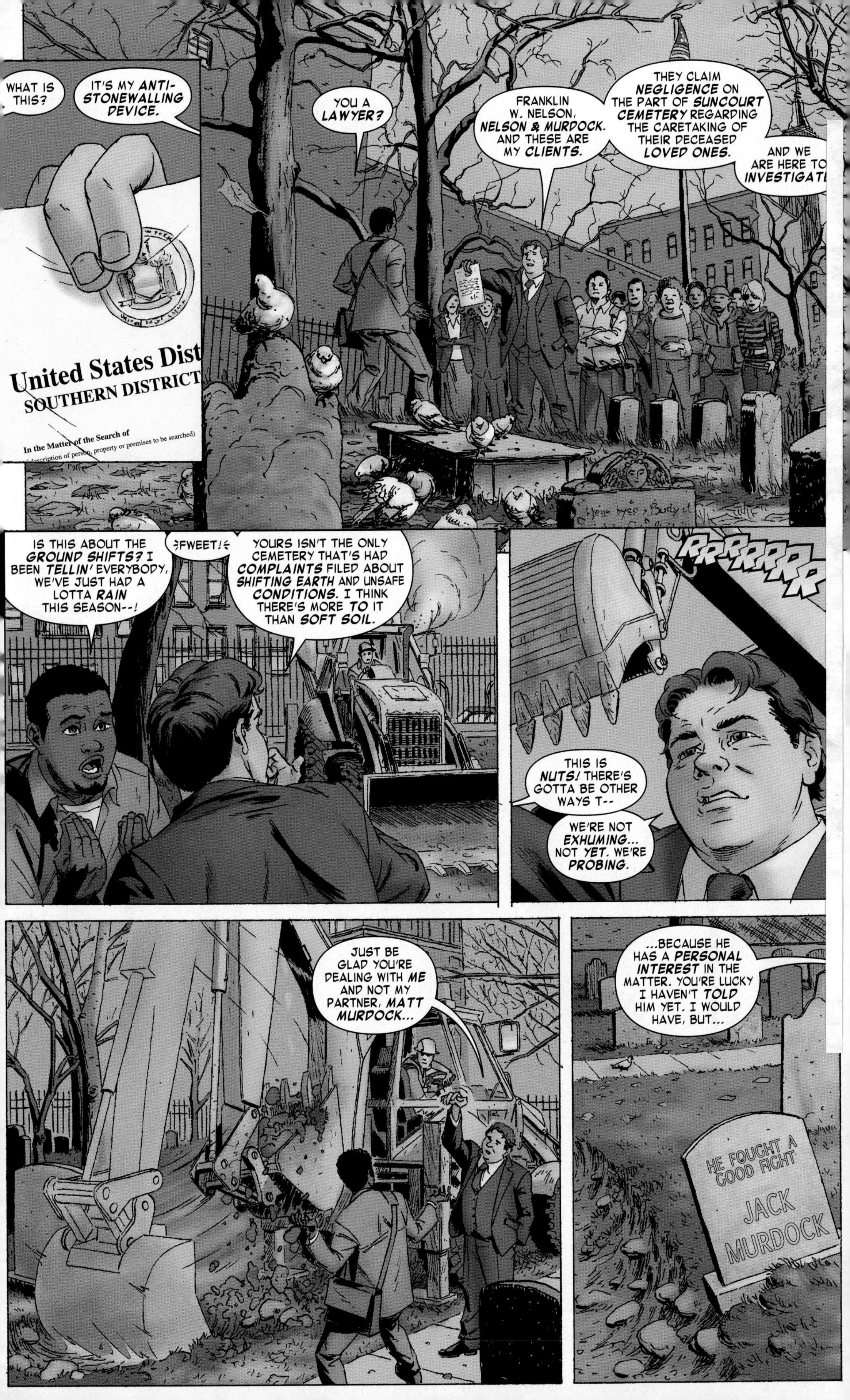
WHAT IS THIS?
IT'S MY ANTI-STONEWALLING DEVICE.
United States Dist
SOUTHERN DISTRICT
In the Matter of the Search of
description of person, property or premises to be searched)
YOU A LAWYER?
FRANKLIN W. NELSON, NELSON & MURDOCK. AND THESE ARE MY CLIENTS.
THEY CLAIM NEGLIGENCE ON THE PART OF SUNCOURT CEMETERY REGARDING THE CARETAKING OF THEIR DECEASED LOVED ONES.
AND WE ARE HERE TO INVESTIGATE
IS THIS ABOUT THE GROUND SHIFTS? I BEEN TELLIN' EVERYBODY, WE'VE JUST HAD A LOTTA RAIN THIS SEASON--!
FWEET!
YOURS ISN'T THE ONLY CEMETERY THAT'S HAD COMPLAINTS FILED ABOUT SHIFTING EARTH AND UNSAFE CONDITIONS. I THINK THERE'S MORE TO IT THAN SOFT SOIL.
RRRRRRR
THIS IS NUTS! THERE'S GOTTA BE OTHER WAYS T--
WE'RE NOT EXHUMING... NOT YET. WE'RE PROBING.
JUST BE GLAD YOU'RE DEALING WITH ME AND NOT MY PARTNER, MATT MURDOCK...
...BECAUSE HE HAS A PERSONAL INTEREST IN THE MATTER. YOU'RE LUCKY I HAVEN'T TOLD HIM YET. I WOULD HAVE, BUT...
HE FOUGHT A GOOD FIGHT
JACK MURDOCK

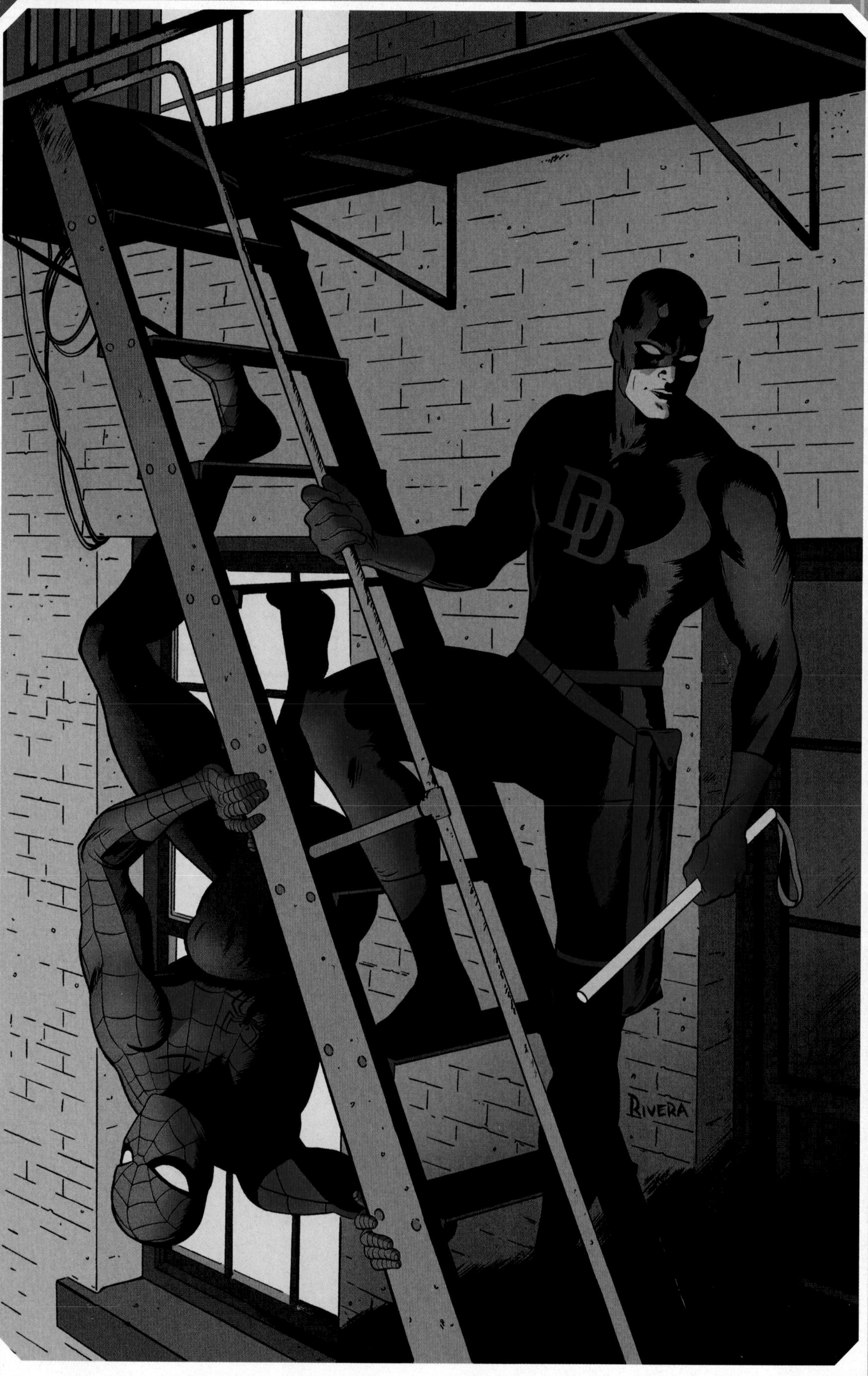
RIVERA

EIGHT

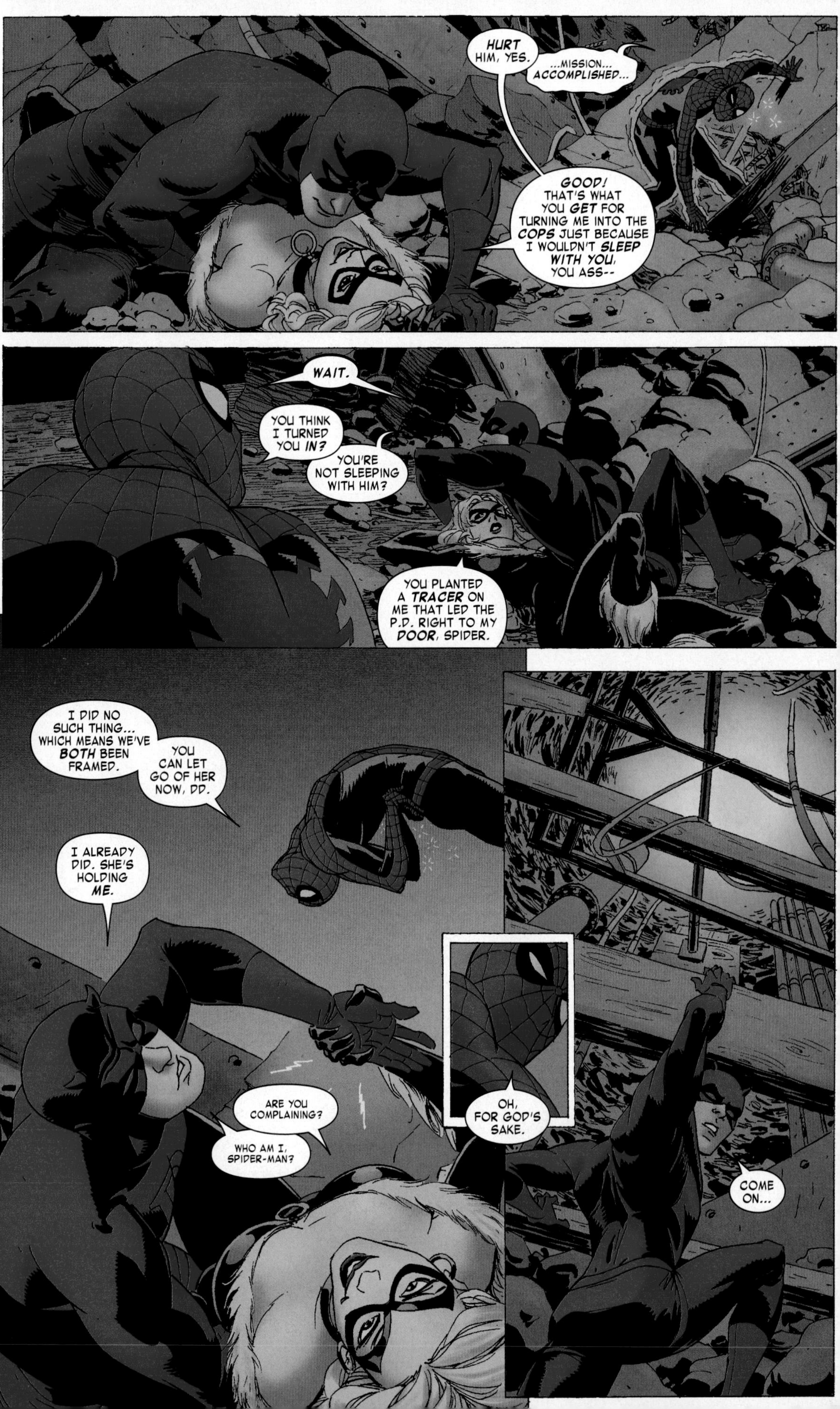
HURT HIM, YES.
...MISSION... ACCOMPLISHED...
GOOD! THAT'S WHAT YOU GET FOR TURNING ME INTO THE COPS JUST BECAUSE I WOULDN'T SLEEP WITH YOU, YOU ASS--
WAIT.
YOU THINK I TURNED YOU IN?
YOU'RE NOT SLEEPING WITH HIM?
YOU PLANTED A TRACER ON ME THAT LED THE P.D. RIGHT TO MY DOOR, SPIDER.
I DID NO SUCH THING... WHICH MEANS WE'VE BOTH BEEN FRAMED.
YOU CAN LET GO OF HER NOW, DD.
I ALREADY DID. SHE'S HOLDING ME.
ARE YOU COMPLAINING?
WHO AM I, SPIDER-MAN?
OH, FOR GOD'S SAKE.
COME ON...

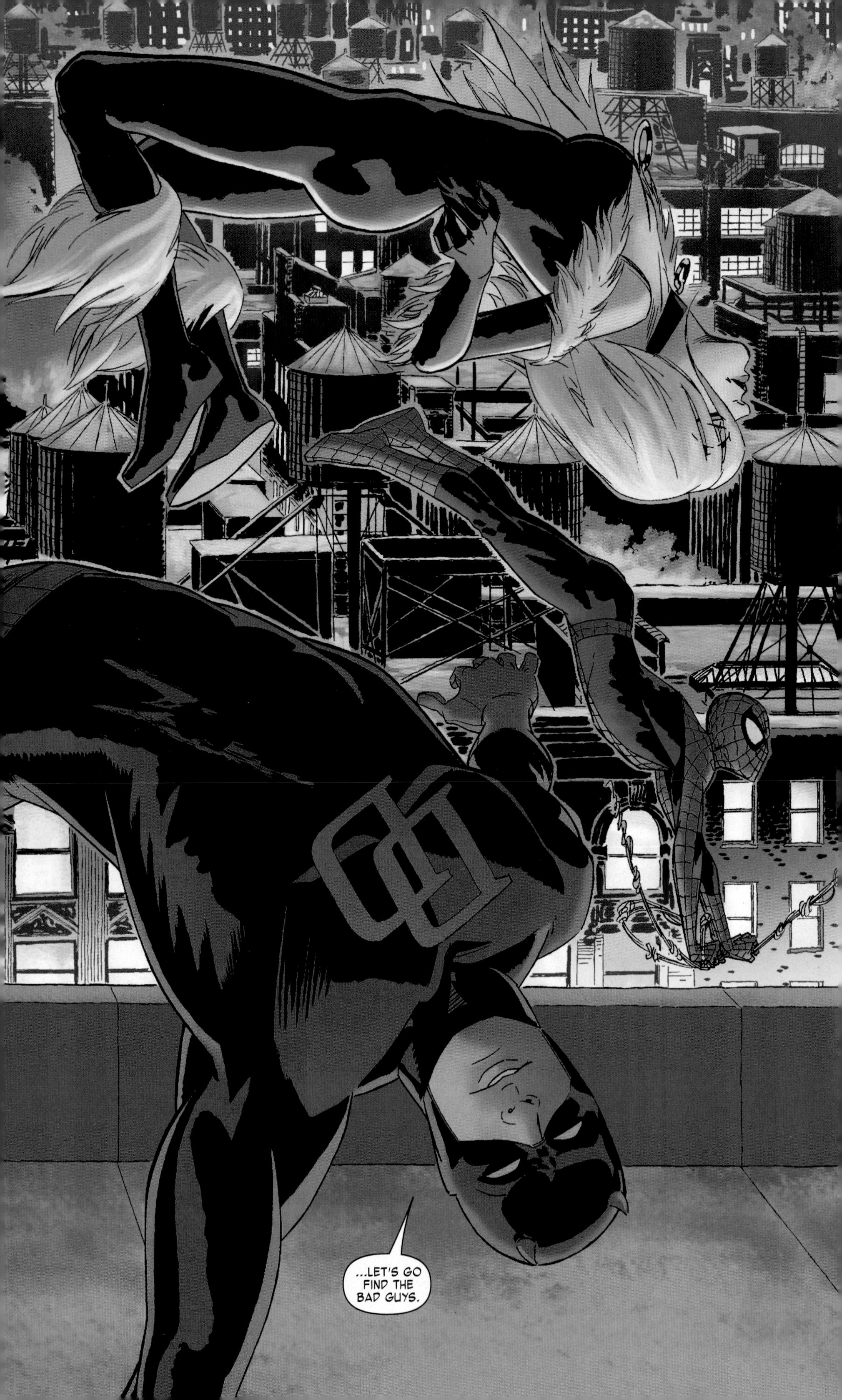
...LET'S GO FIND THE BAD GUYS.

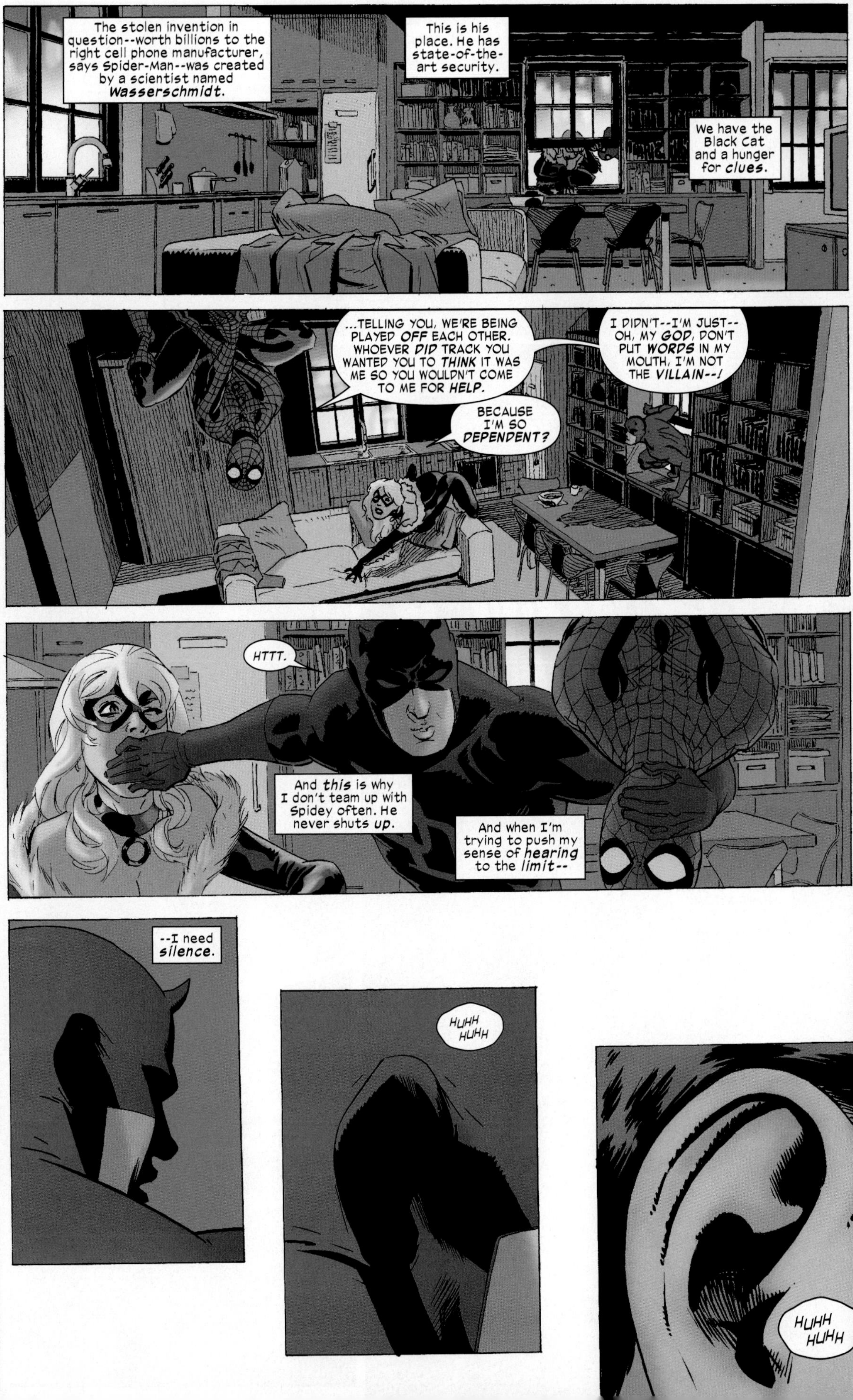

The stolen invention in question--worth billions to the right cell phone manufacturer, says Spider-Man--was created by a scientist named Wasserschmidt.
This is his place. He has state-of-the-art security.
We have the Black Cat and a hunger for clues.
...TELLING YOU, WE'RE BEING PLAYED OFF EACH OTHER. WHOEVER DID TRACK YOU WANTED YOU TO THINK IT WAS ME SO YOU WOULDN'T COME TO ME FOR HELP.
I DIDN'T--I'M JUST--OH, MY GOD, DON'T PUT WORDS IN MY MOUTH, I'M NOT THE VILLAIN--!
BECAUSE I'M SO DEPENDENT?
HTTT.
And this is why I don't team up with Spidey often. He never shuts up.
And when I'm trying to push my sense of hearing to the limit--
--I need silence.
HUHH HUHH
HUHH HUHH

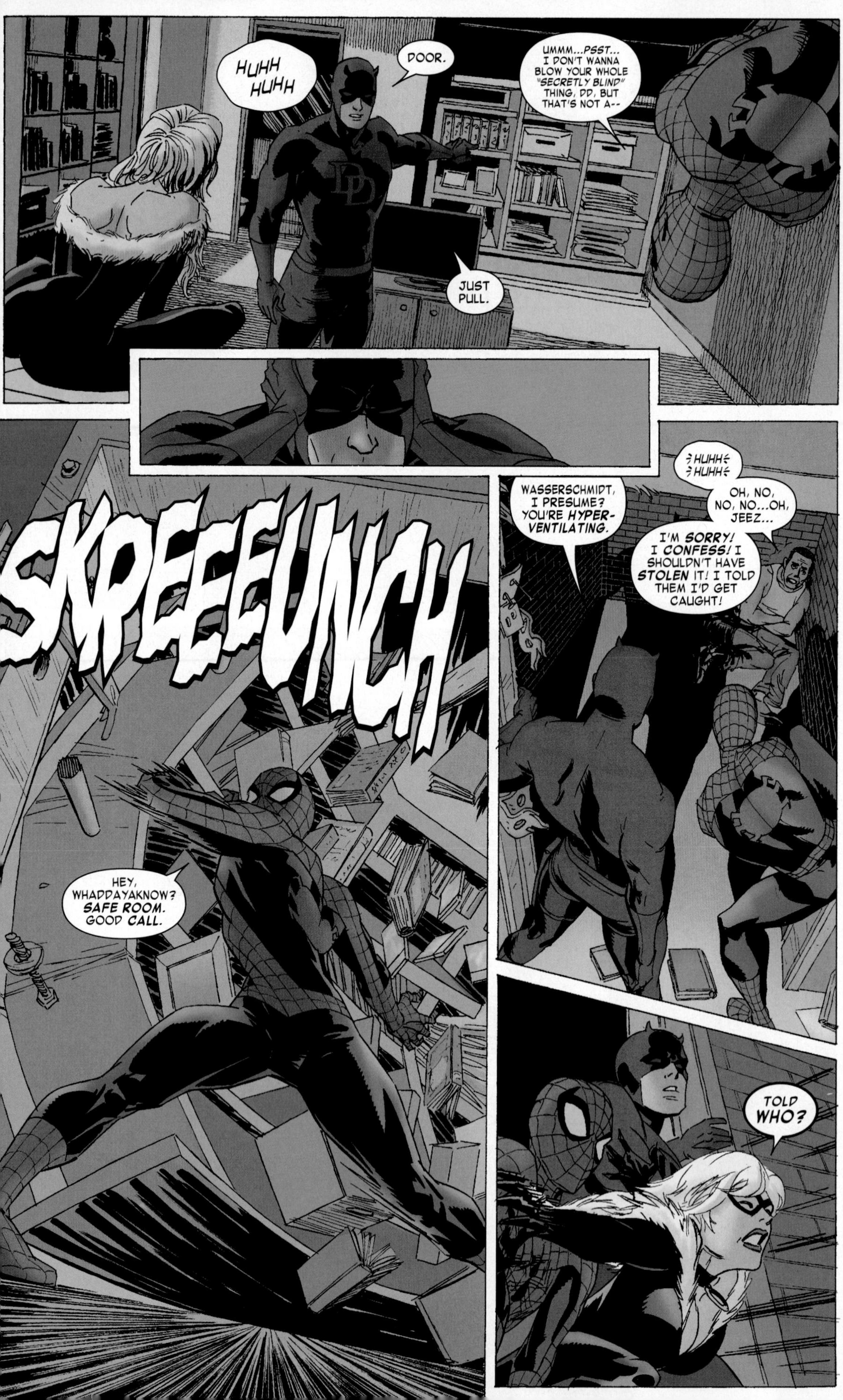
HUHH HUHH
DOOR.
UMMM...PSST... I DON'T WANNA BLOW YOUR WHOLE "SECRETLY BLIND" THING, DD, BUT THAT'S NOT A--
JUST PULL.
SKREEEUNCH
HEY, WHADDAYAKNOW? SAFE ROOM. GOOD CALL.
WASSERSCHMIDT, I PRESUME? YOU'RE HYPER-VENTILATING.
HUHH HUHH
OH, NO, NO, NO...OH, JEEZ...
I'M SORRY! I CONFESS! I SHOULDN'T HAVE STOLEN IT! I TOLD THEM I'D GET CAUGHT!
TOLD WHO?

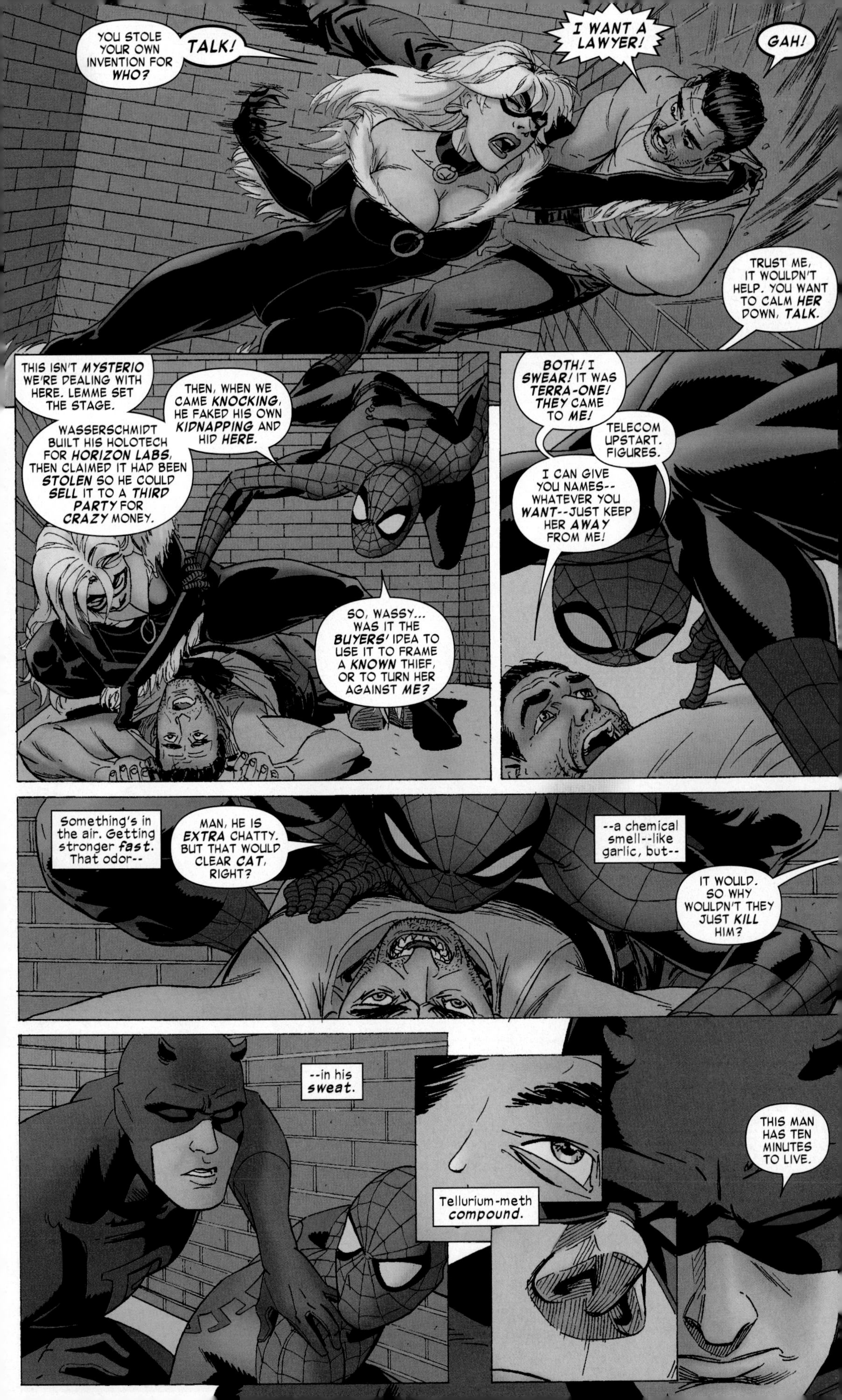
YOU STOLE YOUR OWN INVENTION FOR WHO?
TALK!
I WANT A LAWYER!
GAH!
TRUST ME, IT WOULDN'T HELP. YOU WANT TO CALM HER DOWN, TALK.
THIS ISN'T MYSTERIO WE'RE DEALING WITH HERE. LEMME SET THE STAGE.
WASSERSCHMIDT BUILT HIS HOLOTECH FOR HORIZON LABS, THEN CLAIMED IT HAD BEEN STOLEN SO HE COULD SELL IT TO A THIRD PARTY FOR CRAZY MONEY.
THEN, WHEN WE CAME KNOCKING, HE FAKED HIS OWN KIDNAPPING AND HID HERE.
SO, WASSY... WAS IT THE BUYERS' IDEA TO USE IT TO FRAME A KNOWN THIEF, OR TO TURN HER AGAINST ME?
BOTH! I SWEAR! IT WAS TERRA-ONE! THEY CAME TO ME!
TELECOM UPSTART. FIGURES.
I CAN GIVE YOU NAMES-- WHATEVER YOU WANT--JUST KEEP HER AWAY FROM ME!
Something's in the air. Getting stronger fast. That odor--
MAN, HE IS EXTRA CHATTY. BUT THAT WOULD CLEAR CAT, RIGHT?
--a chemical smell--like garlic, but--
IT WOULD. SO WHY WOULDN'T THEY JUST KILL HIM?
--in his sweat.
Tellurium-meth compound.
THIS MAN HAS TEN MINUTES TO LIVE.

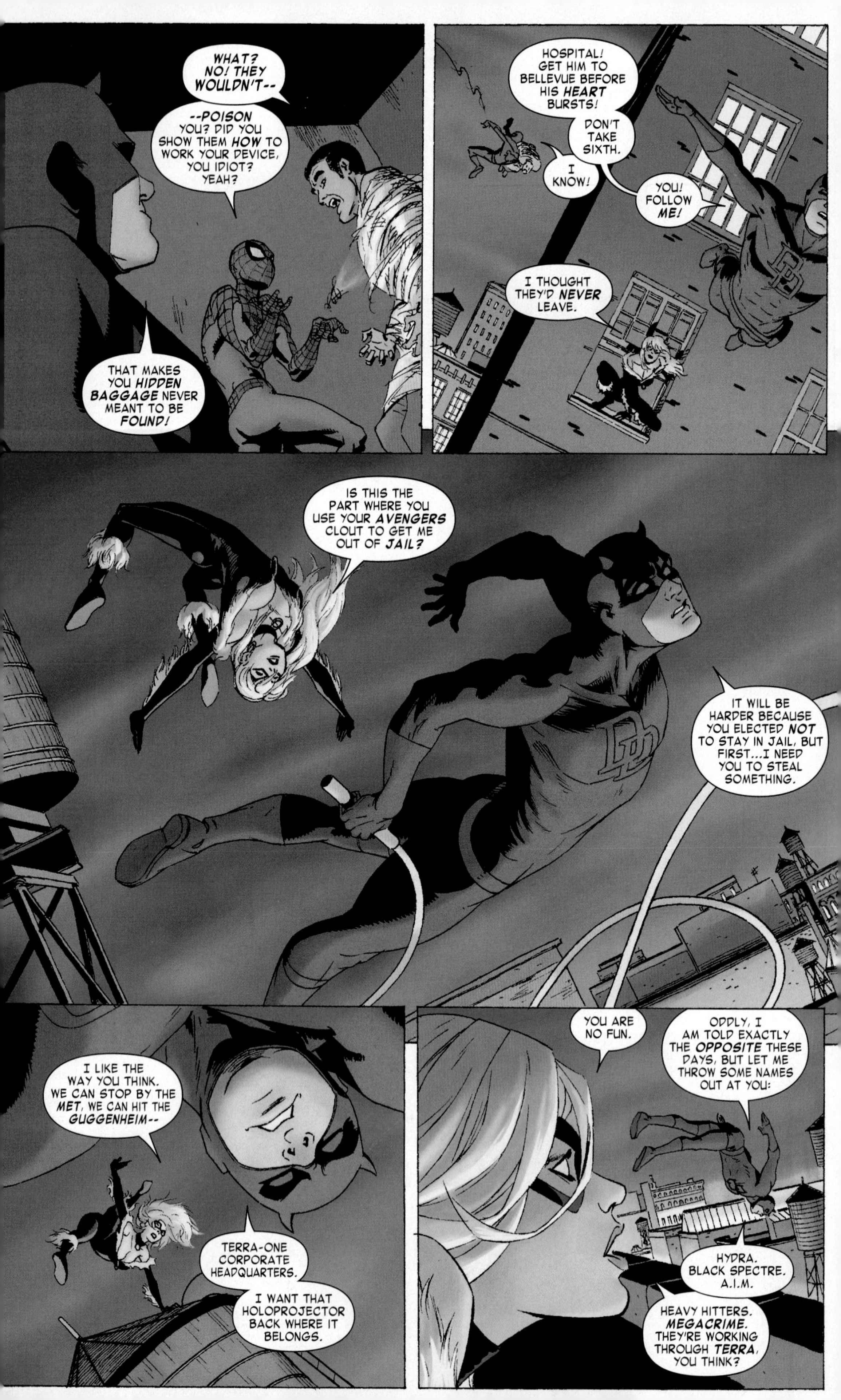
WHAT? NO! THEY WOULDN'T--
--POISON YOU? DID YOU SHOW THEM HOW TO WORK YOUR DEVICE, YOU IDIOT? YEAH?
THAT MAKES YOU HIDDEN BAGGAGE NEVER MEANT TO BE FOUND!
HOSPITAL! GET HIM TO BELLEVUE BEFORE HIS HEART BURSTS!
DON'T TAKE SIXTH.
I KNOW!
YOU! FOLLOW ME!
I THOUGHT THEY'D NEVER LEAVE.
IS THIS THE PART WHERE YOU USE YOUR AVENGERS CLOUT TO GET ME OUT OF JAIL?
IT WILL BE HARDER BECAUSE YOU ELECTED NOT TO STAY IN JAIL, BUT FIRST...I NEED YOU TO STEAL SOMETHING.
I LIKE THE WAY YOU THINK. WE CAN STOP BY THE MET, WE CAN HIT THE GUGGENHEIM--
TERRA-ONE CORPORATE HEADQUARTERS.
I WANT THAT HOLOPROJECTOR BACK WHERE IT BELONGS.
YOU ARE NO FUN.
ODDLY, I AM TOLD EXACTLY THE OPPOSITE THESE DAYS, BUT LET ME THROW SOME NAMES OUT AT YOU:
HYDRA. BLACK SPECTRE. A.I.M.
HEAVY HITTERS. MEGACRIME. THEY'RE WORKING THROUGH TERRA, YOU THINK?

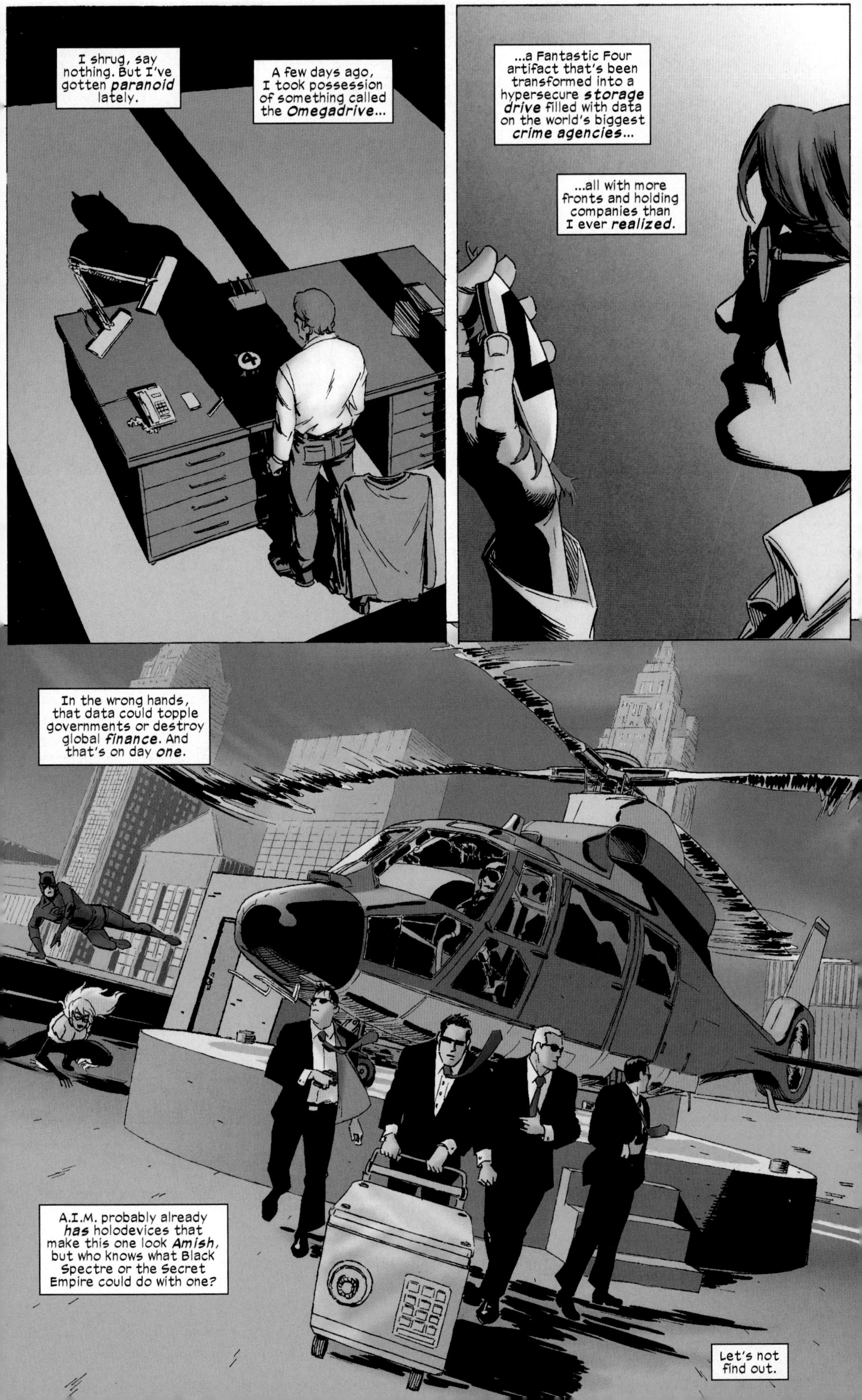
I shrug, say nothing. But I've gotten *paranoid* lately.
A few days ago, I took possession of something called the *Omegadrive*...
...a Fantastic Four artifact that's been transformed into a hypersecure *storage drive* filled with data on the world's biggest *crime agencies*...
...all with more fronts and holding companies than I ever *realized*.
In the wrong hands, that data could topple governments or destroy global *finance*. And that's on day *one*.
A.I.M. probably already *has* holodevices that make this one look *Amish*, but who knows what Black Spectre or the Secret Empire could do with one?
Let's not find out.

INCOMING!

OPEN FIRE!

HEY, I THINK WE FOUND YOUR *HOLOGIZMO.*

ON THAT *CART,* THAT IS, NOT *SHOOTING* AT US. YOU HAVE A *PLAN?*

PLANNING IS OVERRATED.

IT'S ALWAYS MORE EXCITING TO BE SURPRISED.

YOU NEVER KNOW WHAT NEW TOOLS YOU MIGHT DISCOVER.

FWWP-P-p

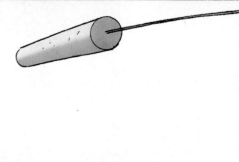

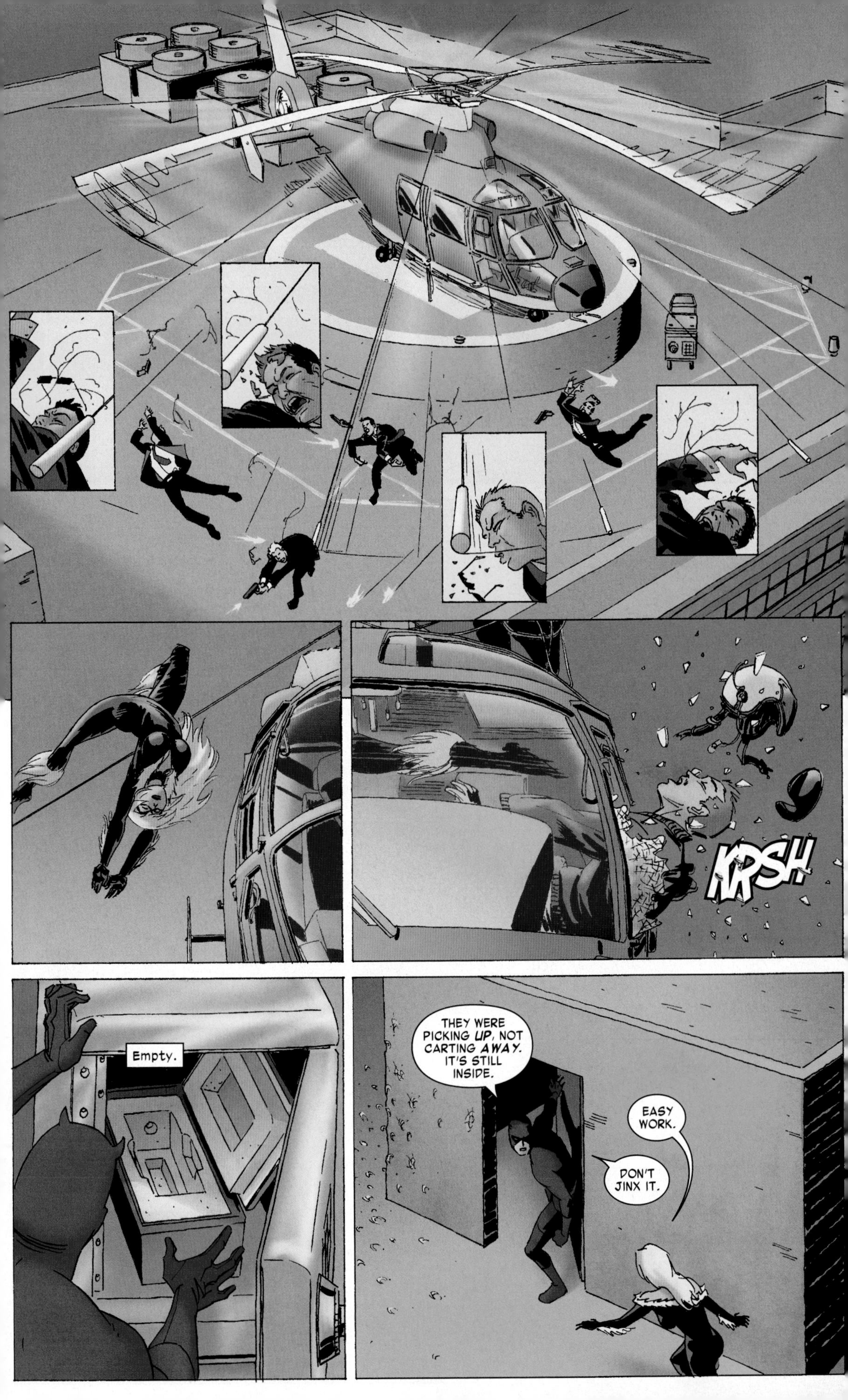
KRSH
Empty.
THEY WERE PICKING UP, NOT CARTING AWAY. IT'S STILL INSIDE.
EASY WORK.
DON'T JINX IT.

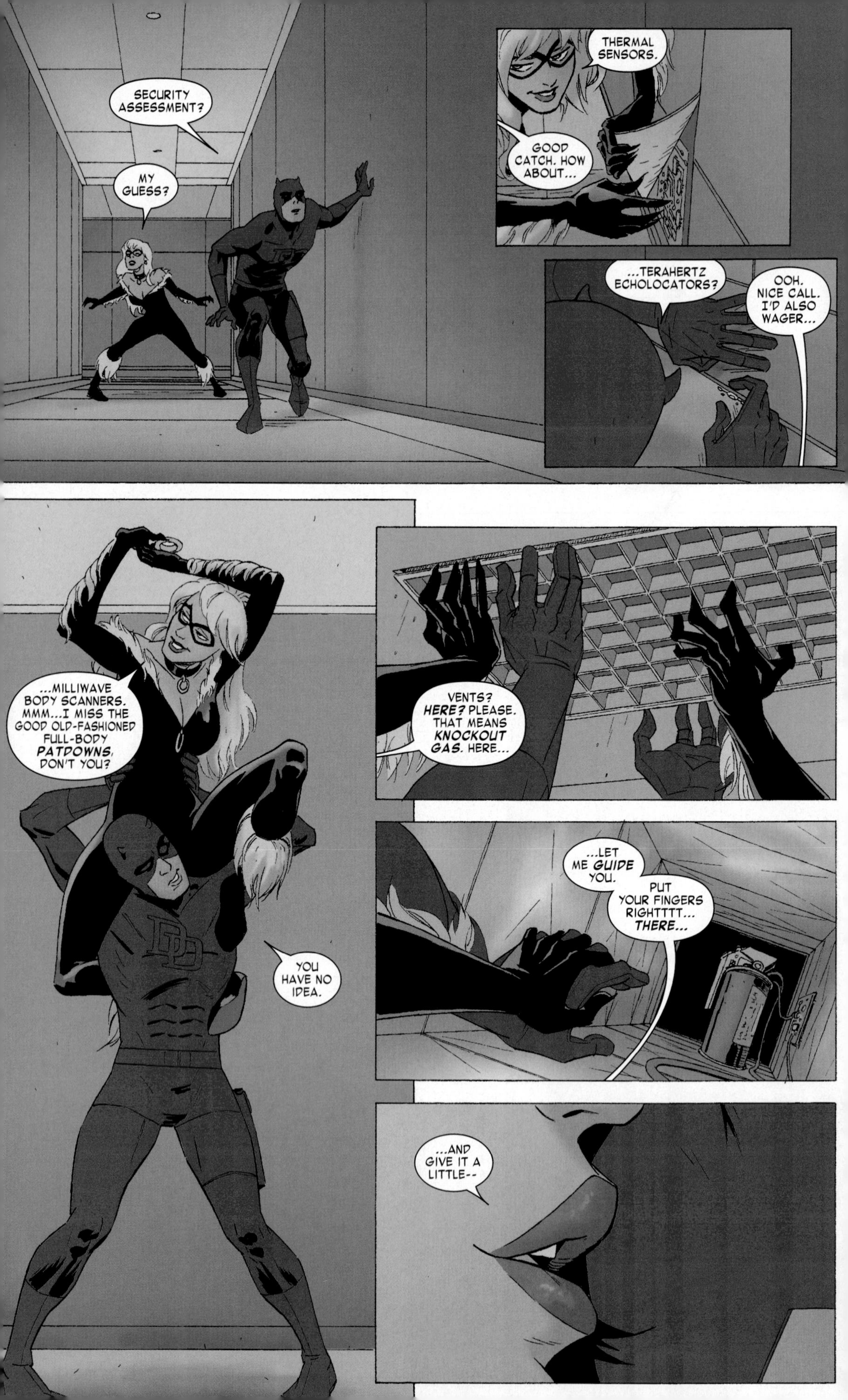
SECURITY ASSESSMENT?
MY GUESS?
THERMAL SENSORS.
GOOD CATCH. HOW ABOUT...
...TERAHERTZ ECHOLOCATORS?
OOH. NICE CALL. I'D ALSO WAGER...
...MILLIWAVE BODY SCANNERS. MMM...I MISS THE GOOD OLD-FASHIONED FULL-BODY *PATDOWNS*, DON'T YOU?
YOU HAVE NO IDEA.
VENTS? *HERE?* PLEASE. THAT MEANS *KNOCKOUT GAS*. HERE...
...LET ME *GUIDE* YOU.
PUT YOUR FINGERS RIGHTTTT... *THERE...*
...AND GIVE IT A LITTLE--

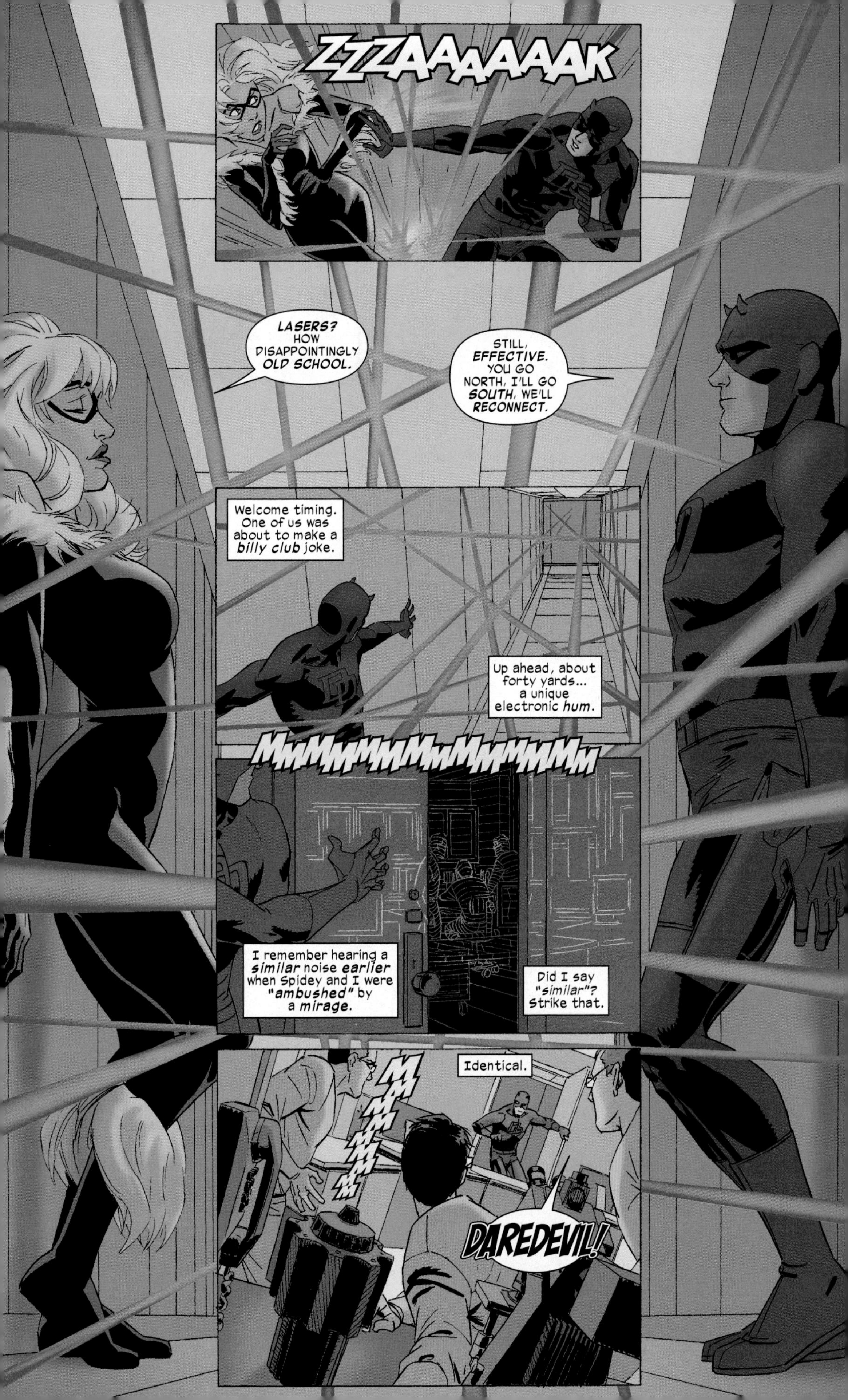
ZZZAAAAAAK
LASERS? HOW DISAPPOINTINGLY OLD SCHOOL.
STILL, EFFECTIVE. YOU GO NORTH, I'LL GO SOUTH, WE'LL RECONNECT.
Welcome timing. One of us was about to make a billy club joke.
Up ahead, about forty yards... a unique electronic hum.
MMMMMMMMMMMMMMMMMM
I remember hearing a similar noise earlier when Spidey and I were "ambushed" by a mirage.
Did I say "similar"? Strike that.
Identical.
MMMMMMMMM
DAREDEVIL!

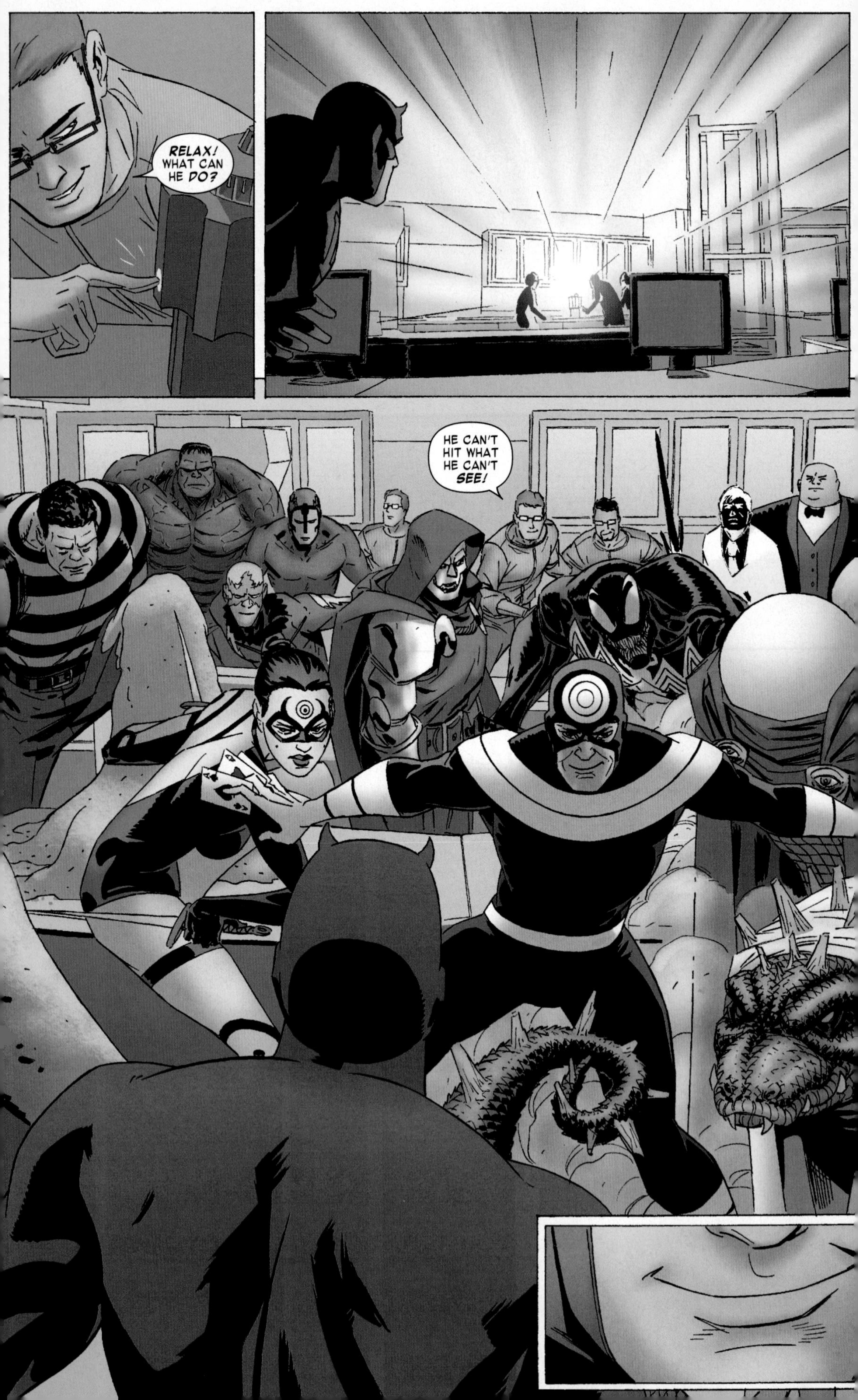
RELAX! WHAT CAN HE DO?
HE CAN'T HIT WHAT HE CAN'T SEE!

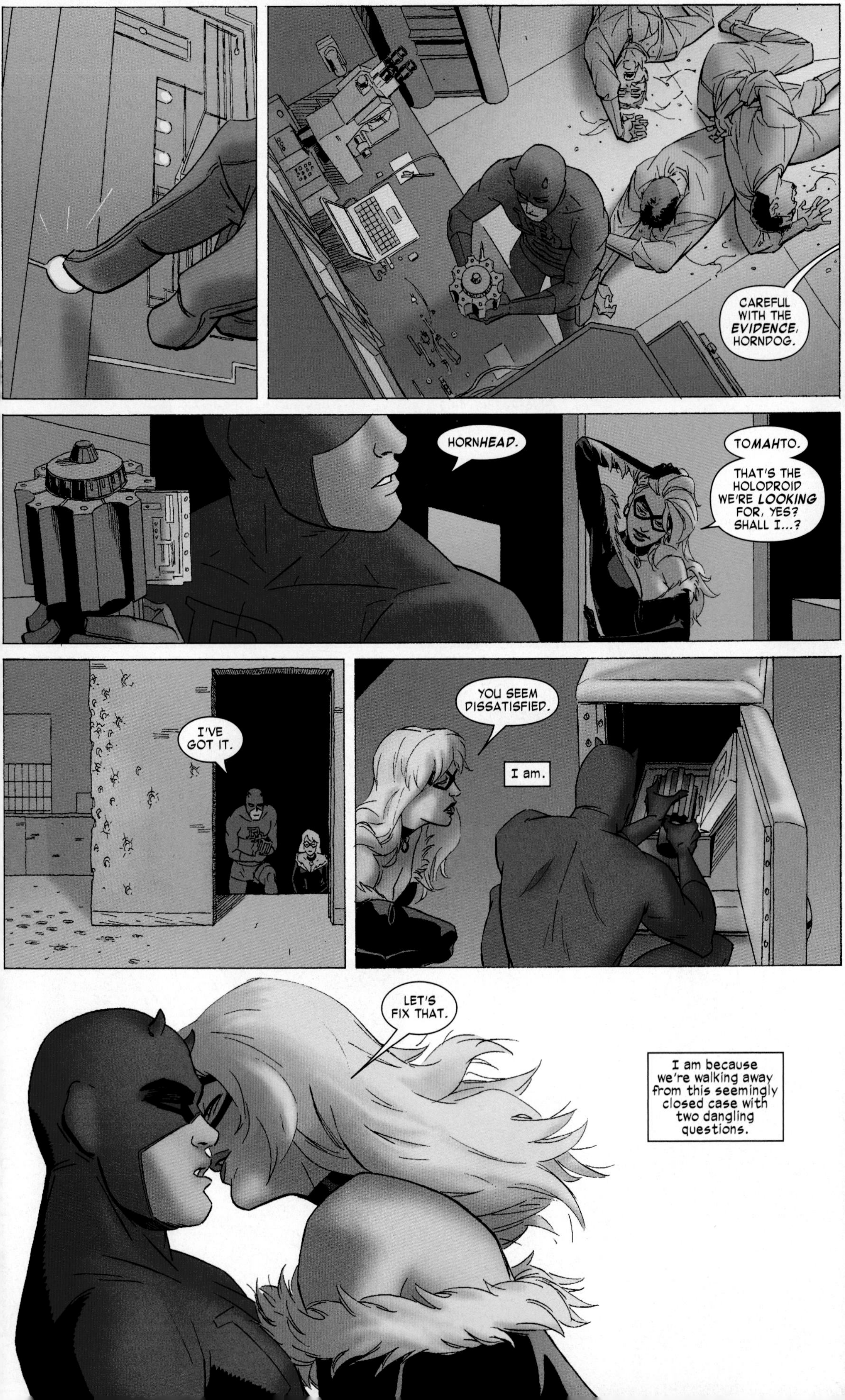
CAREFUL WITH THE EVIDENCE, HORNDOG.
HORNHEAD.
TOMAHTO.
THAT'S THE HOLODROID WE'RE LOOKING FOR, YES? SHALL I...?
I'VE GOT IT.
YOU SEEM DISSATISFIED.
I am.
LET'S FIX THAT.
I am because we're walking away from this seemingly closed case with two dangling questions.

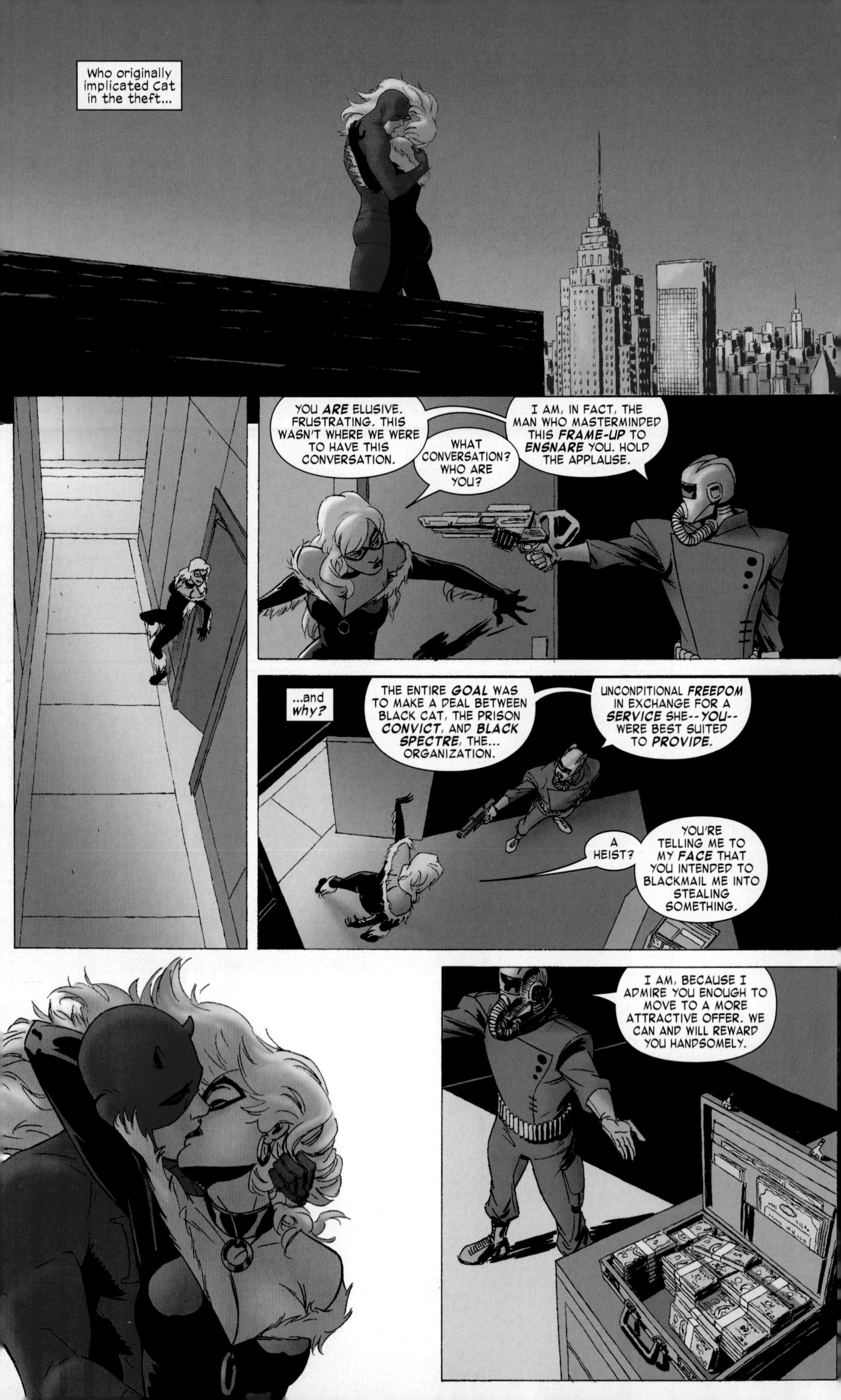
Who originally implicated Cat in the theft...
YOU ARE ELUSIVE. FRUSTRATING. THIS WASN'T WHERE WE WERE TO HAVE THIS CONVERSATION.
WHAT CONVERSATION? WHO ARE YOU?
I AM, IN FACT, THE MAN WHO MASTERMINDED THIS FRAME-UP TO ENSNARE YOU. HOLD THE APPLAUSE.
...and why?
THE ENTIRE GOAL WAS TO MAKE A DEAL BETWEEN BLACK CAT, THE PRISON CONVICT, AND BLACK SPECTRE, THE... ORGANIZATION.
UNCONDITIONAL FREEDOM IN EXCHANGE FOR A SERVICE SHE--YOU--WERE BEST SUITED TO PROVIDE.
A HEIST?
YOU'RE TELLING ME TO MY FACE THAT YOU INTENDED TO BLACKMAIL ME INTO STEALING SOMETHING.
I AM, BECAUSE I ADMIRE YOU ENOUGH TO MOVE TO A MORE ATTRACTIVE OFFER. WE CAN AND WILL REWARD YOU HANDSOMELY.

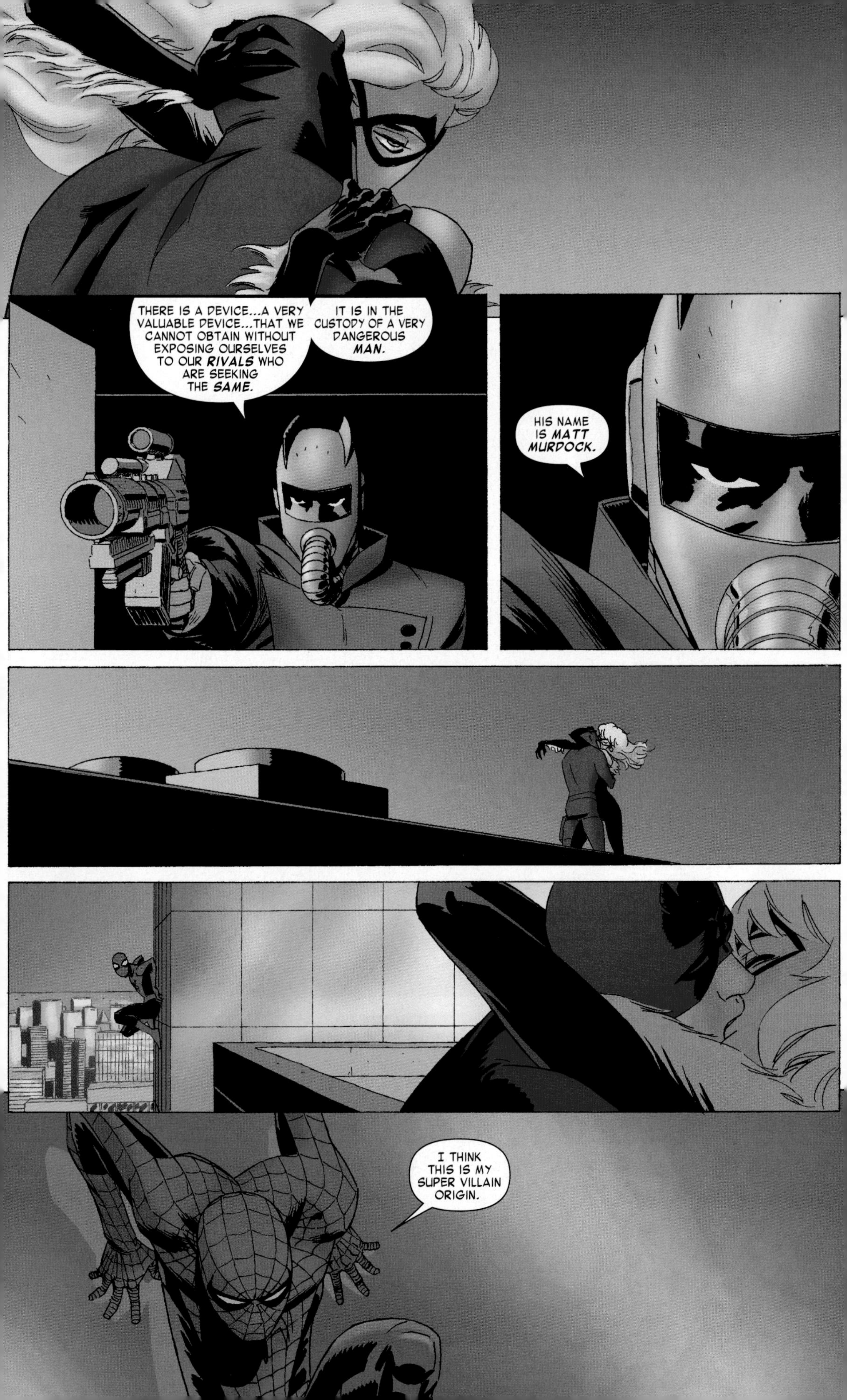
THERE IS A DEVICE...A VERY VALUABLE DEVICE...THAT WE CANNOT OBTAIN WITHOUT EXPOSING OURSELVES TO OUR RIVALS WHO ARE SEEKING THE SAME.
IT IS IN THE CUSTODY OF A VERY DANGEROUS MAN.
HIS NAME IS MATT MURDOCK.
I THINK THIS IS MY SUPER VILLAIN ORIGIN.

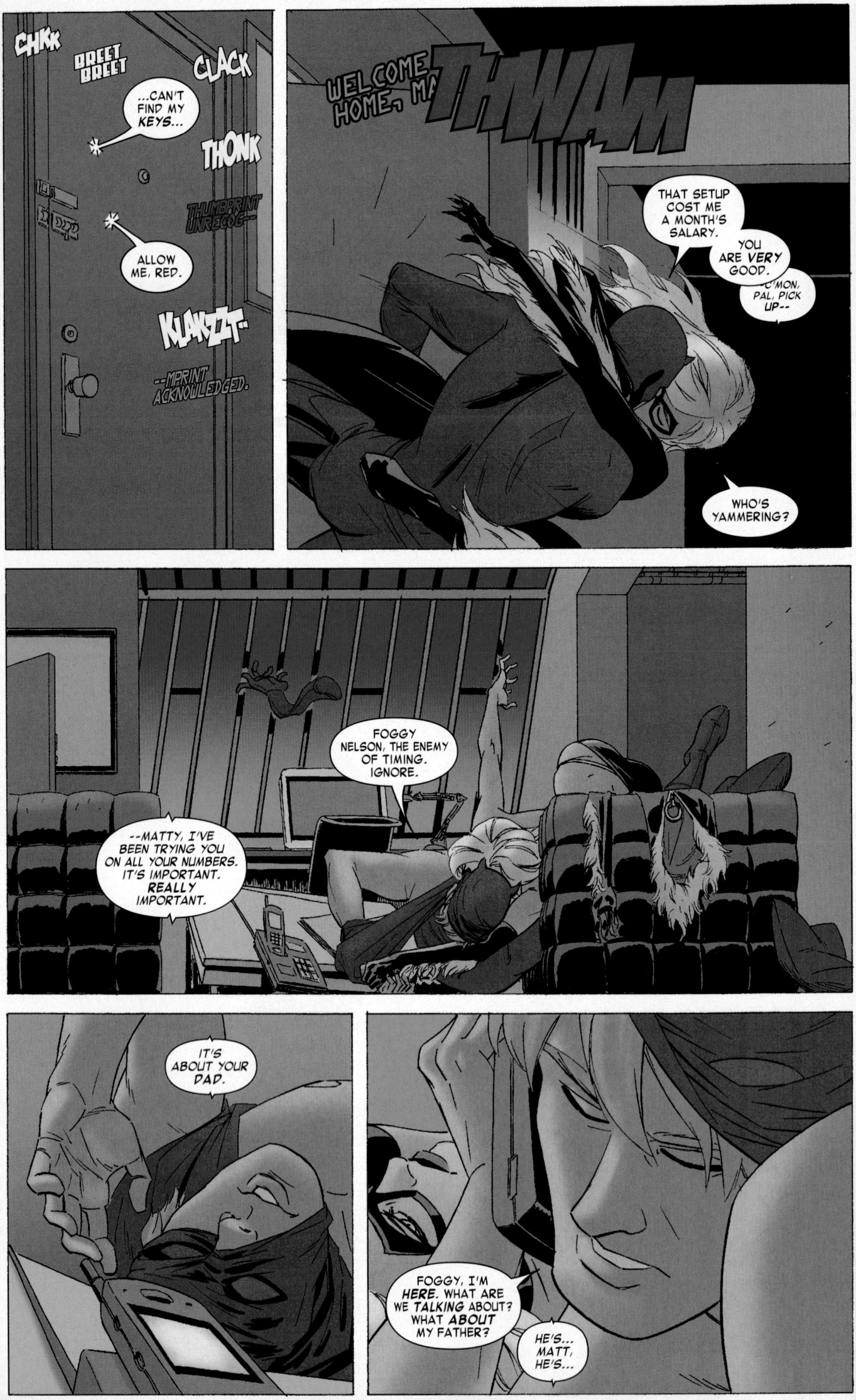
CHKK
BREET BREET
CLACK
...CAN'T FIND MY KEYS...
THONK
THUMBPRINT UNRECOG--
ALLOW ME, RED.
KLAKZZT-
--MPRINT ACKNOWLEDGED.
WELCOME HOME, MA
THWAM
THAT SETUP COST ME A MONTH'S SALARY.
YOU ARE VERY GOOD.
C'MON, PAL, PICK UP--
WHO'S YAMMERING?
FOGGY NELSON, THE ENEMY OF TIMING. IGNORE.
--MATTY, I'VE BEEN TRYING YOU ON ALL YOUR NUMBERS. IT'S IMPORTANT. REALLY IMPORTANT.
IT'S ABOUT YOUR DAD.
FOGGY, I'M HERE. WHAT ARE WE TALKING ABOUT? WHAT ABOUT MY FATHER?
HE'S... MATT, HE'S...

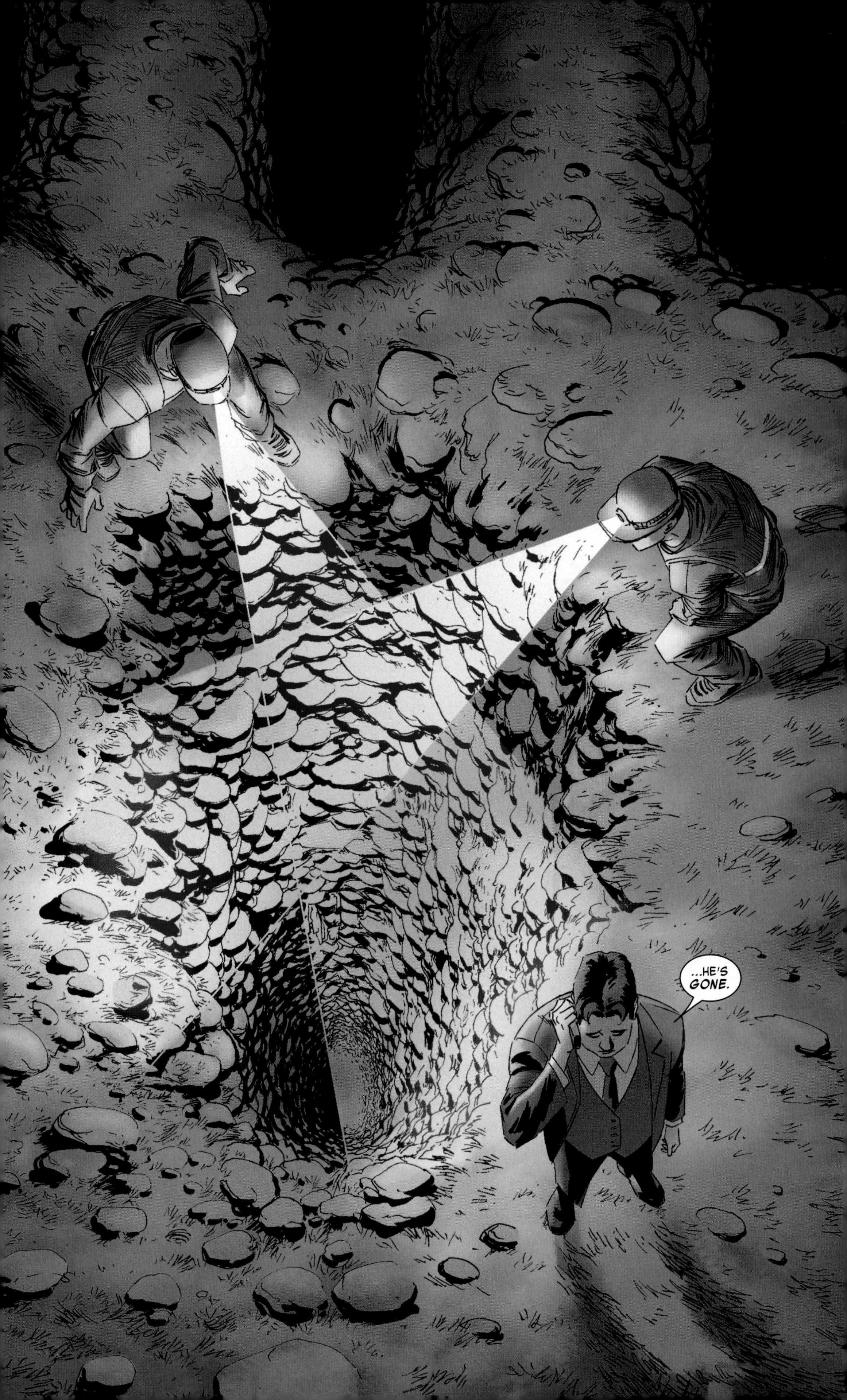
...HE'S GONE.

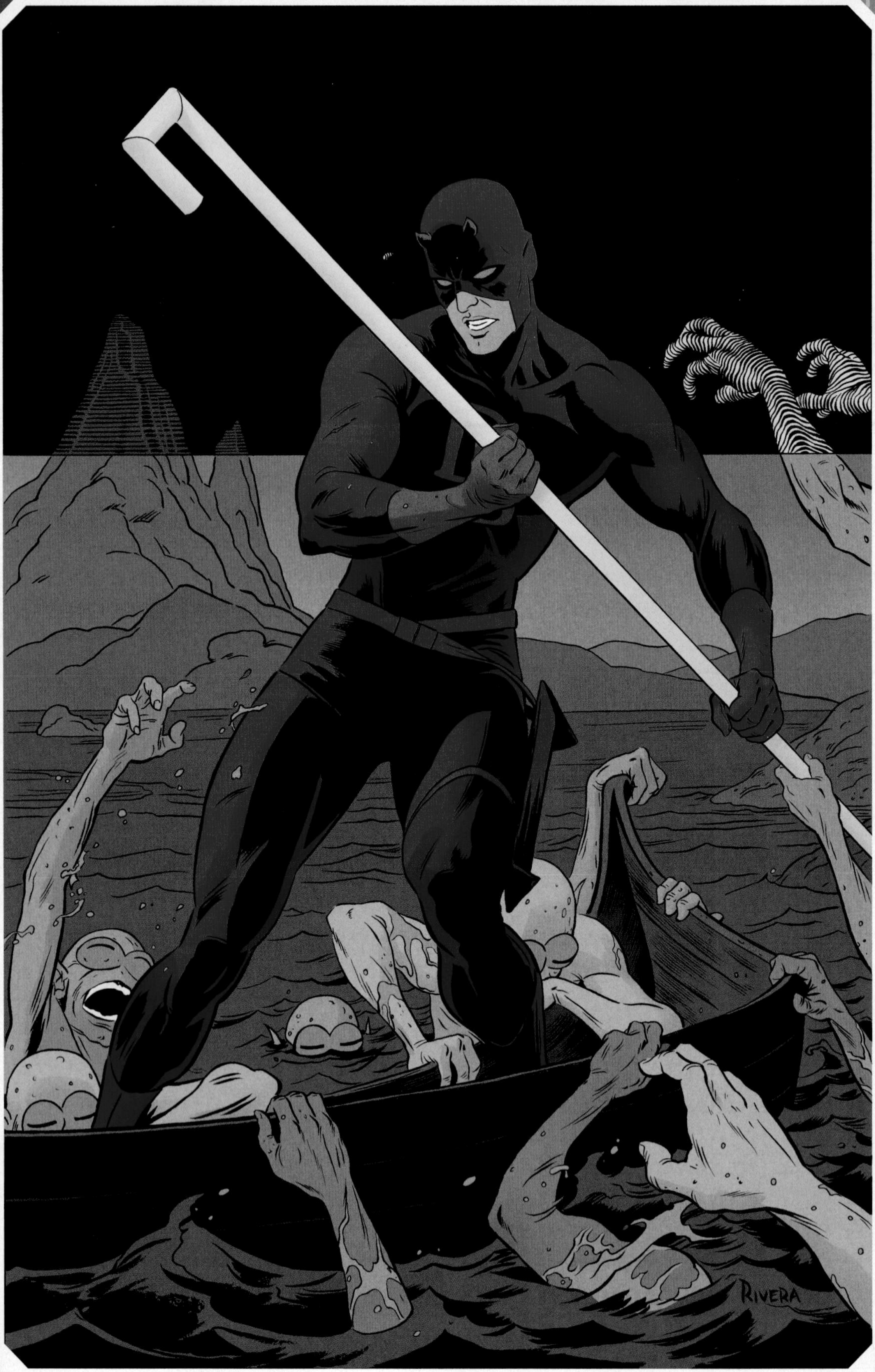
RIVERA

NINE

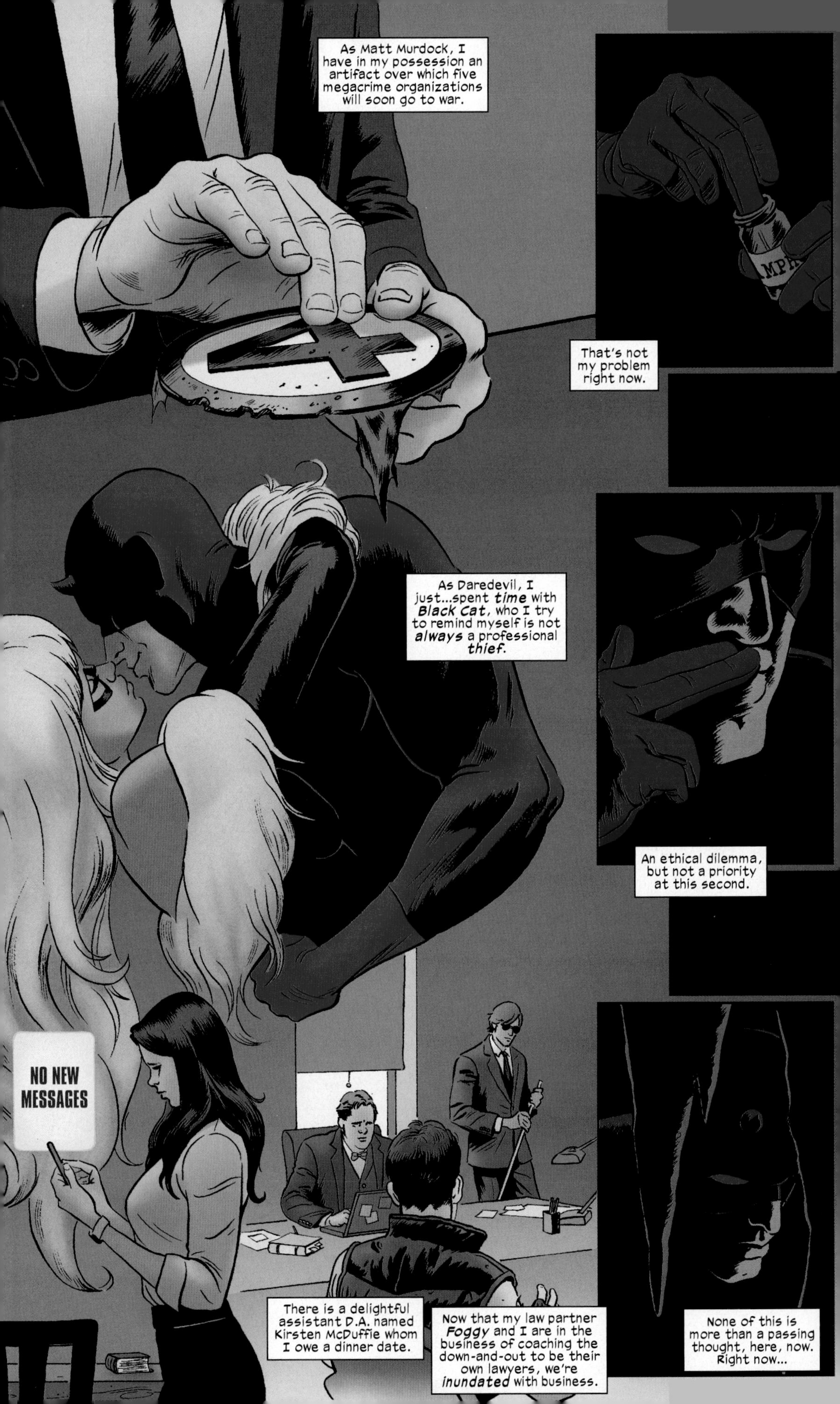

As Matt Murdock, I have in my possession an artifact over which five megacrime organizations will soon go to war.
That's not my problem right now.
As Daredevil, I just...spent *time* with *Black Cat*, who I try to remind myself is not *always* a professional *thief*.
An ethical dilemma, but not a priority at this second.
NO NEW MESSAGES
There is a delightful assistant D.A. named Kirsten McDuffie whom I owe a dinner date.
Now that my law partner *Foggy* and I are in the business of coaching the down-and-out to be their own lawyers, we're *inundated* with business.
None of this is more than a passing thought, here, now. Right now...

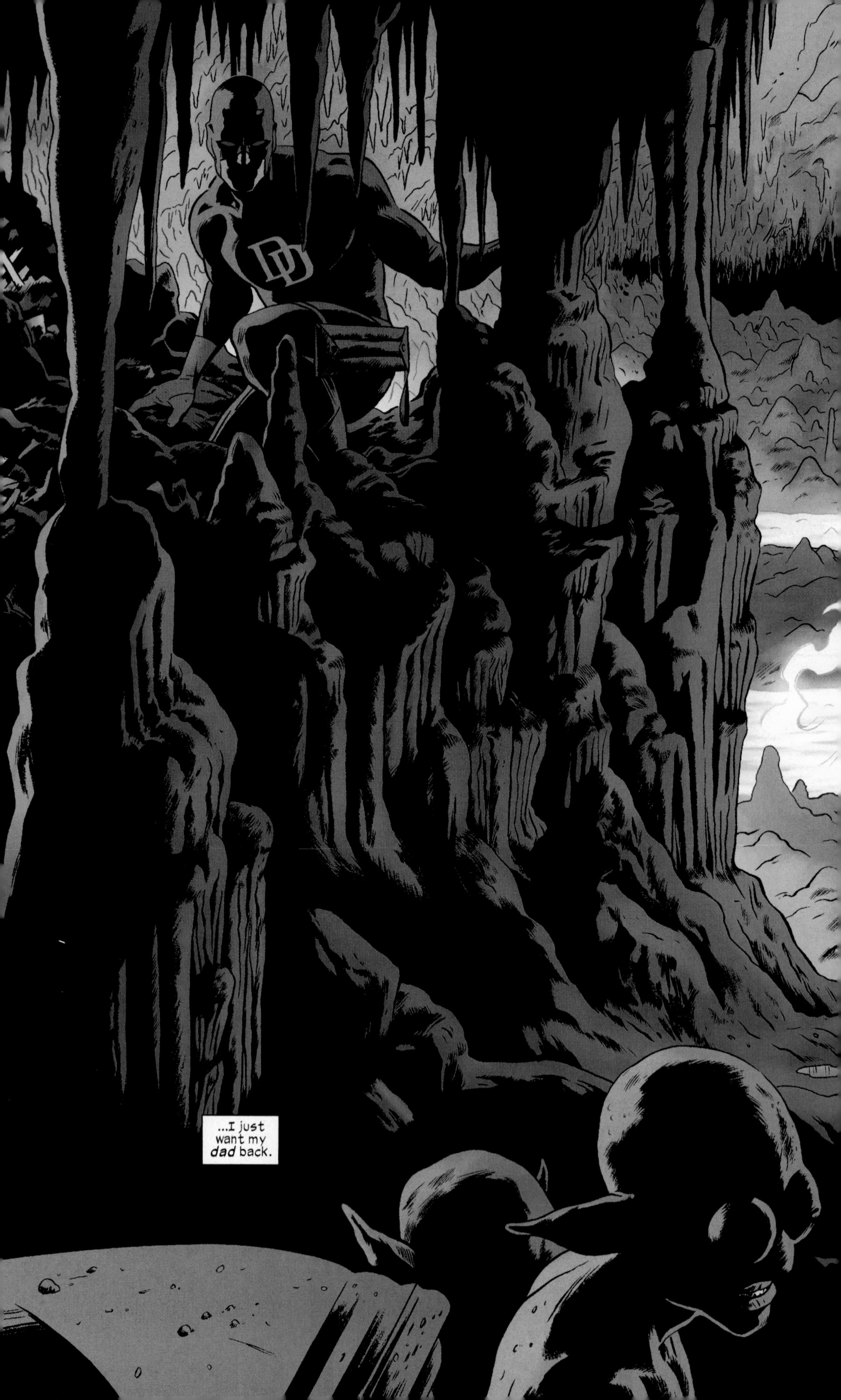
...I just want my *dad* back.

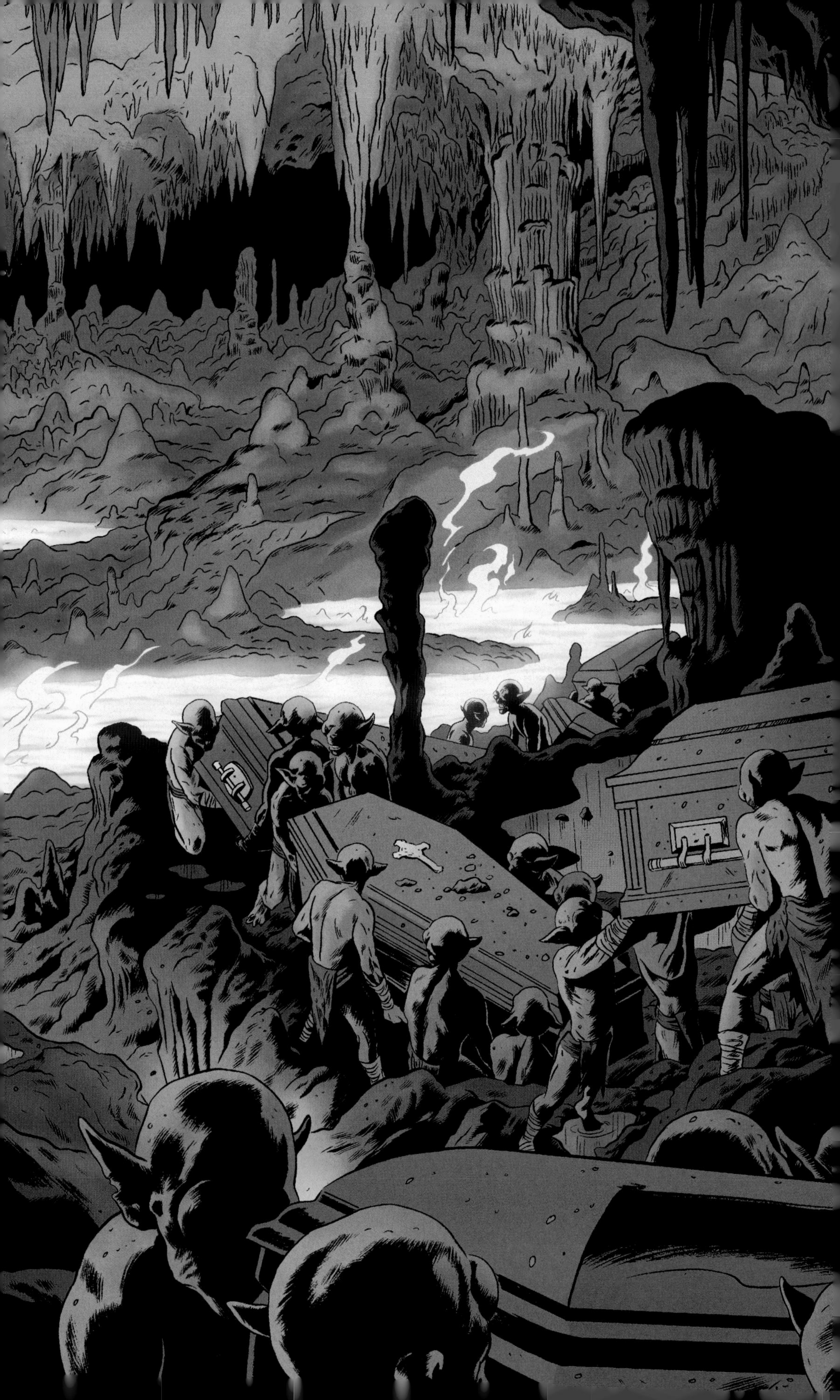

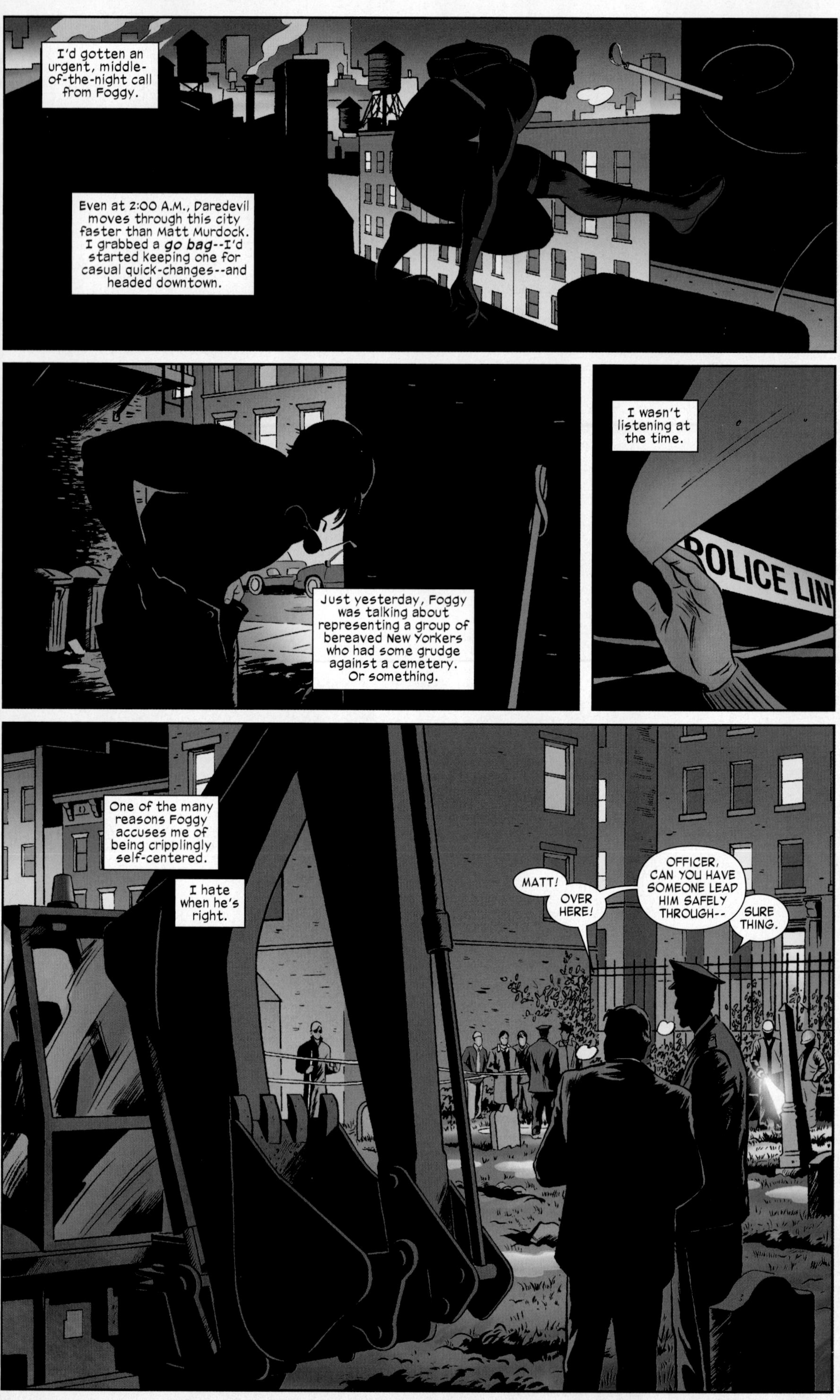
I'd gotten an urgent, middle-of-the-night call from Foggy.
Even at 2:00 A.M., Daredevil moves through this city faster than Matt Murdock. I grabbed a *go bag*--I'd started keeping one for casual quick-changes--and headed downtown.
Just yesterday, Foggy was talking about representing a group of bereaved New Yorkers who had some grudge against a cemetery. Or something.
I wasn't listening at the time.
POLICE LIN
One of the many reasons Foggy accuses me of being cripplingly self-centered.
I hate when he's right.
MATT!
OVER HERE!
OFFICER, CAN YOU HAVE SOMEONE LEAD HIM SAFELY THROUGH--
SURE THING.

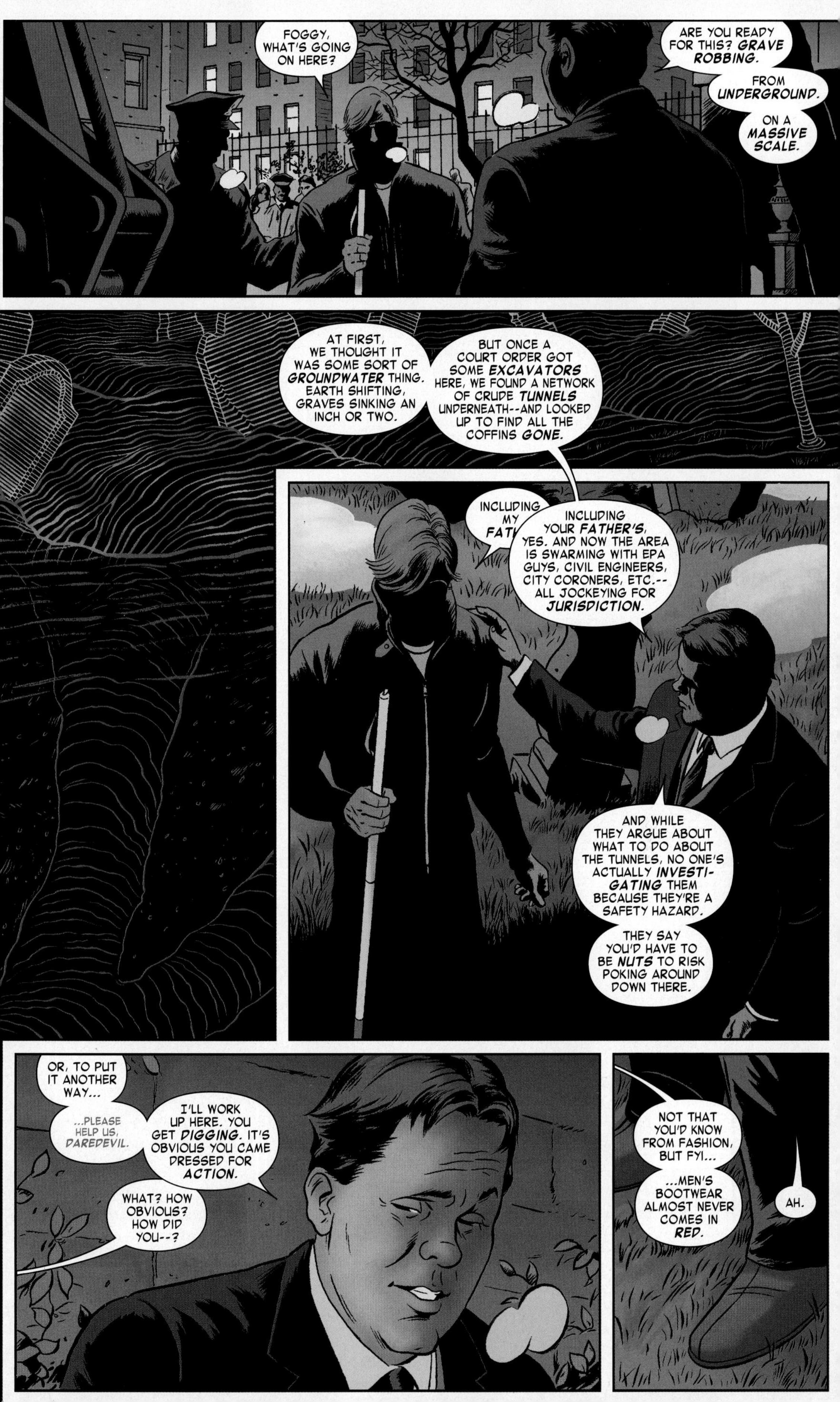
FOGGY, WHAT'S GOING ON HERE?
ARE YOU READY FOR THIS? GRAVE ROBBING.
FROM UNDERGROUND.
ON A MASSIVE SCALE.
AT FIRST, WE THOUGHT IT WAS SOME SORT OF GROUNDWATER THING. EARTH SHIFTING, GRAVES SINKING AN INCH OR TWO.
BUT ONCE A COURT ORDER GOT SOME EXCAVATORS HERE, WE FOUND A NETWORK OF CRUDE TUNNELS UNDERNEATH--AND LOOKED UP TO FIND ALL THE COFFINS GONE.
INCLUDING MY FAT
INCLUDING YOUR FATHER'S, YES. AND NOW THE AREA IS SWARMING WITH EPA GUYS, CIVIL ENGINEERS, CITY CORONERS, ETC.--ALL JOCKEYING FOR JURISDICTION.
AND WHILE THEY ARGUE ABOUT WHAT TO DO ABOUT THE TUNNELS, NO ONE'S ACTUALLY INVESTI-GATING THEM BECAUSE THEY'RE A SAFETY HAZARD.
THEY SAY YOU'D HAVE TO BE NUTS TO RISK POKING AROUND DOWN THERE.
OR, TO PUT IT ANOTHER WAY...
...PLEASE HELP US, DAREDEVIL.
I'LL WORK UP HERE. YOU GET DIGGING. IT'S OBVIOUS YOU CAME DRESSED FOR ACTION.
WHAT? HOW OBVIOUS? HOW DID YOU--?
NOT THAT YOU'D KNOW FROM FASHION, BUT FYI...
...MEN'S BOOTWEAR ALMOST NEVER COMES IN RED.
AH.

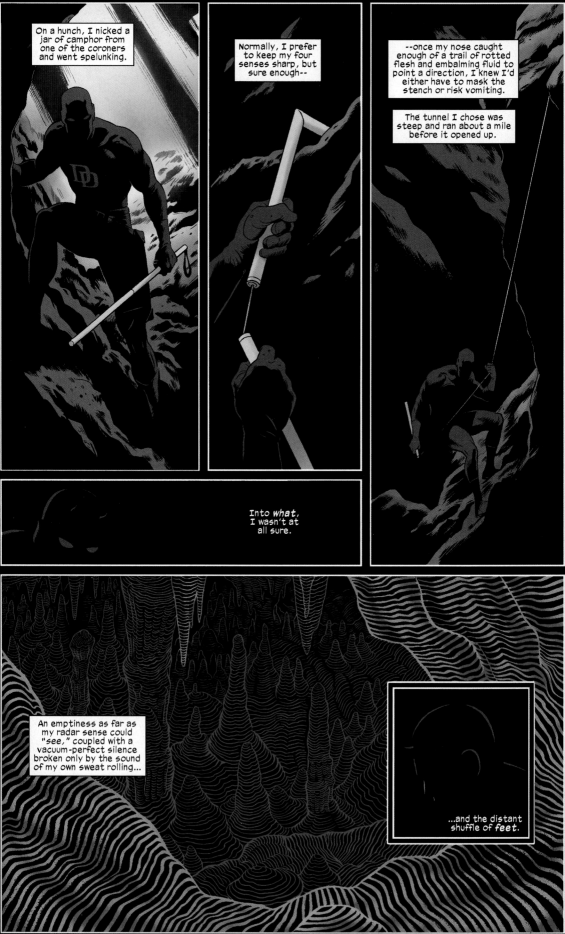

On a hunch, I nicked a jar of camphor from one of the coroners and went spelunking.

Normally, I prefer to keep my four senses sharp, but sure enough--

--once my nose caught enough of a trail of rotted flesh and embalming fluid to point a direction, I knew I'd either have to mask the stench or risk vomiting.

The tunnel I chose was steep and ran about a mile before it opened up.

Into *what*, I wasn't at all sure.

An emptiness as far as my radar sense could "*see*," coupled with a vacuum-perfect silence broken only by the sound of my own sweat rolling...

...and the distant shuffle of *feet*.

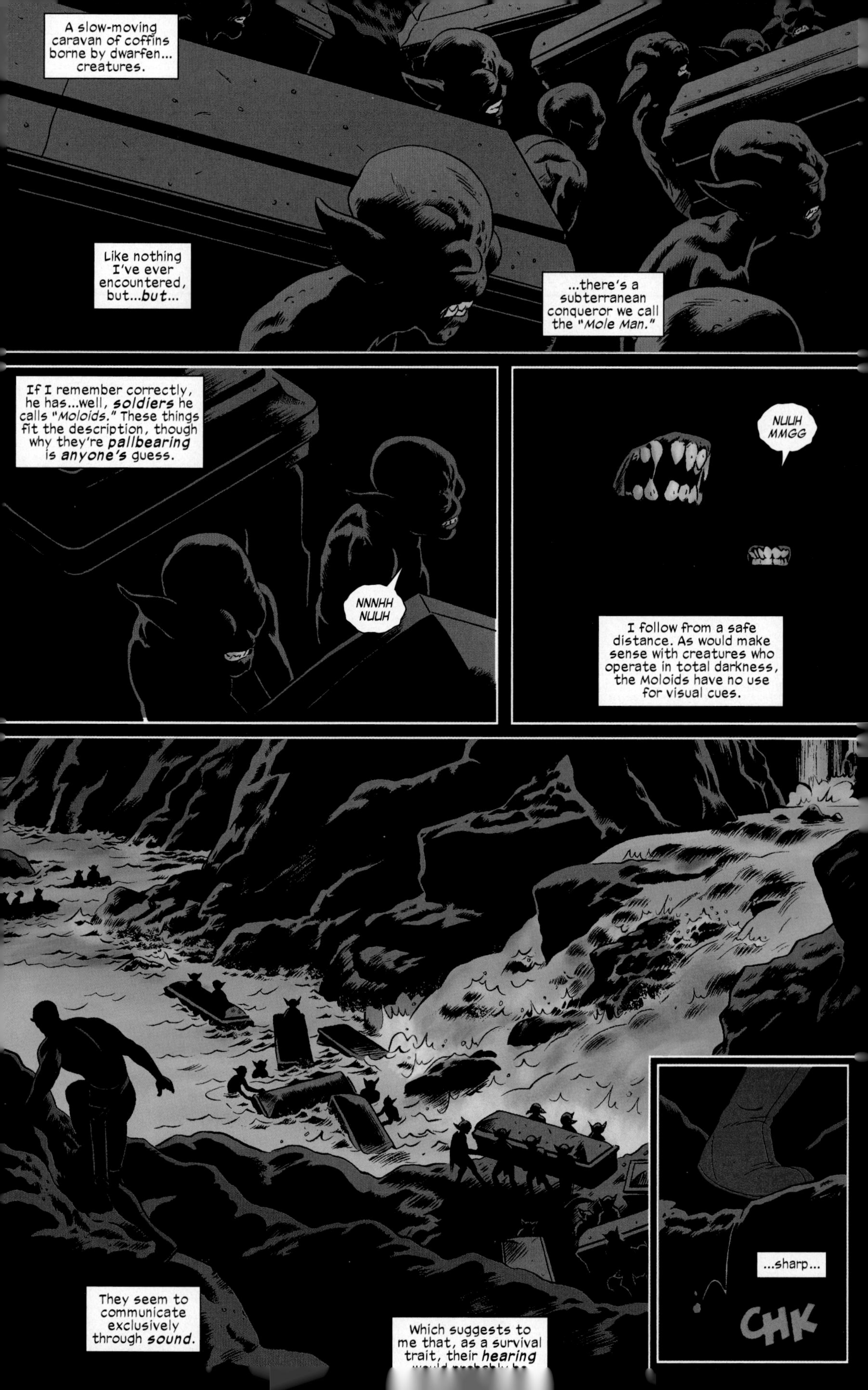
A slow-moving caravan of coffins borne by dwarfen... creatures.
Like nothing I've ever encountered, but...*but*...
...there's a subterranean conqueror we call the "*Mole Man*."
If I remember correctly, he has...well, *soldiers* he calls "*Moloids*." These things fit the description, though why they're *pallbearing* is *anyone's* guess.
NNNHH NUUH
NUUH MMGG
I follow from a safe distance. As would make sense with creatures who operate in total darkness, the Moloids have no use for visual cues.
They seem to communicate exclusively through *sound*.
Which suggests to me that, as a survival trait, their *hearing*
...sharp...
CHK

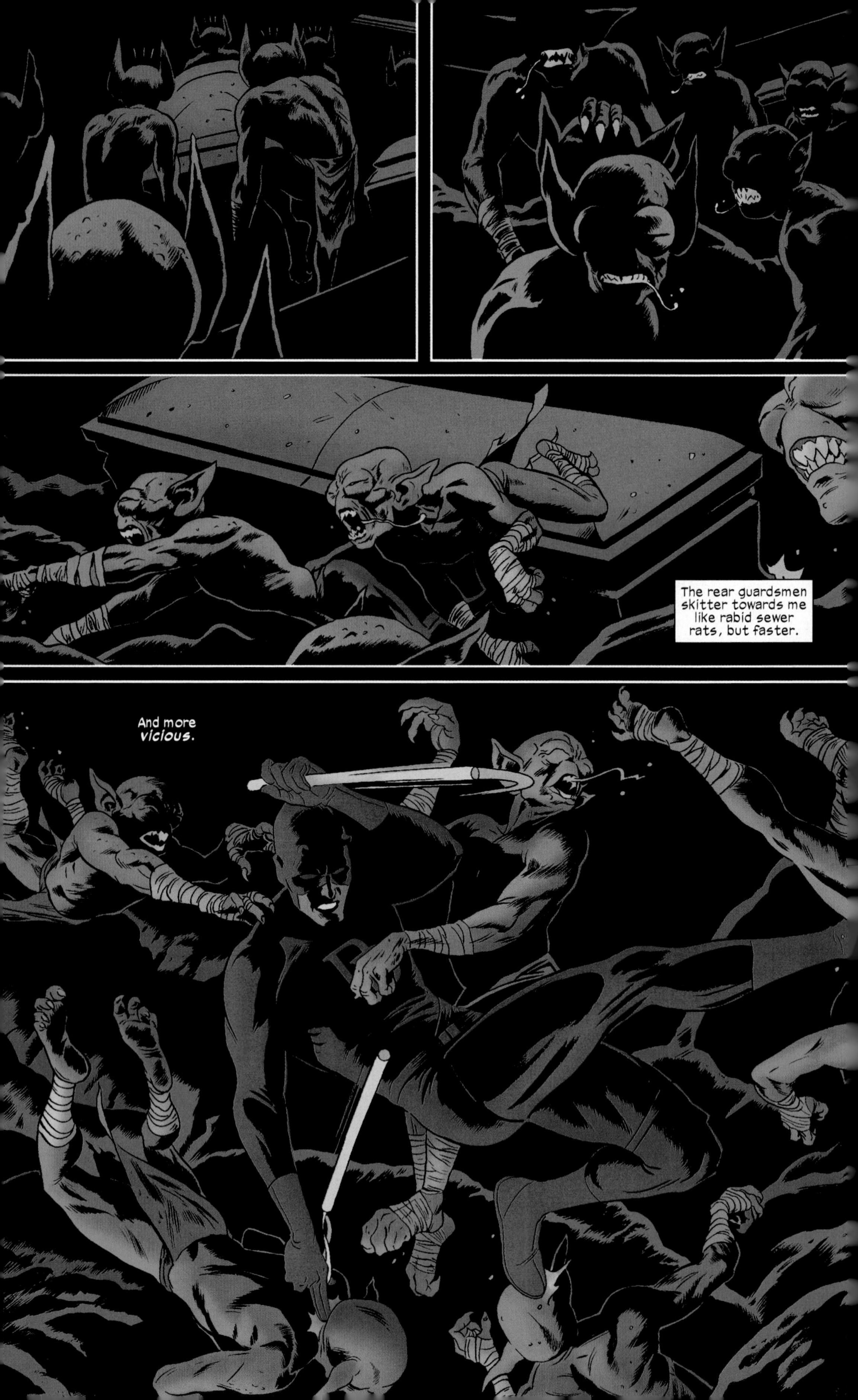

The rear guardsmen skitter towards me like rabid sewer rats, but faster.
And more *vicious*.

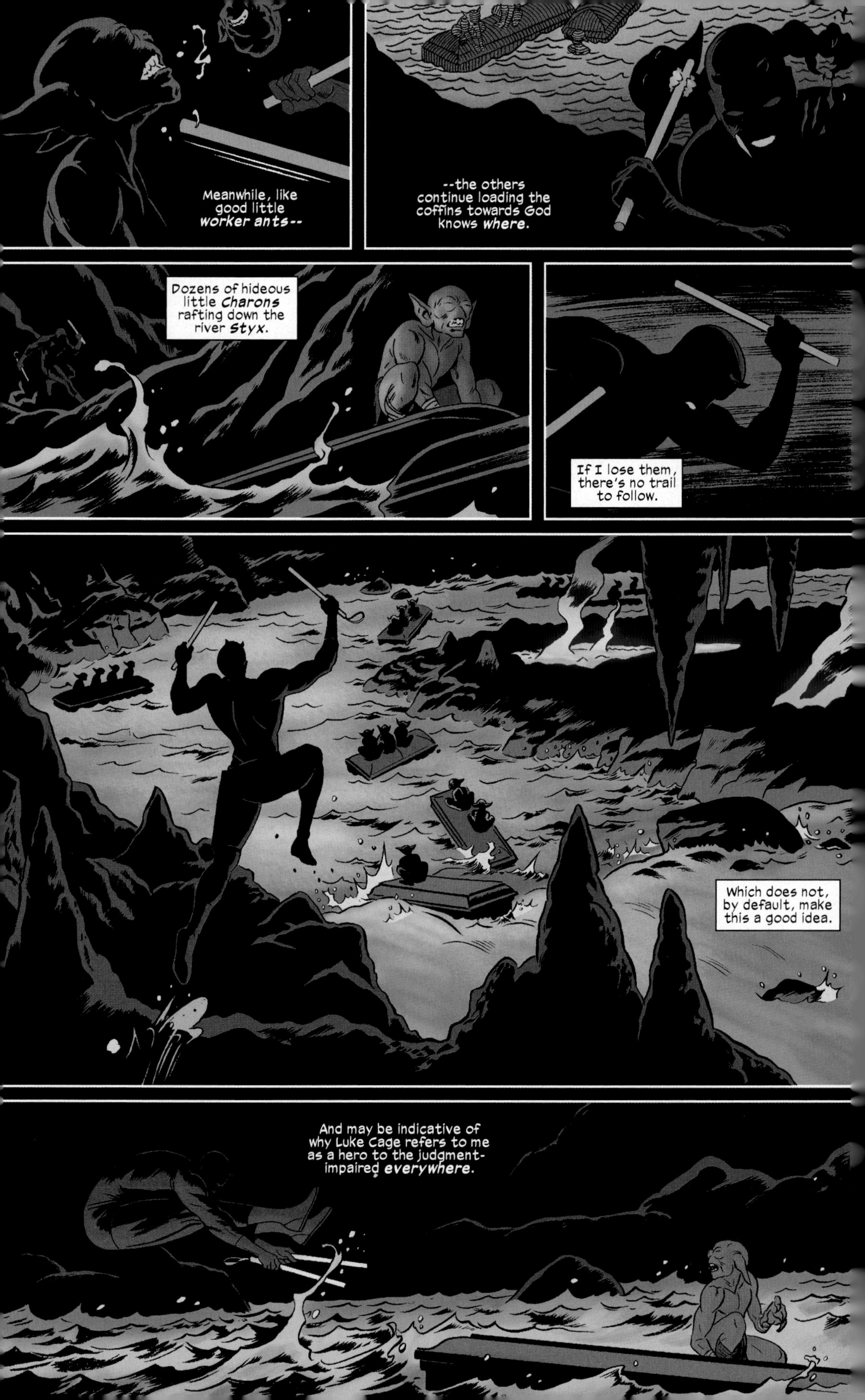

Meanwhile, like good little worker ants--
--the others continue loading the coffins towards God knows where.
Dozens of hideous little Charons rafting down the river Styx.
If I lose them, there's no trail to follow.
Which does not, by default, make this a good idea.
And may be indicative of why Luke Cage refers to me as a hero to the judgment-impaired everywhere.

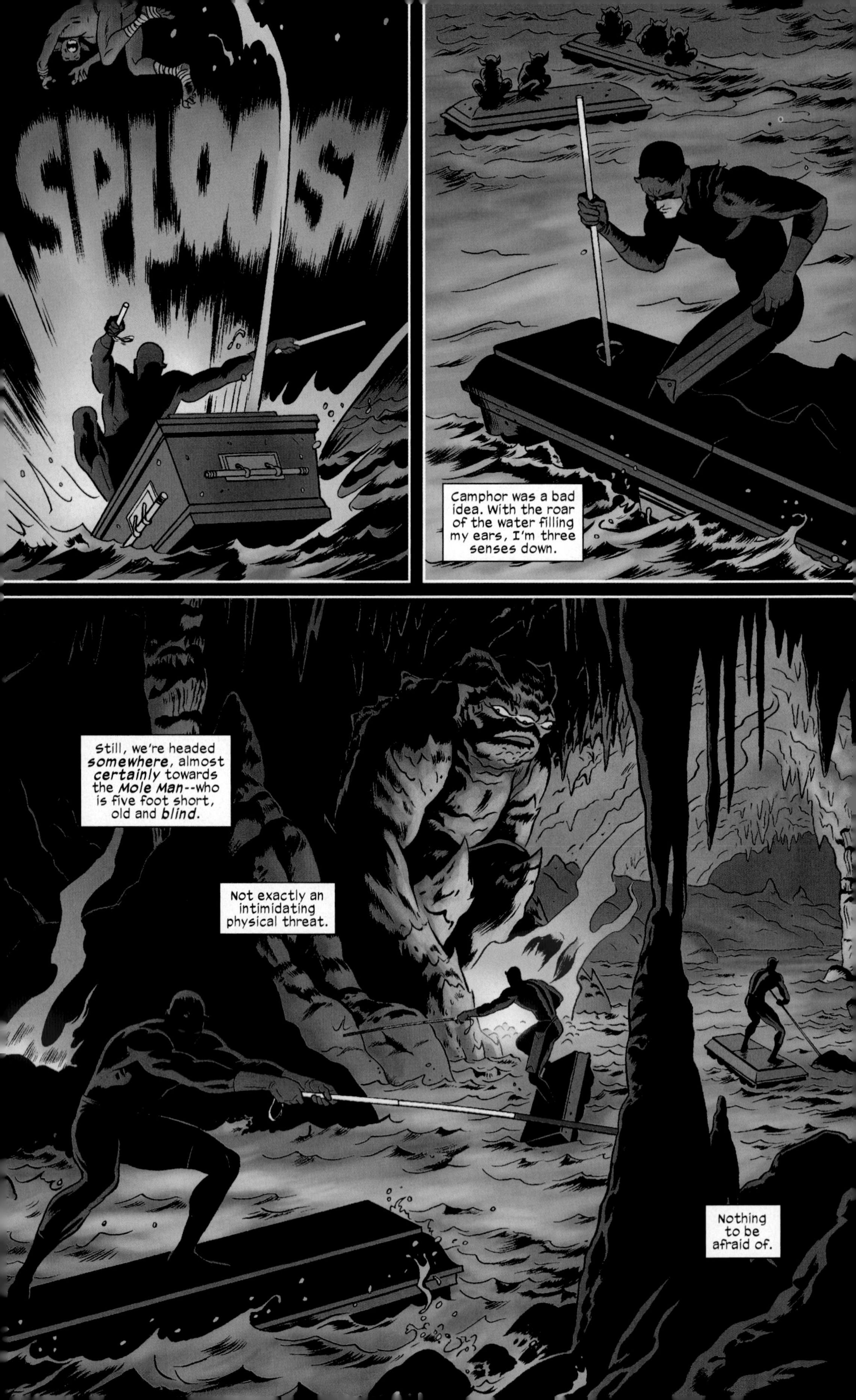

SPLOOSH
Camphor was a bad idea. With the roar of the water filling my ears, I'm three senses down.
Still, we're headed *somewhere*, almost *certainly* towards the *Mole Man*--who is five foot short, old and *blind*.
Not exactly an intimidating physical threat.
Nothing to be afraid of.

Just caves.

This leg of the journey comes to an end as the river slows.

KLAK

CHFF

SCHK

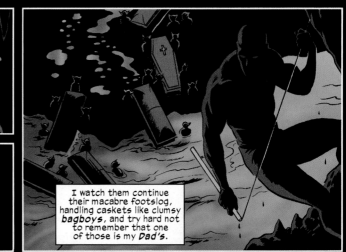

I watch them continue their macabre footslog, handling caskets like clumsy *bagboys*, and try hard not to remember that one of those is my *Dad's*.

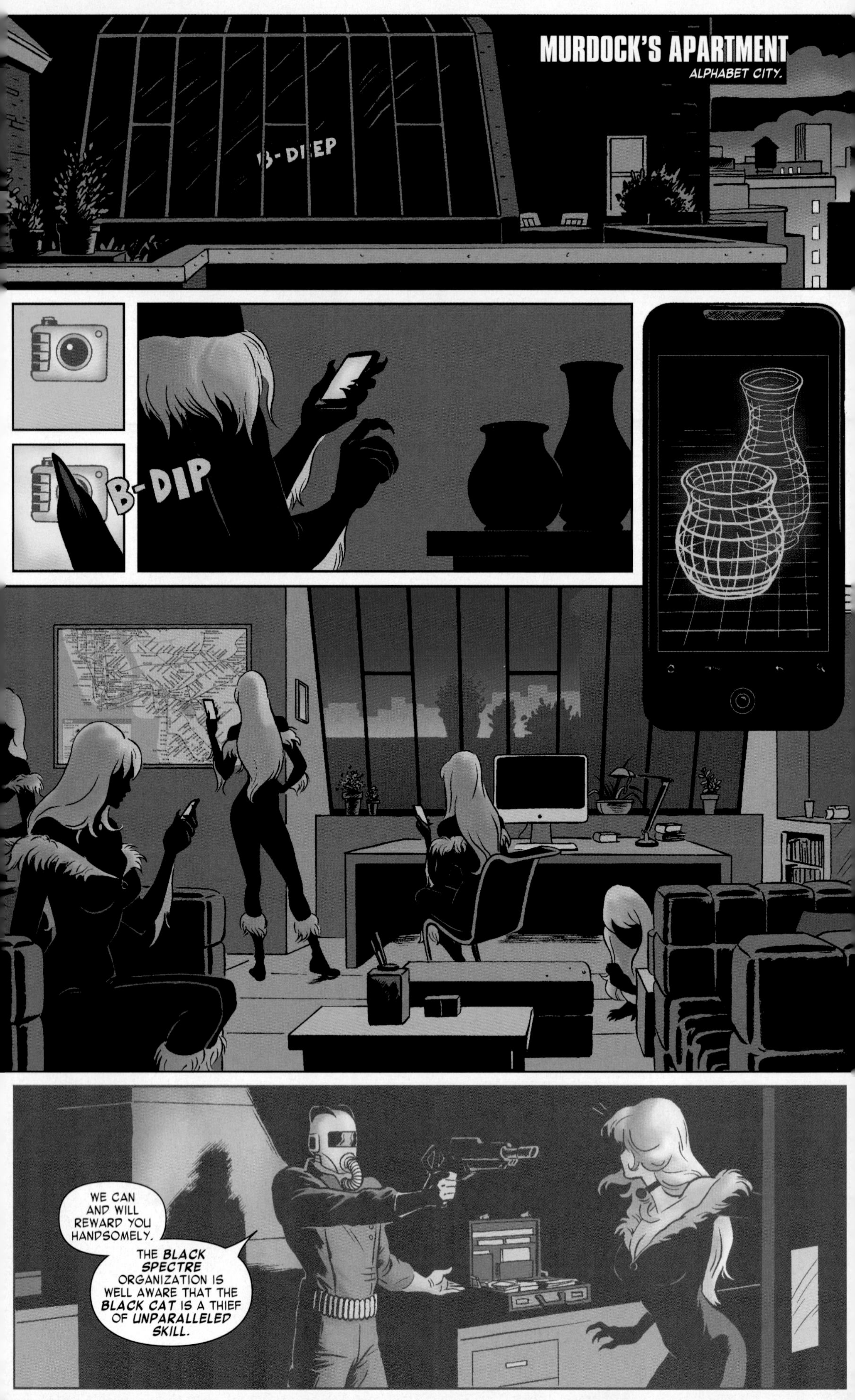
MURDOCK'S APARTMENT
ALPHABET CITY.
B-DEEP
B-DIP
WE CAN AND WILL REWARD YOU HANDSOMELY.
THE BLACK SPECTRE ORGANIZATION IS WELL AWARE THAT THE BLACK CAT IS A THIEF OF UNPARALLELED SKILL.

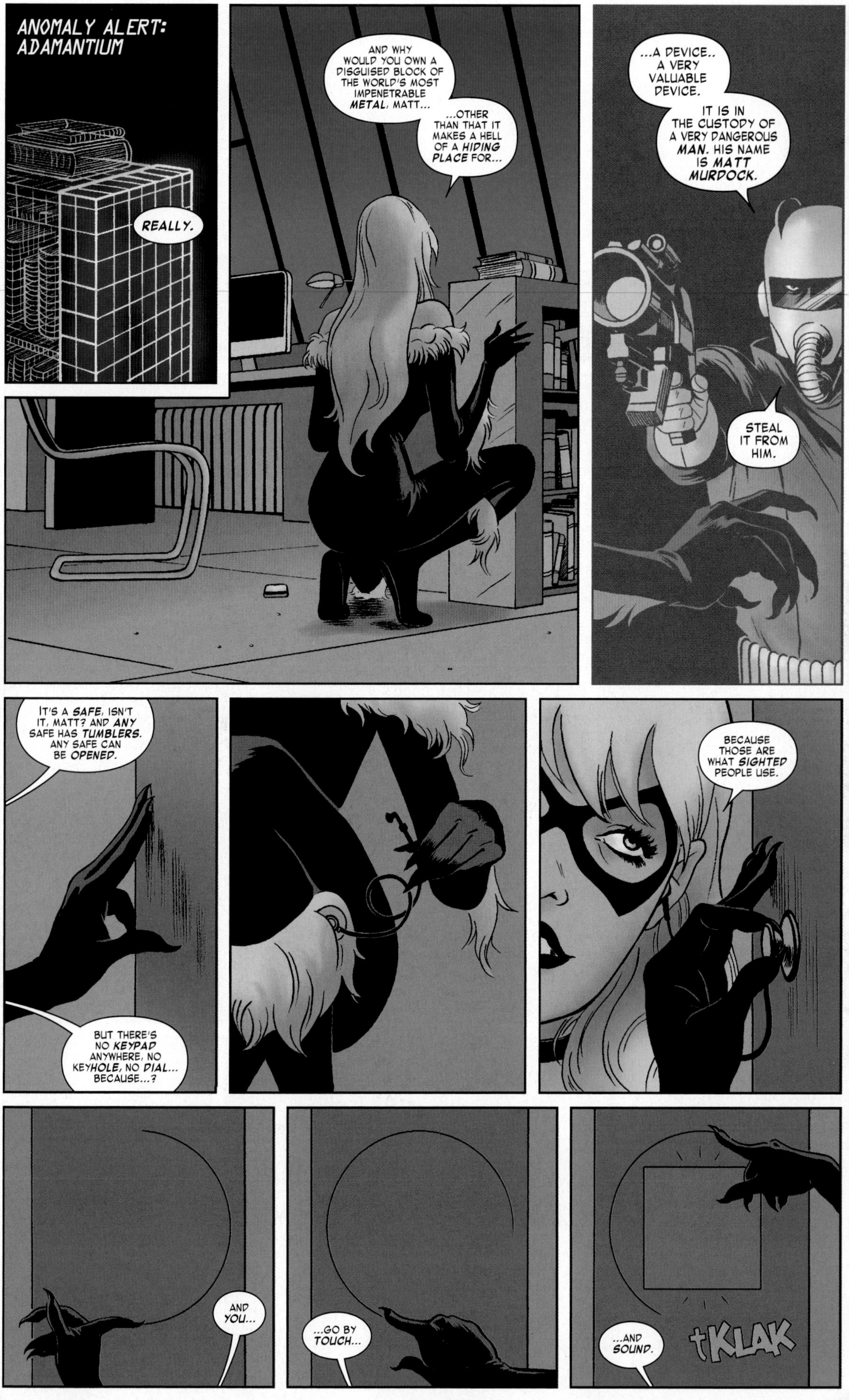
ANOMALY ALERT: ADAMANTIUM
REALLY.
AND WHY WOULD YOU OWN A DISGUISED BLOCK OF THE WORLD'S MOST IMPENETRABLE METAL, MATT...
...OTHER THAN THAT IT MAKES A HELL OF A HIDING PLACE FOR...
...A DEVICE.. A VERY VALUABLE DEVICE.
IT IS IN THE CUSTODY OF A VERY DANGEROUS MAN. HIS NAME IS MATT MURDOCK.
STEAL IT FROM HIM.
IT'S A SAFE, ISN'T IT, MATT? AND ANY SAFE HAS TUMBLERS. ANY SAFE CAN BE OPENED.
BUT THERE'S NO KEYPAD ANYWHERE, NO KEYHOLE, NO DIAL... BECAUSE...?
BECAUSE THOSE ARE WHAT SIGHTED PEOPLE USE.
AND YOU...
...GO BY TOUCH...
...AND SOUND.
tKLAK

 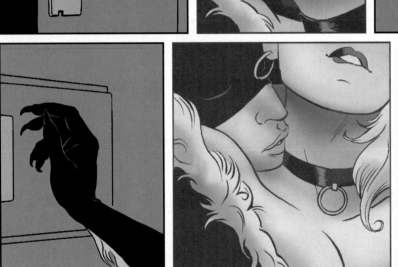 

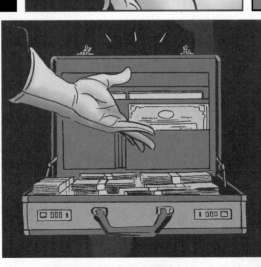

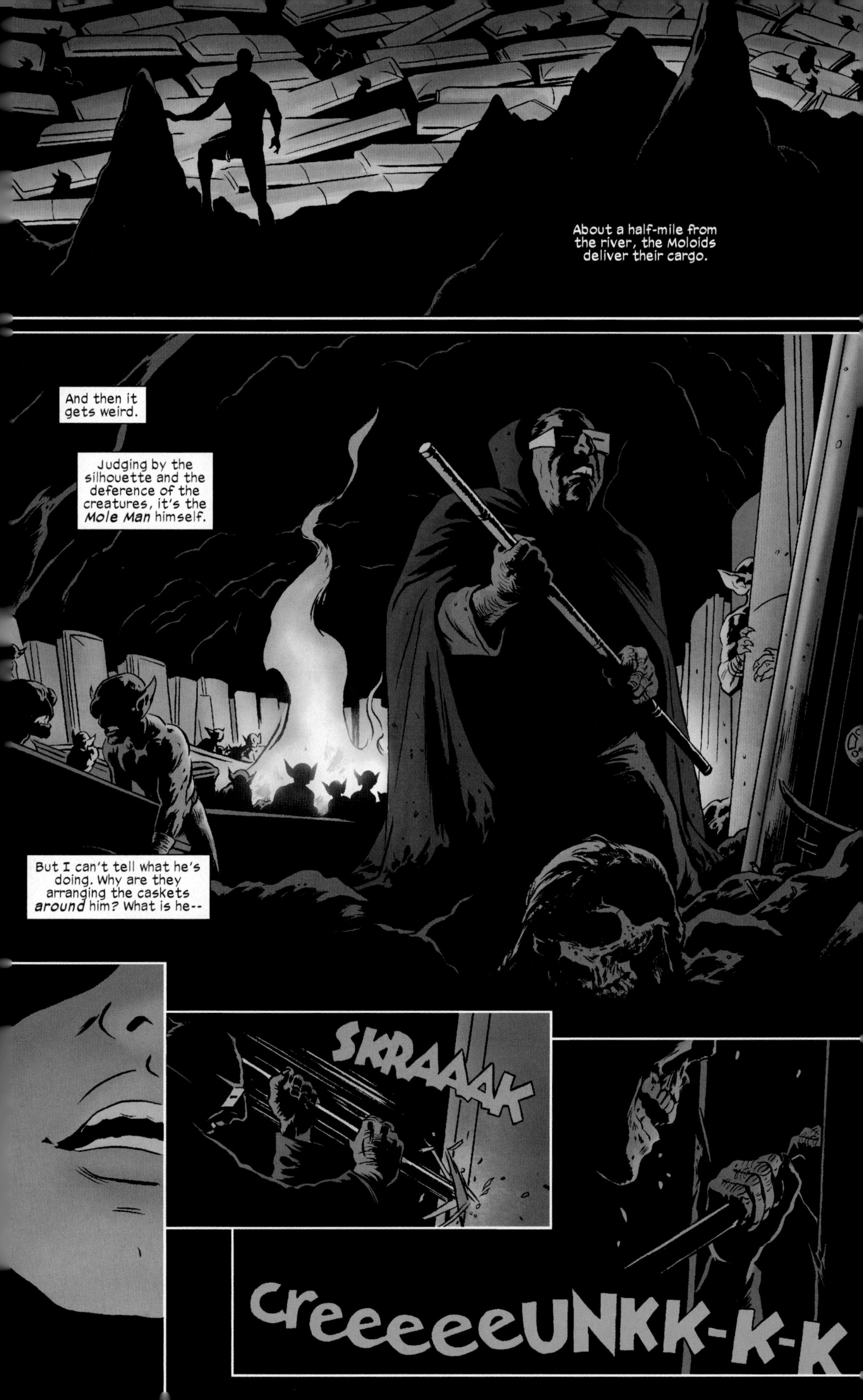
About a half-mile from the river, the Moloids deliver their cargo.
And then it gets weird.
Judging by the silhouette and the deference of the creatures, it's the *Mole Man* himself.
But I can't tell what he's doing. Why are they arranging the caskets *around* him? What is he--
SKRAAAK
CreeeeeeUNKK-K-K

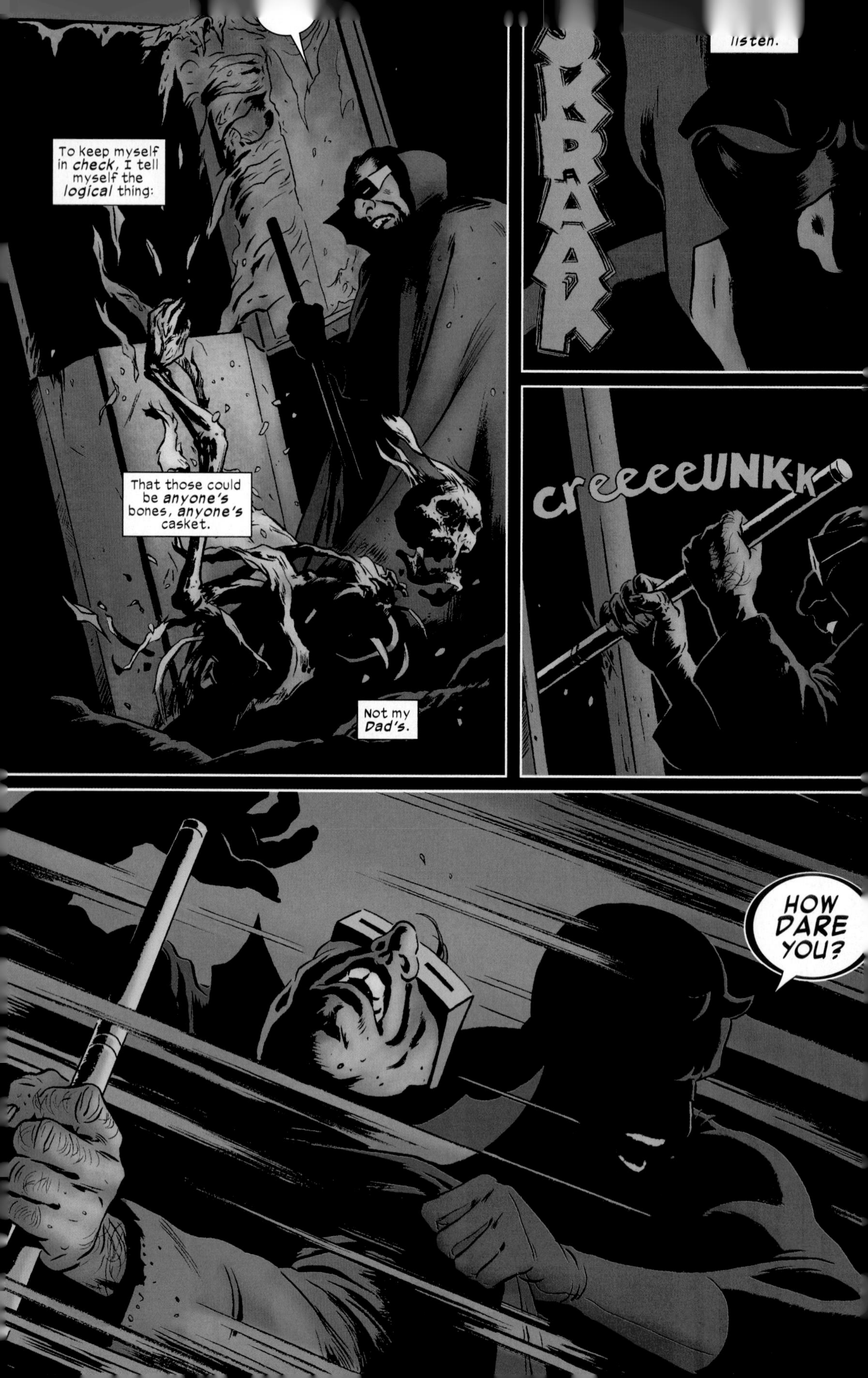

To keep myself in *check*, I tell myself the *logical* thing:
That those could be *anyone's* bones, *anyone's* casket.
Not my *Dad's*.
KRAAK
listen.
creeeeUNK-K
HOW DARE YOU?

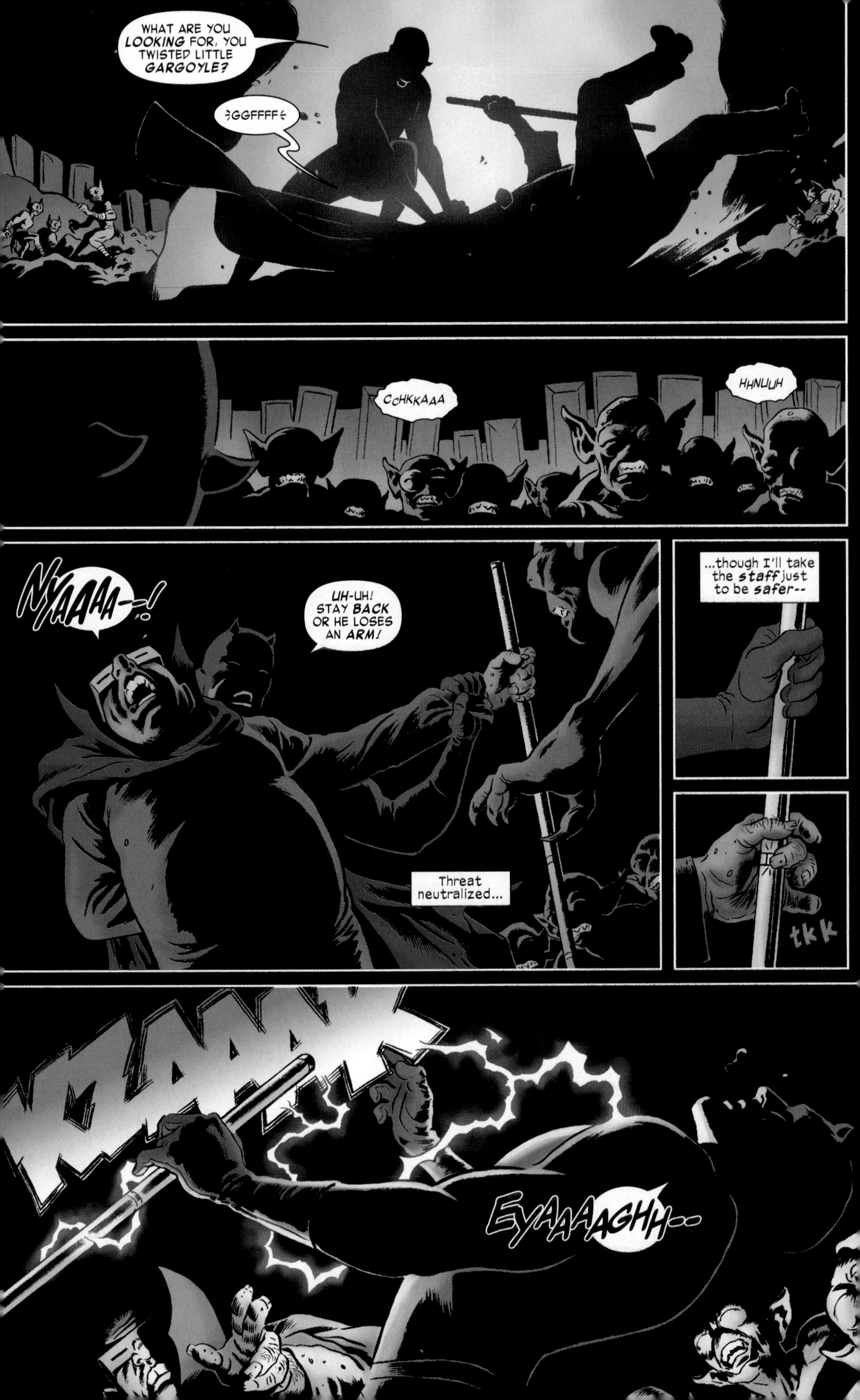
WHAT ARE YOU LOOKING FOR, YOU TWISTED LITTLE GARGOYLE?
GGFFFF
CCHKKAAA
HHNUUH
NYAAAA--!
UH-UH! STAY BACK OR HE LOSES AN ARM!
Threat neutralized...
...though I'll take the staff just to be safer--
tkk
EYAAAAGHH--

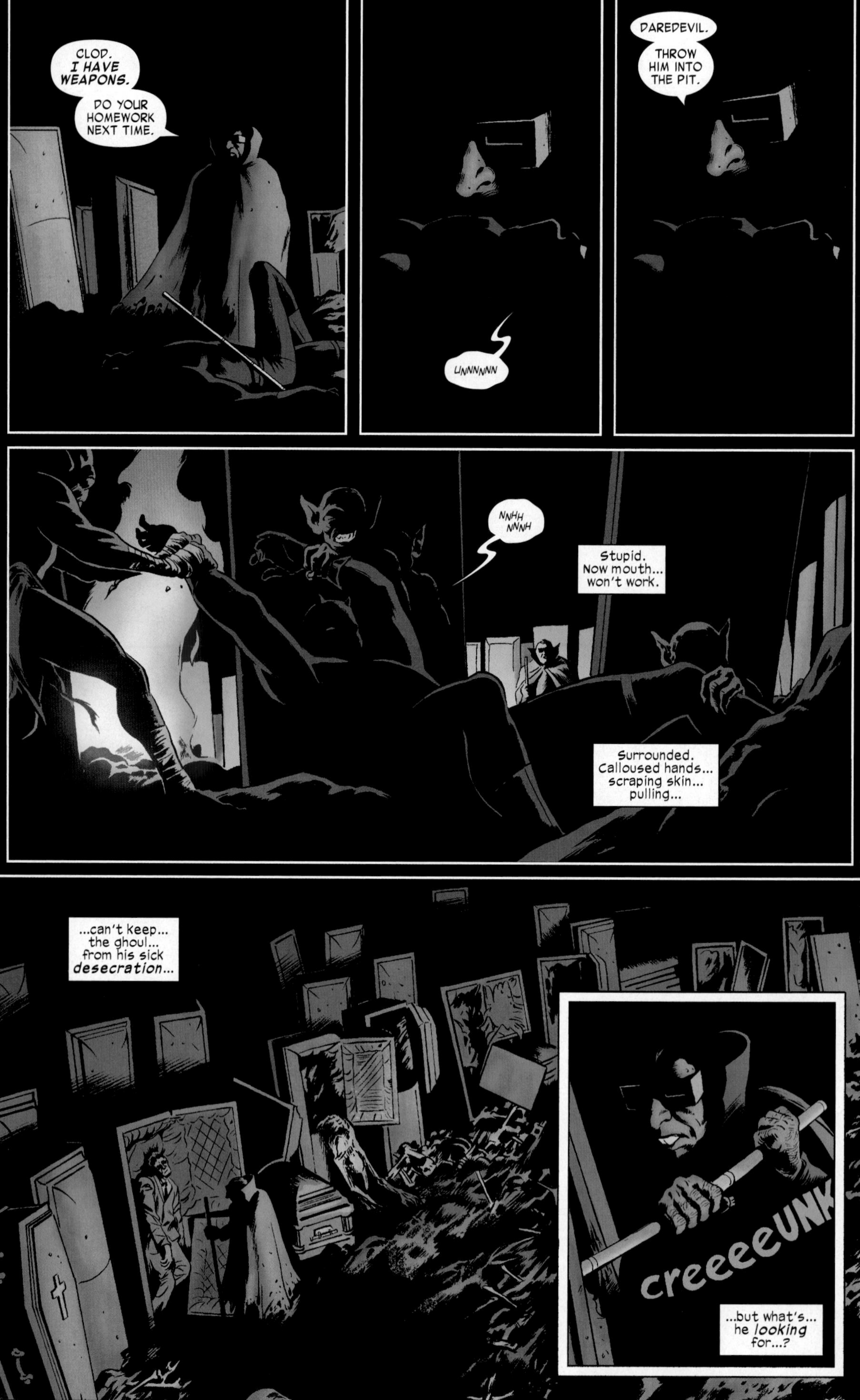
CLOD. I HAVE WEAPONS.
DO YOUR HOMEWORK NEXT TIME.
UNNNNNN
DAREDEVIL.
THROW HIM INTO THE PIT.
NNHH NNNH
Stupid. Now mouth... won't work.
Surrounded. Calloused hands... scraping skin... pulling...
...can't keep... the ghoul... from his sick desecration...
creeeeUNK
...but what's... he looking for...?

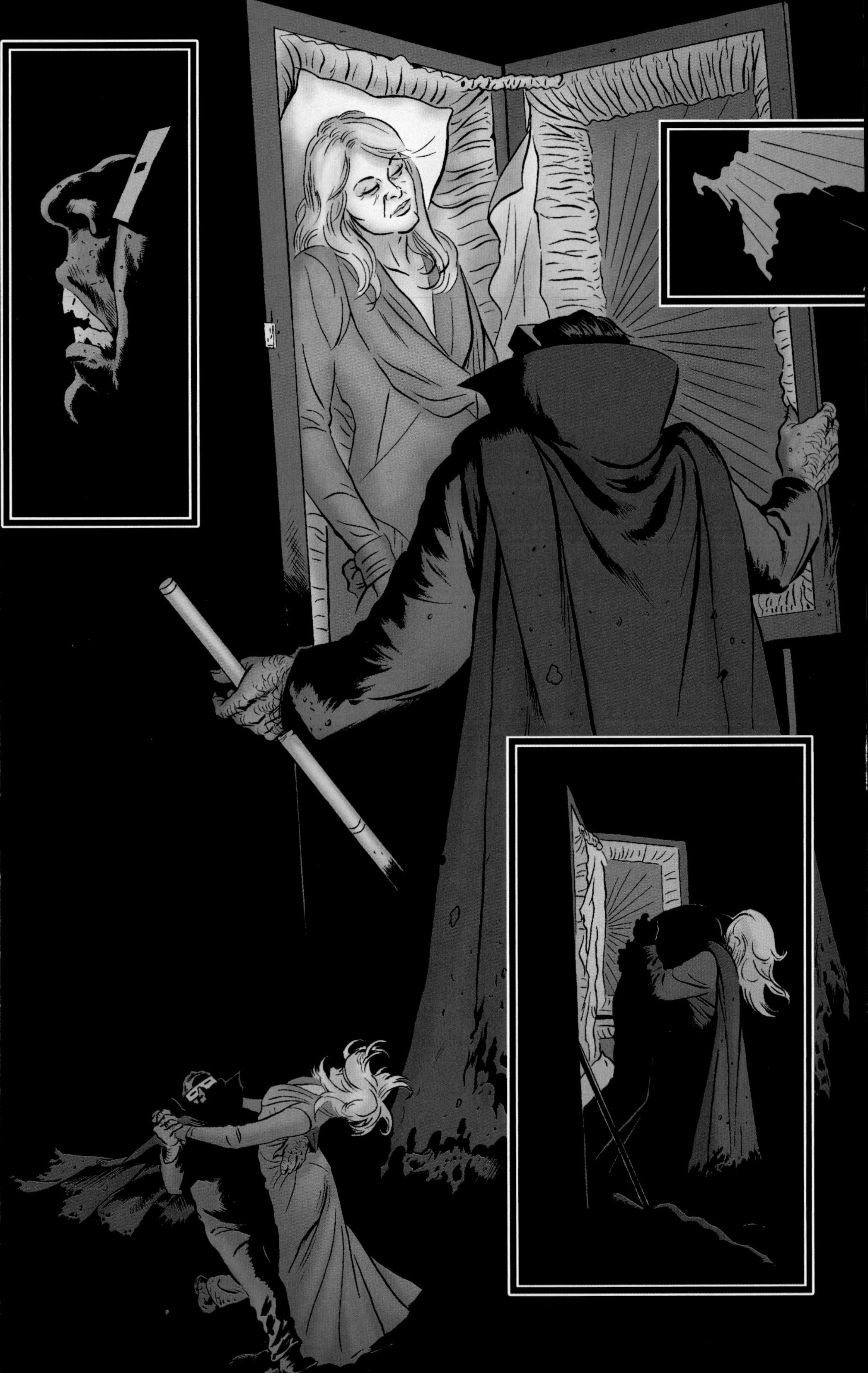

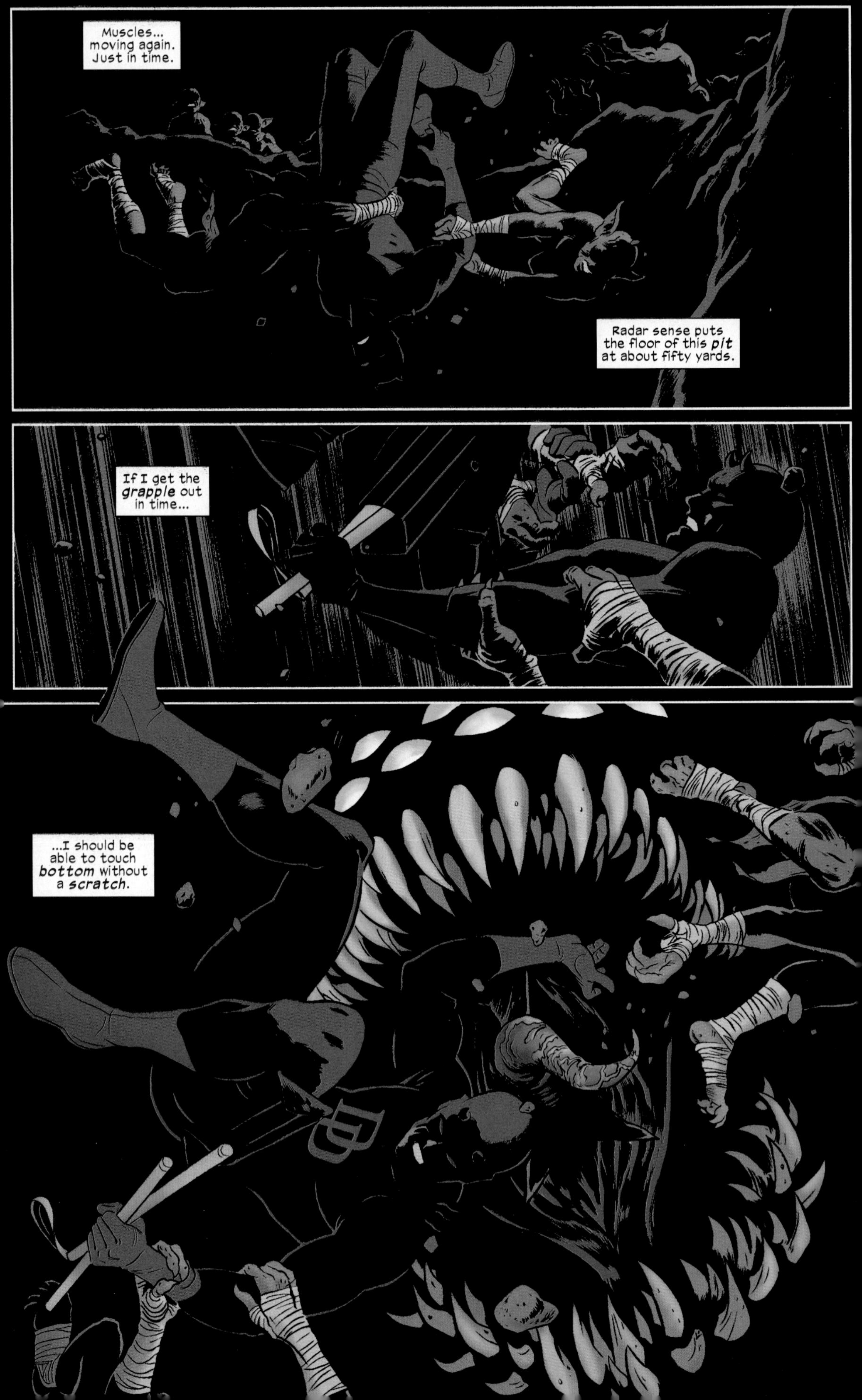
Muscles... moving again. Just in time.
Radar sense puts the floor of this pit at about fifty yards.
If I get the grapple out in time...
...I should be able to touch bottom without a scratch.

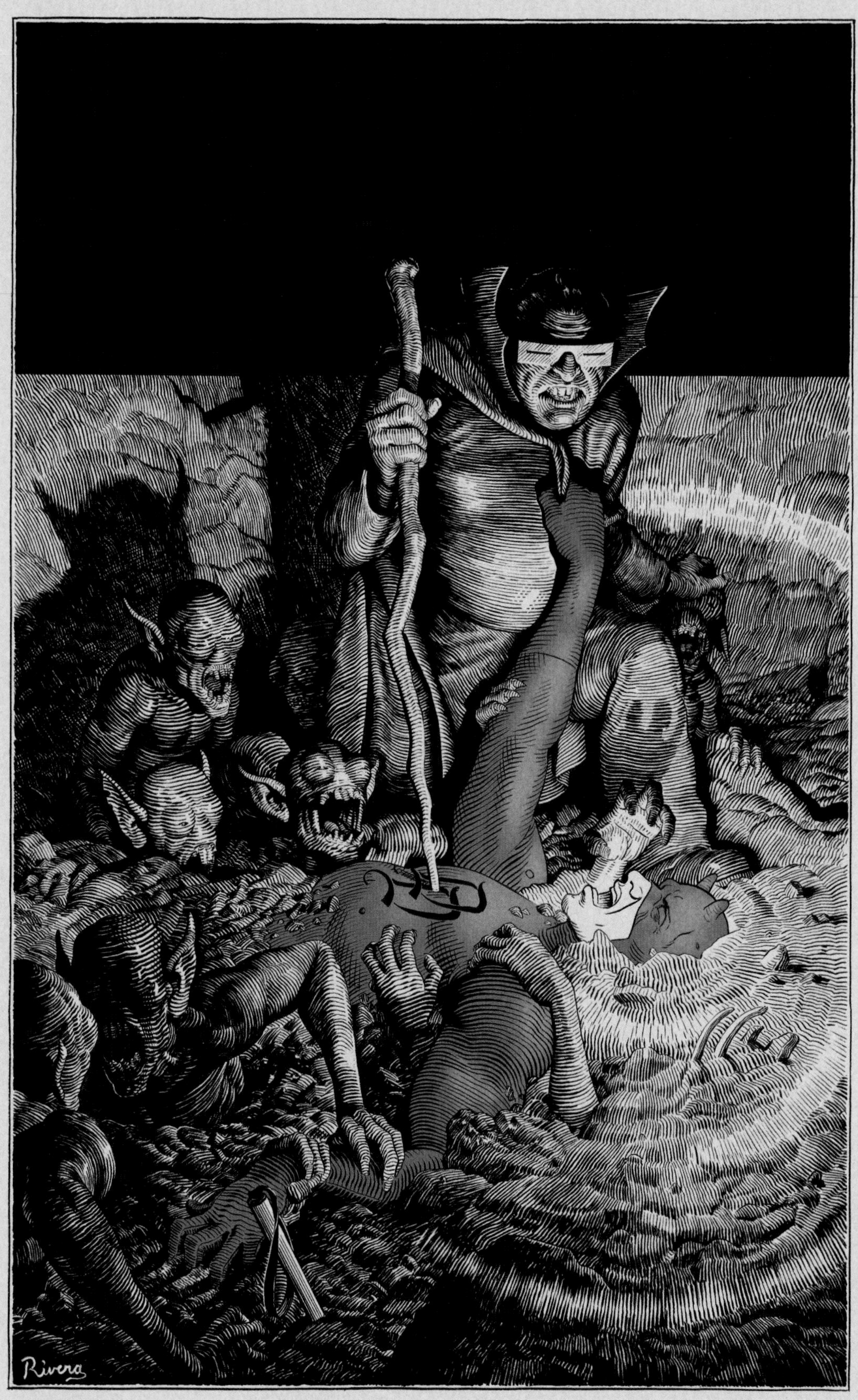
Rivera

TEN

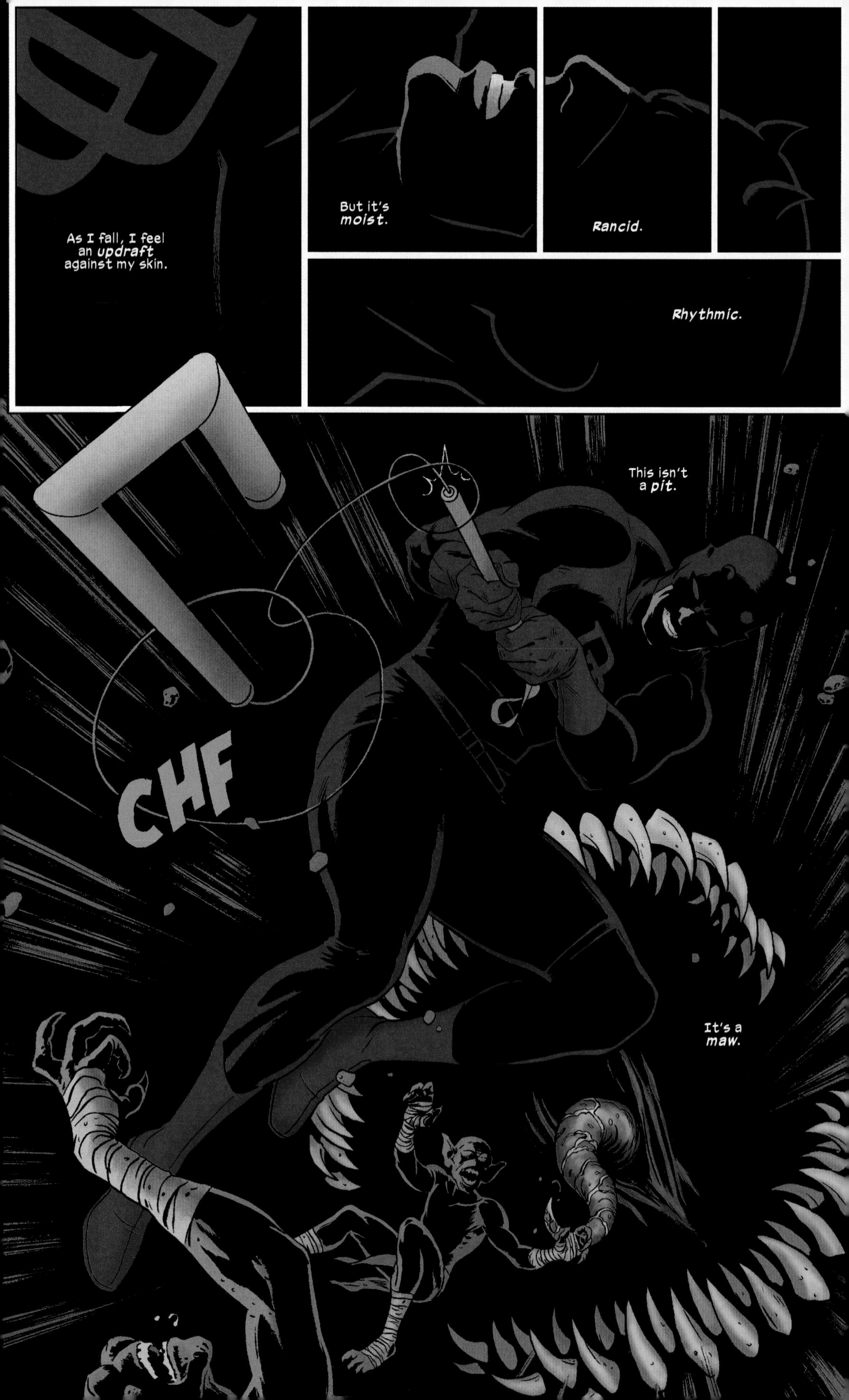
As I fall, I feel an updraft against my skin.
But it's moist.
Rancid.
Rhythmic.
This isn't a pit.
CHF
It's a maw.

SCHKK

SNAP

I don't know what this thing is. I don't want to know. Doesn't matter.

Despite what we heard as kids, neither *Jonah* nor *Pinocchio* could really survive inside a *giant beast*. Not for *ten seconds*.

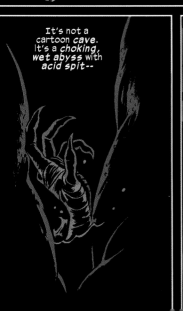

It's not a cartoon *cave*. It's a *choking, wet abyss* with *acid spit*--

--and *teeth*--

--and an *appetite*.

Time for *one move*.

All that can **save** me--

FWIP FWIP

--is if its *tongue* is even half as sensitive as *mine.*

FWAP

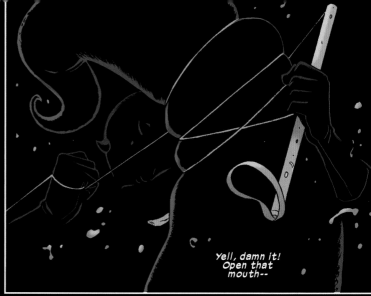

Yell, damn it! Open that *mouth*--

--and **YELL!**

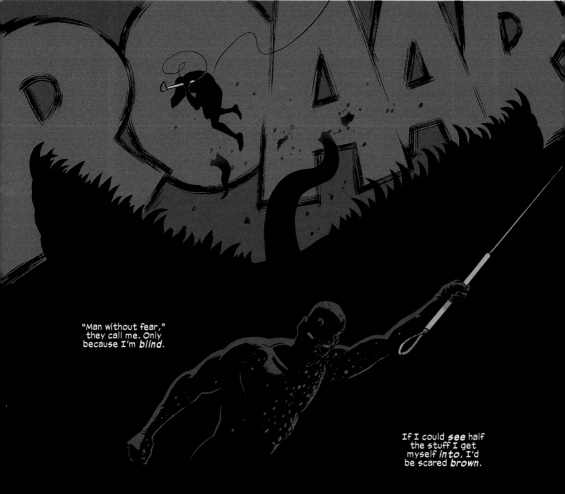

"Man without fear," they call me. Only because I'm *blind.*

If I could *see* half the stuff I get myself *into,* I'd be scared *brown.*

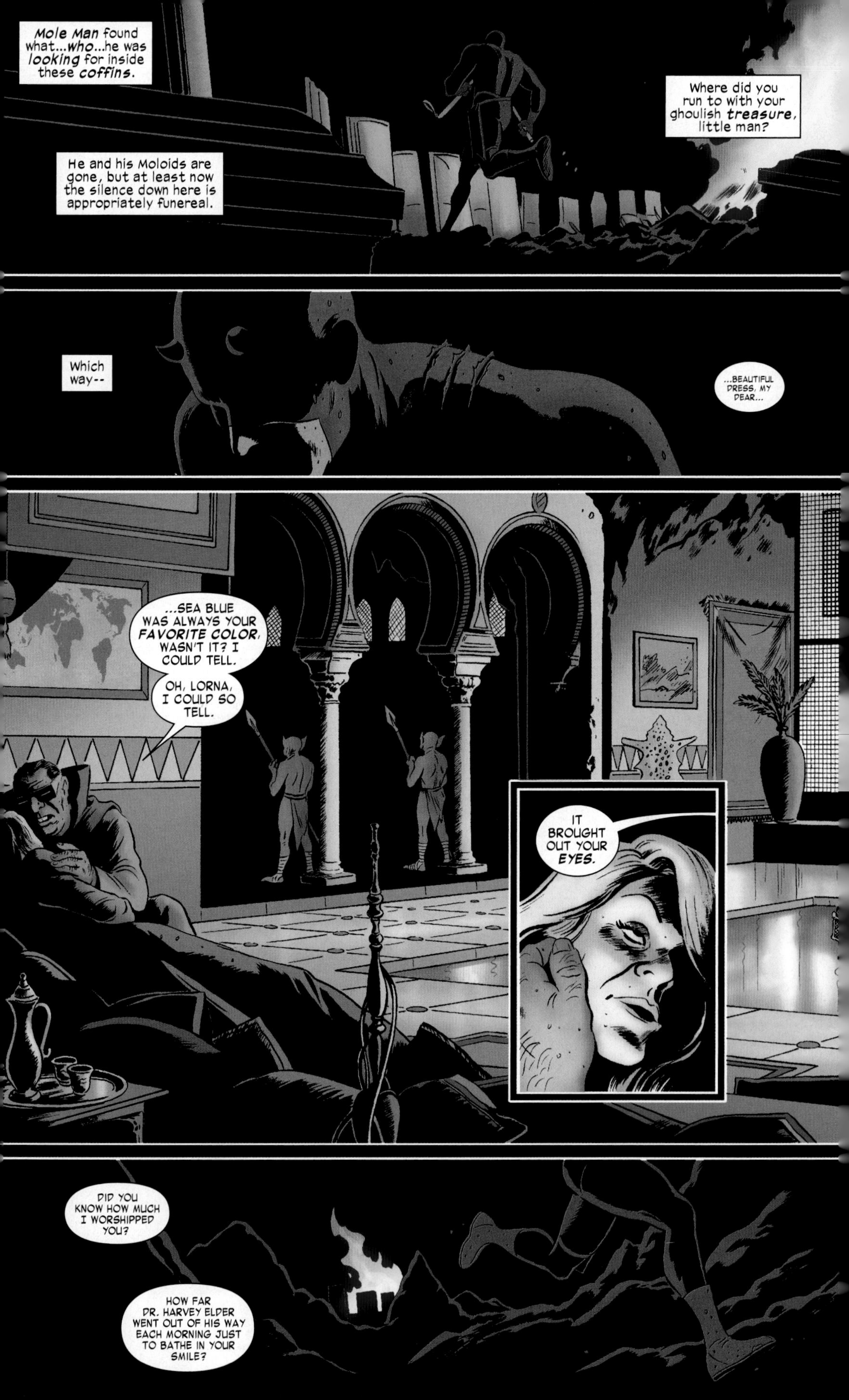
Mole Man found what...who...he was looking for inside these coffins.
He and his Moloids are gone, but at least now the silence down here is appropriately funereal.
Where did you run to with your ghoulish treasure, little man?
Which way--
...BEAUTIFUL DRESS, MY DEAR...
...SEA BLUE WAS ALWAYS YOUR FAVORITE COLOR, WASN'T IT? I COULD TELL.
OH, LORNA, I COULD SO TELL.
IT BROUGHT OUT YOUR EYES.
DID YOU KNOW HOW MUCH I WORSHIPPED YOU?
HOW FAR DR. HARVEY ELDER WENT OUT OF HIS WAY EACH MORNING JUST TO BATHE IN YOUR SMILE?

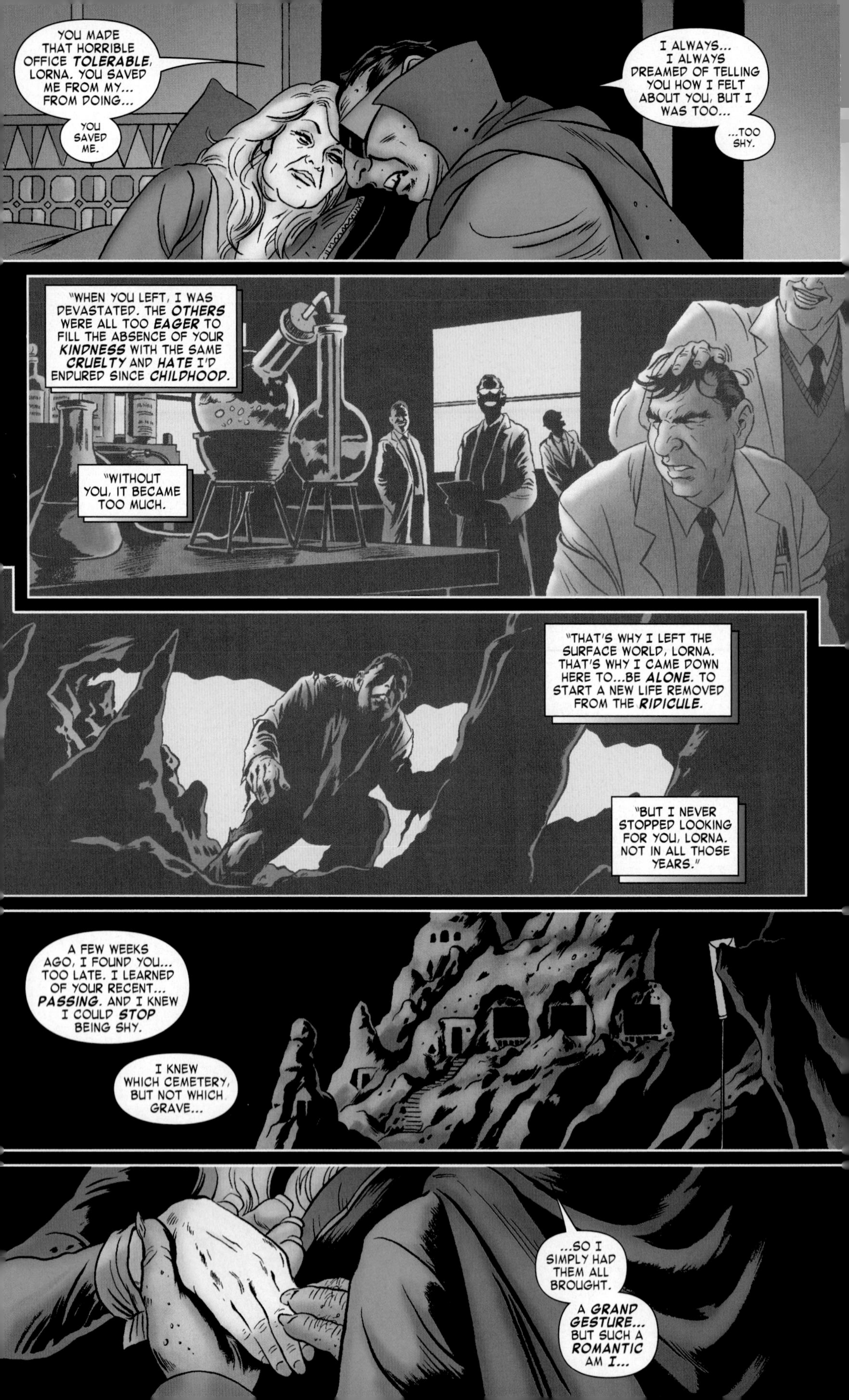
YOU MADE THAT HORRIBLE OFFICE TOLERABLE, LORNA. YOU SAVED ME FROM MY... FROM DOING...
YOU SAVED ME.
I ALWAYS... I ALWAYS DREAMED OF TELLING YOU HOW I FELT ABOUT YOU, BUT I WAS TOO...
...TOO SHY.
"WHEN YOU LEFT, I WAS DEVASTATED. THE OTHERS WERE ALL TOO EAGER TO FILL THE ABSENCE OF YOUR KINDNESS WITH THE SAME CRUELTY AND HATE I'D ENDURED SINCE CHILDHOOD.
"WITHOUT YOU, IT BECAME TOO MUCH.
"THAT'S WHY I LEFT THE SURFACE WORLD, LORNA. THAT'S WHY I CAME DOWN HERE TO...BE ALONE. TO START A NEW LIFE REMOVED FROM THE RIDICULE.
"BUT I NEVER STOPPED LOOKING FOR YOU, LORNA. NOT IN ALL THOSE YEARS."
A FEW WEEKS AGO, I FOUND YOU... TOO LATE. I LEARNED OF YOUR RECENT... PASSING. AND I KNEW I COULD STOP BEING SHY.
I KNEW WHICH CEMETERY, BUT NOT WHICH GRAVE...
...SO I SIMPLY HAD THEM ALL BROUGHT.
A GRAND GESTURE... BUT SUCH A ROMANTIC AM I...

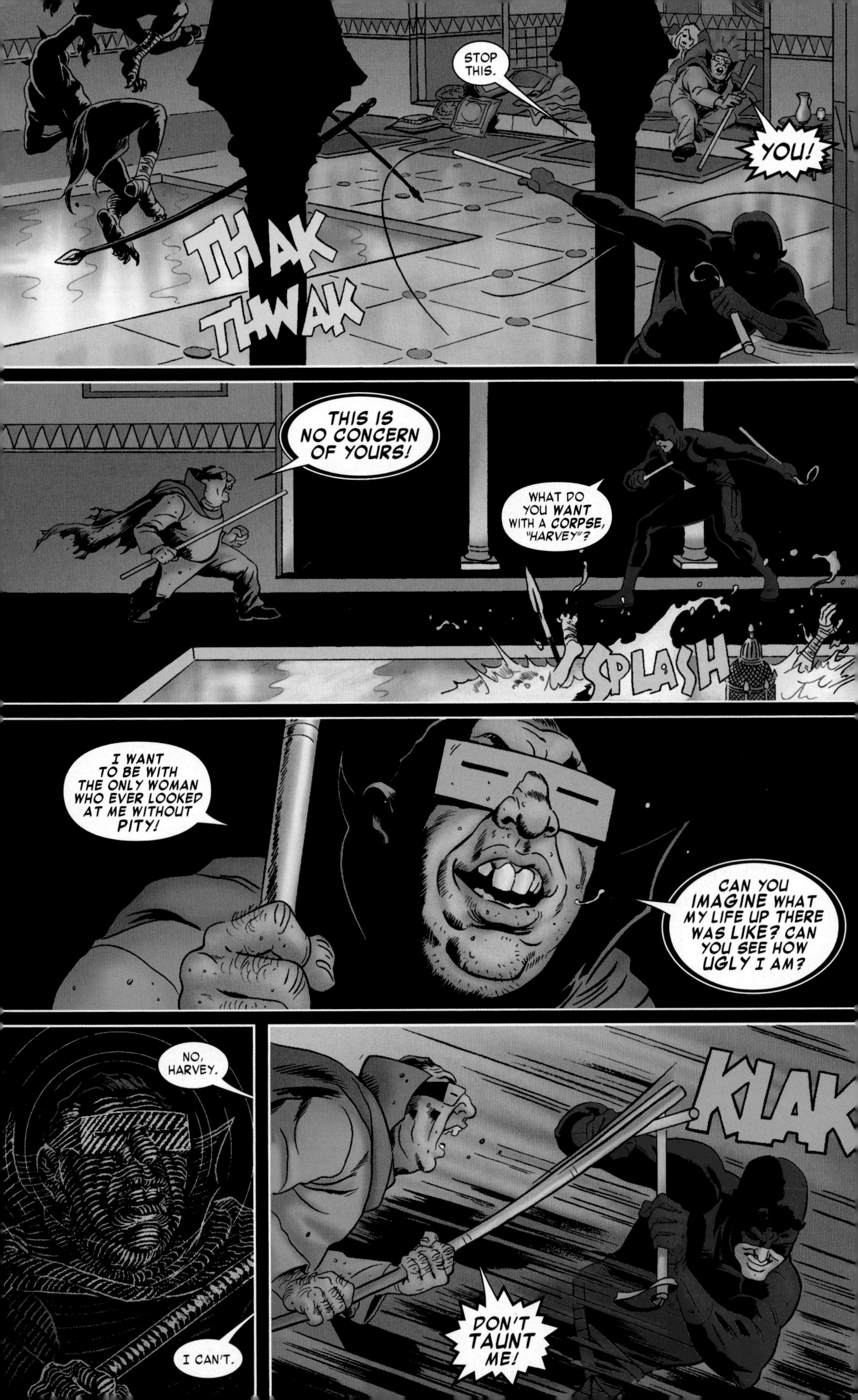
STOP THIS.
YOU!
THAK
THWAK
THIS IS NO CONCERN OF YOURS!
WHAT DO YOU WANT WITH A CORPSE, "HARVEY"?
SPLASH
I WANT TO BE WITH THE ONLY WOMAN WHO EVER LOOKED AT ME WITHOUT PITY!
CAN YOU IMAGINE WHAT MY LIFE UP THERE WAS LIKE? CAN YOU SEE HOW UGLY I AM?
NO, HARVEY.
I CAN'T.
KLAK
DON'T TAUNT ME!

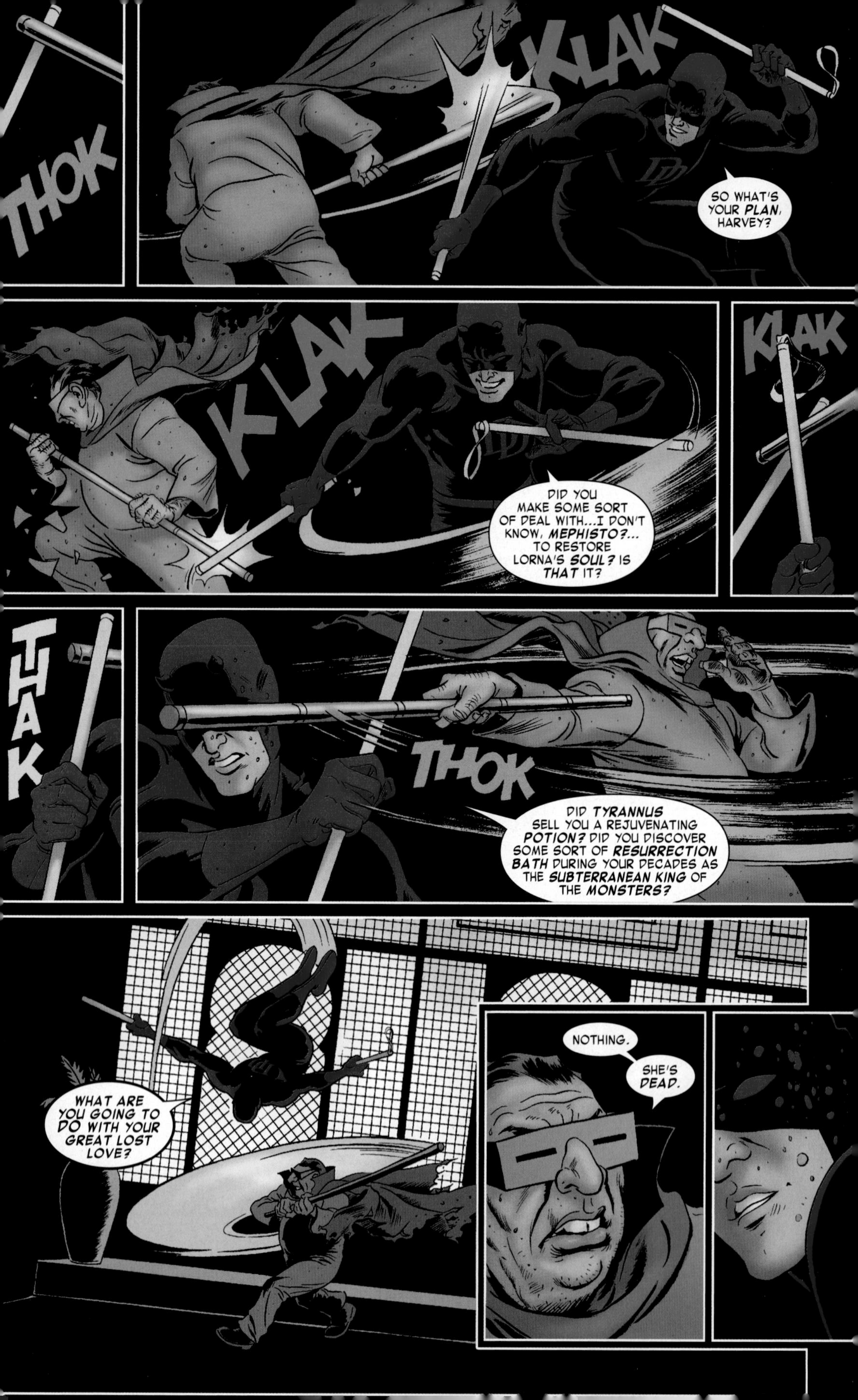
THOK
KLAK
SO WHAT'S YOUR PLAN, HARVEY?
KLAK
KLAK
DID YOU MAKE SOME SORT OF DEAL WITH...I DON'T KNOW, MEPHISTO?... TO RESTORE LORNA'S SOUL? IS THAT IT?
THAK
THOK
DID TYRANNUS SELL YOU A REJUVENATING POTION? DID YOU DISCOVER SOME SORT OF RESURRECTION BATH DURING YOUR DECADES AS THE SUBTERRANEAN KING OF THE MONSTERS?
WHAT ARE YOU GOING TO DO WITH YOUR GREAT LOST LOVE?
NOTHING.
SHE'S DEAD.

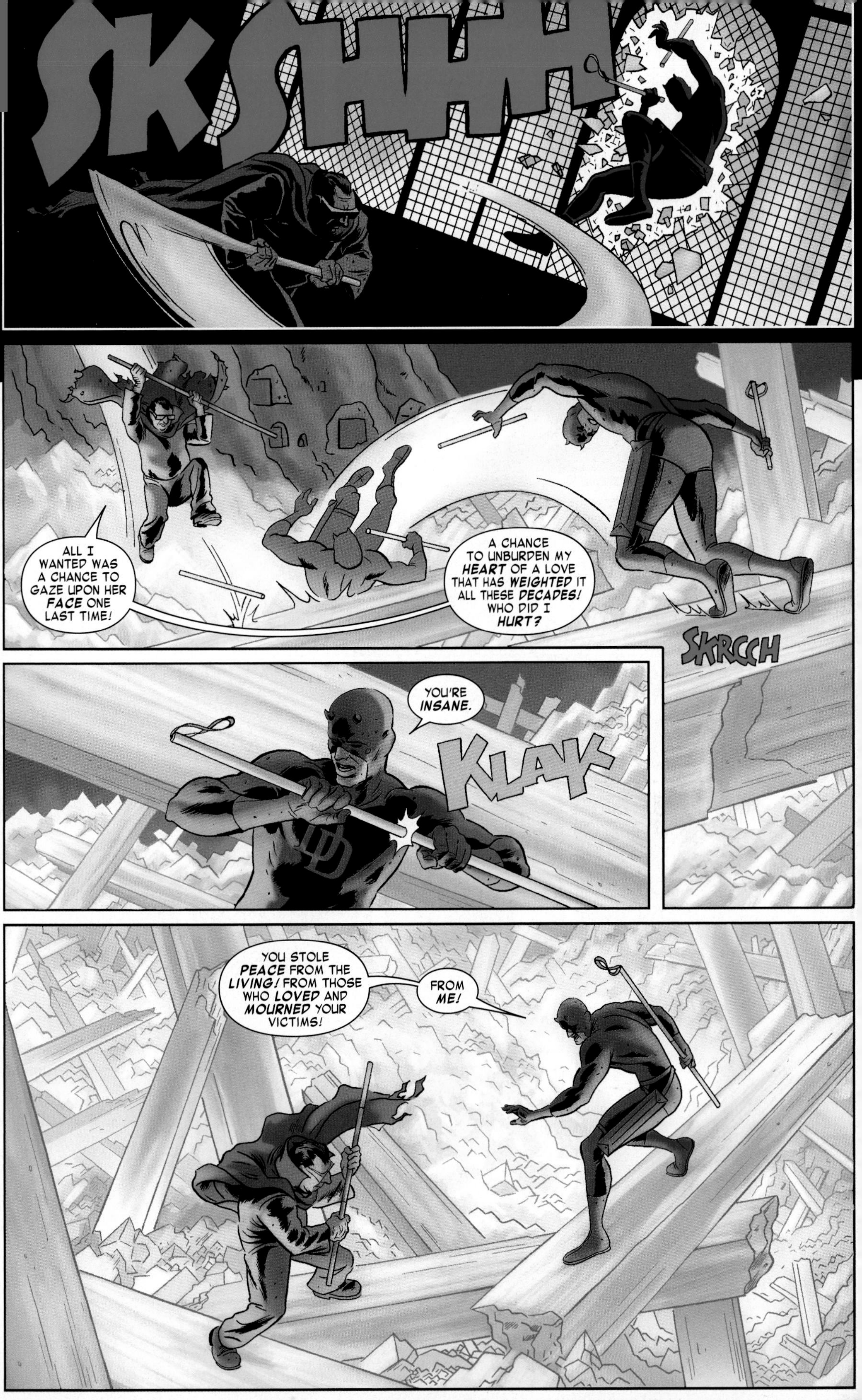
SKSHHH
ALL I WANTED WAS A CHANCE TO GAZE UPON HER FACE ONE LAST TIME!
A CHANCE TO UNBURDEN MY HEART OF A LOVE THAT HAS WEIGHTED IT ALL THESE DECADES! WHO DID I HURT?
SKRCCH
YOU'RE INSANE.
KLAK
YOU STOLE PEACE FROM THE LIVING! FROM THOSE WHO LOVED AND MOURNED YOUR VICTIMS!
FROM ME!

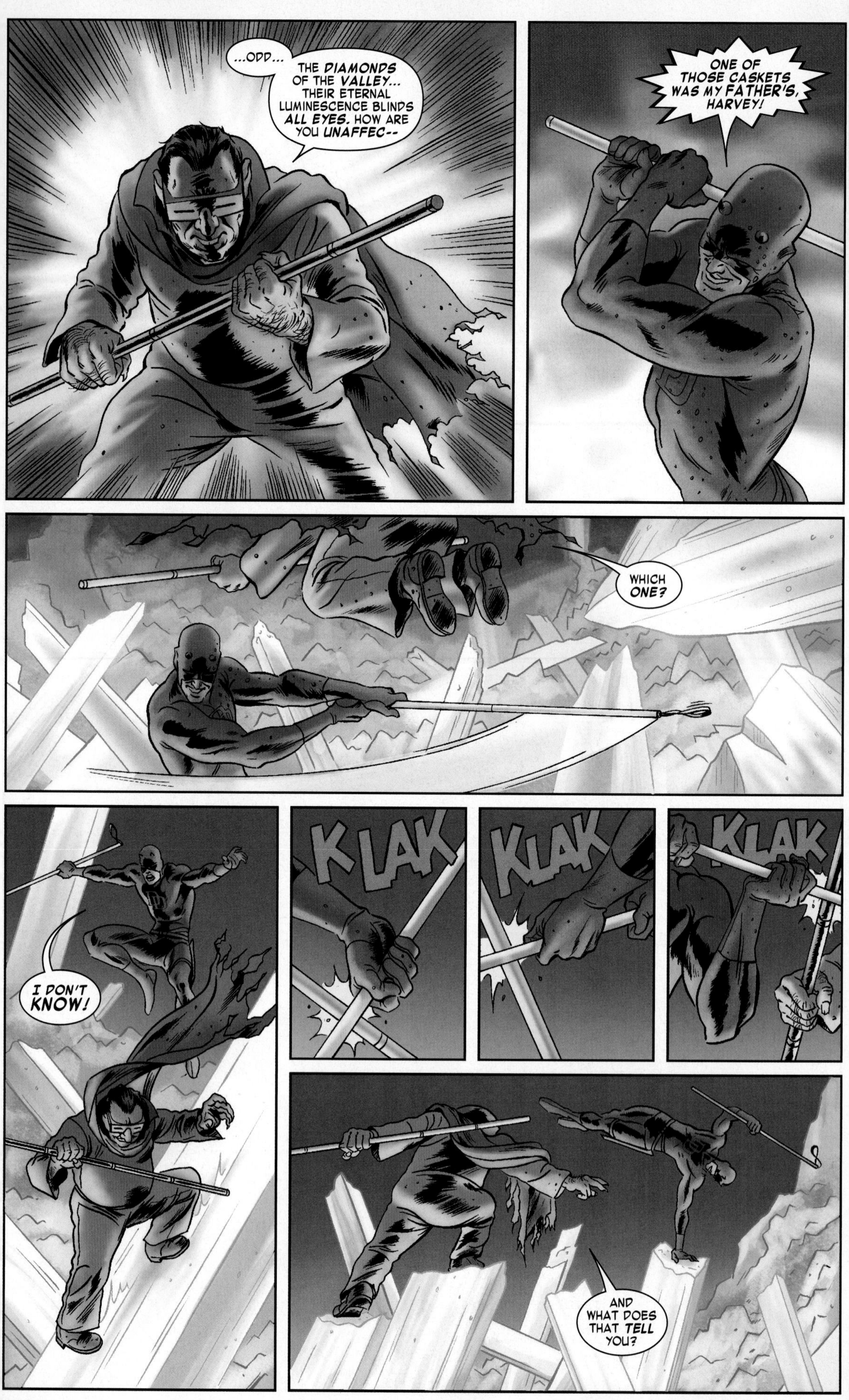
...ODD...
THE DIAMONDS OF THE VALLEY... THEIR ETERNAL LUMINESCENCE BLINDS ALL EYES. HOW ARE YOU UNAFFEC--
ONE OF THOSE CASKETS WAS MY FATHER'S, HARVEY!
WHICH ONE?
I DON'T KNOW!
KLAK
KLAK
KLAK
AND WHAT DOES THAT TELL YOU?

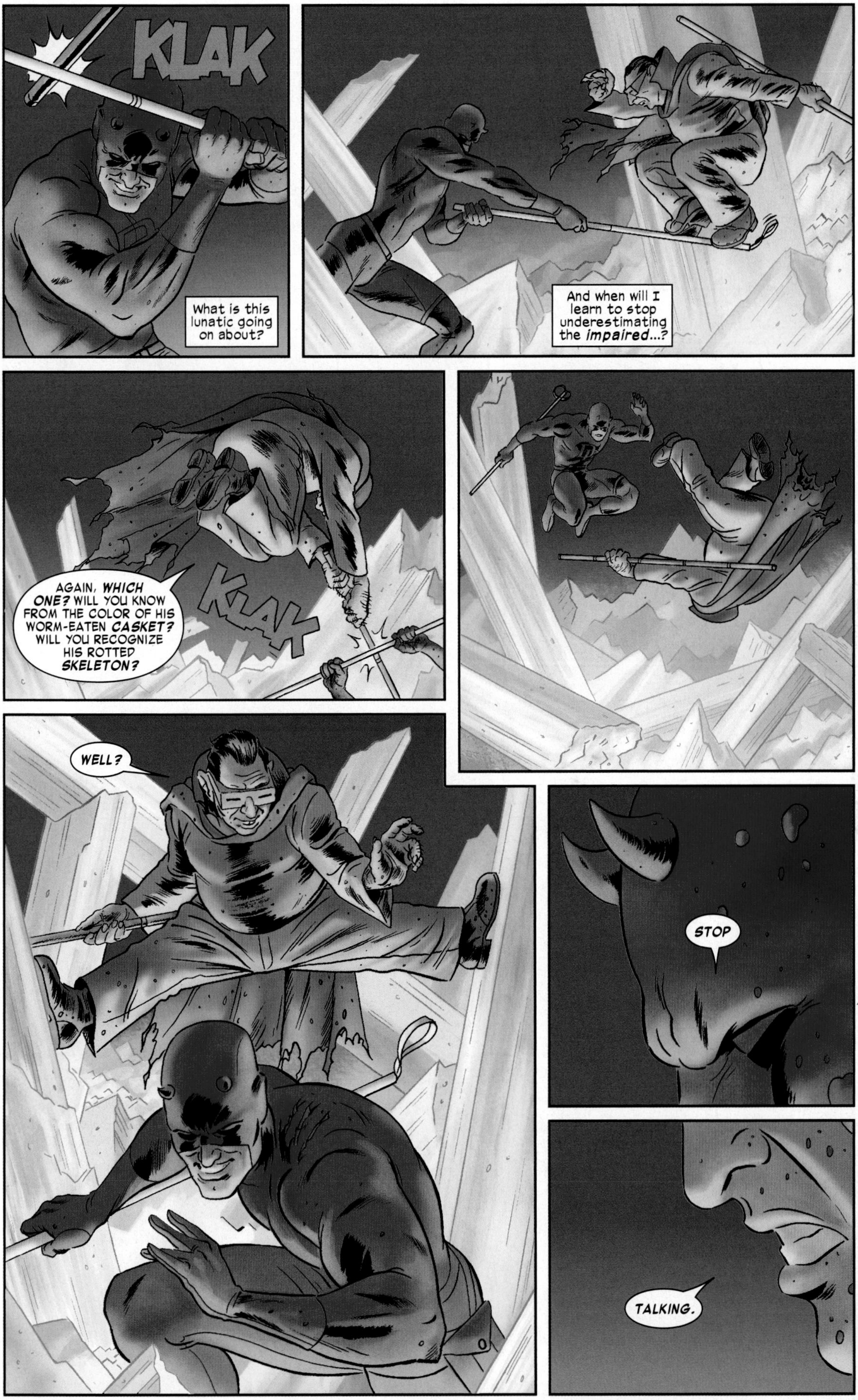
KLAK
What is this lunatic going on about?
And when will I learn to stop underestimating the *impaired*...?
AGAIN, ***WHICH ONE?*** WILL YOU KNOW FROM THE COLOR OF HIS WORM-EATEN ***CASKET?*** WILL YOU RECOGNIZE HIS ROTTED ***SKELETON?***
KLAK
WELL?
STOP
TALKING.

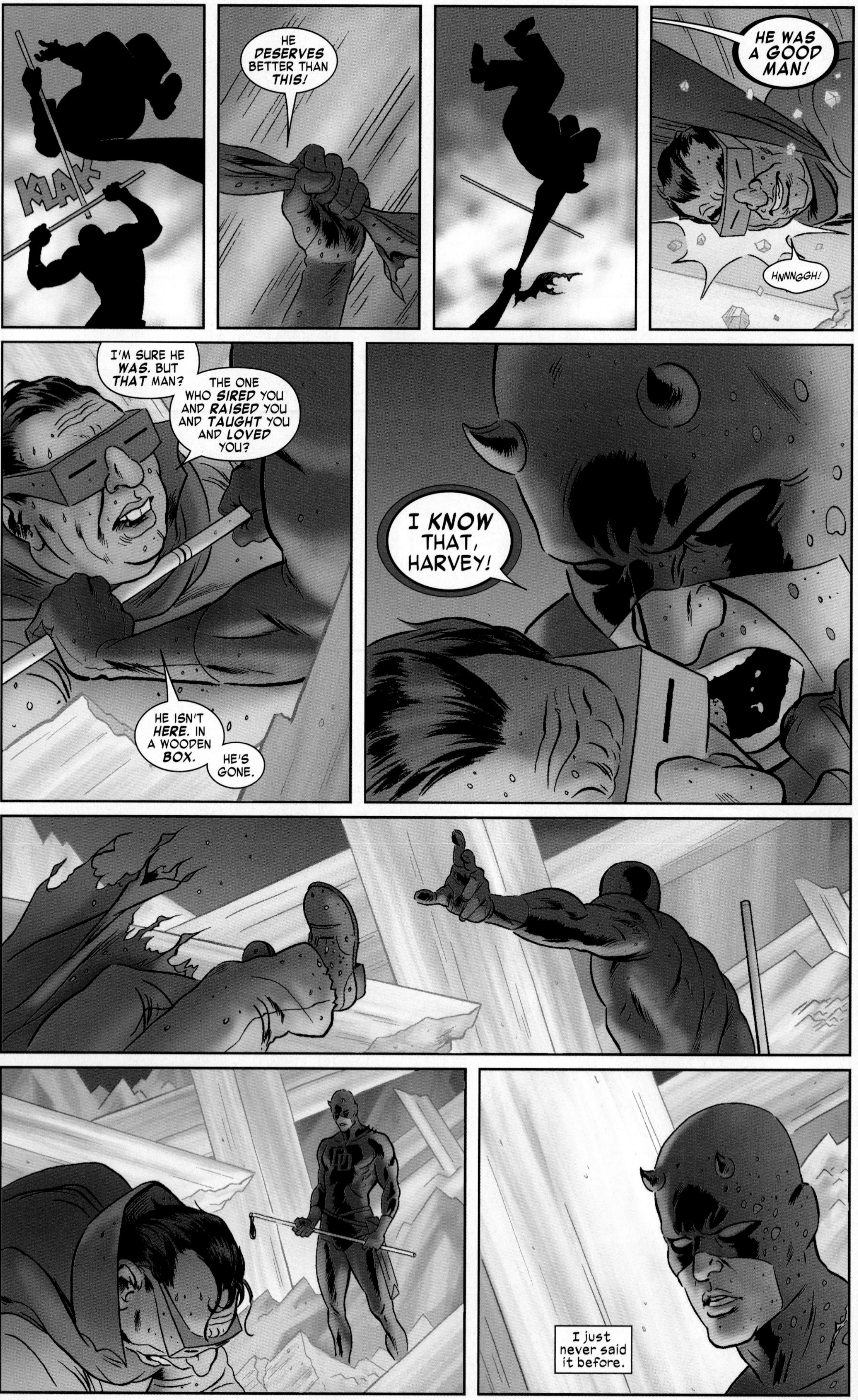
KLAK
HE DESERVES BETTER THAN THIS!
HE WAS A GOOD MAN!
HNNNGGH!
I'M SURE HE WAS. BUT THAT MAN?
THE ONE WHO SIRED YOU AND RAISED YOU AND TAUGHT YOU AND LOVED YOU?
HE ISN'T HERE. IN A WOODEN BOX.
HE'S GONE.
I KNOW THAT, HARVEY!
I just never said it before.

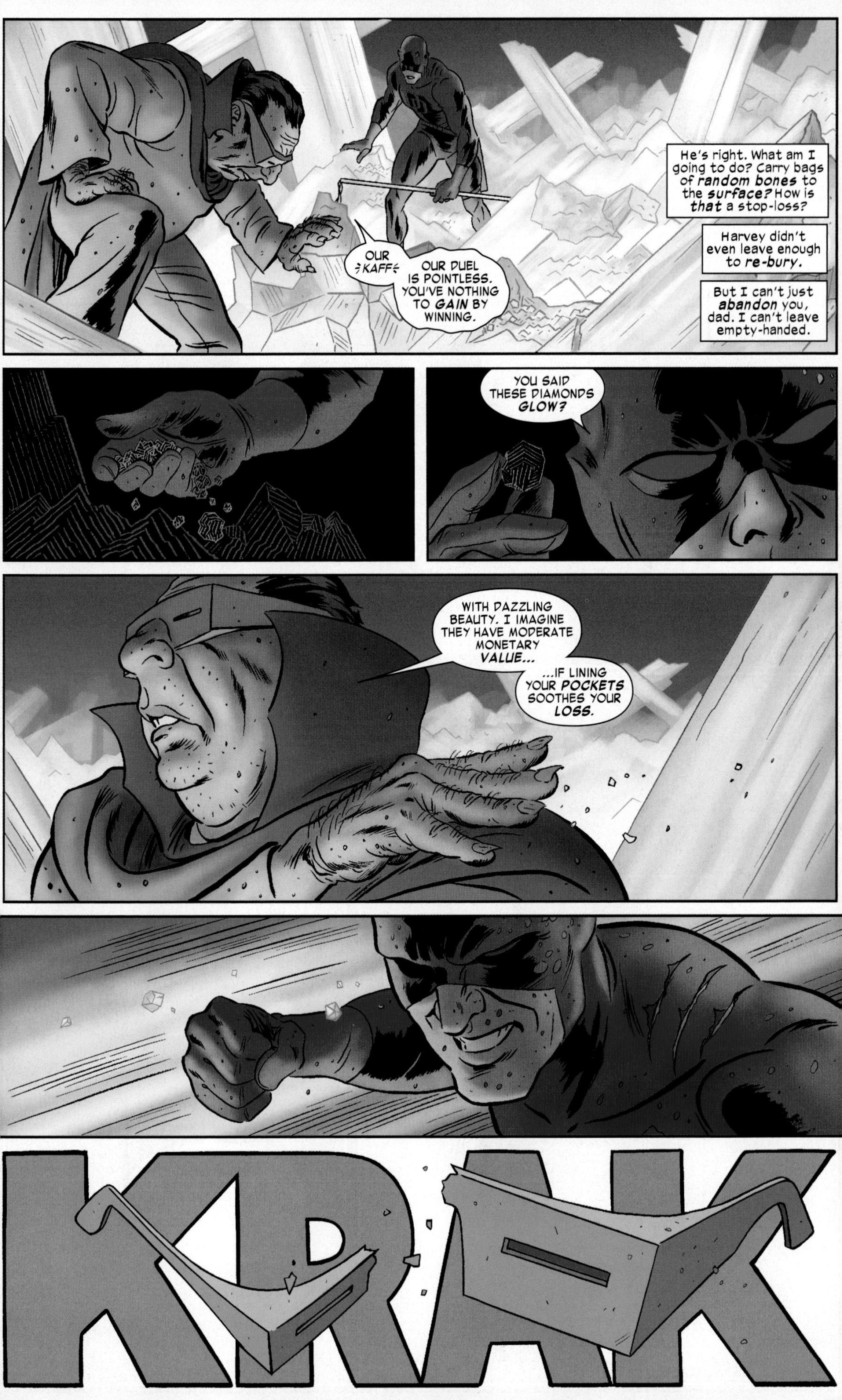
He's right. What am I going to do? Carry bags of *random bones* to the *surface?* How is *that* a stop-loss?
Harvey didn't even leave enough to *re-bury.*
But I can't just *abandon* you, dad. I can't leave empty-handed.
OUR *KAFF* OUR DUEL IS POINTLESS. YOU'VE NOTHING TO *GAIN* BY WINNING.
YOU SAID THESE DIAMONDS *GLOW?*
WITH DAZZLING BEAUTY. I IMAGINE THEY HAVE MODERATE MONETARY *VALUE...*
...IF LINING YOUR *POCKETS* SOOTHES YOUR *LOSS.*
KRAK

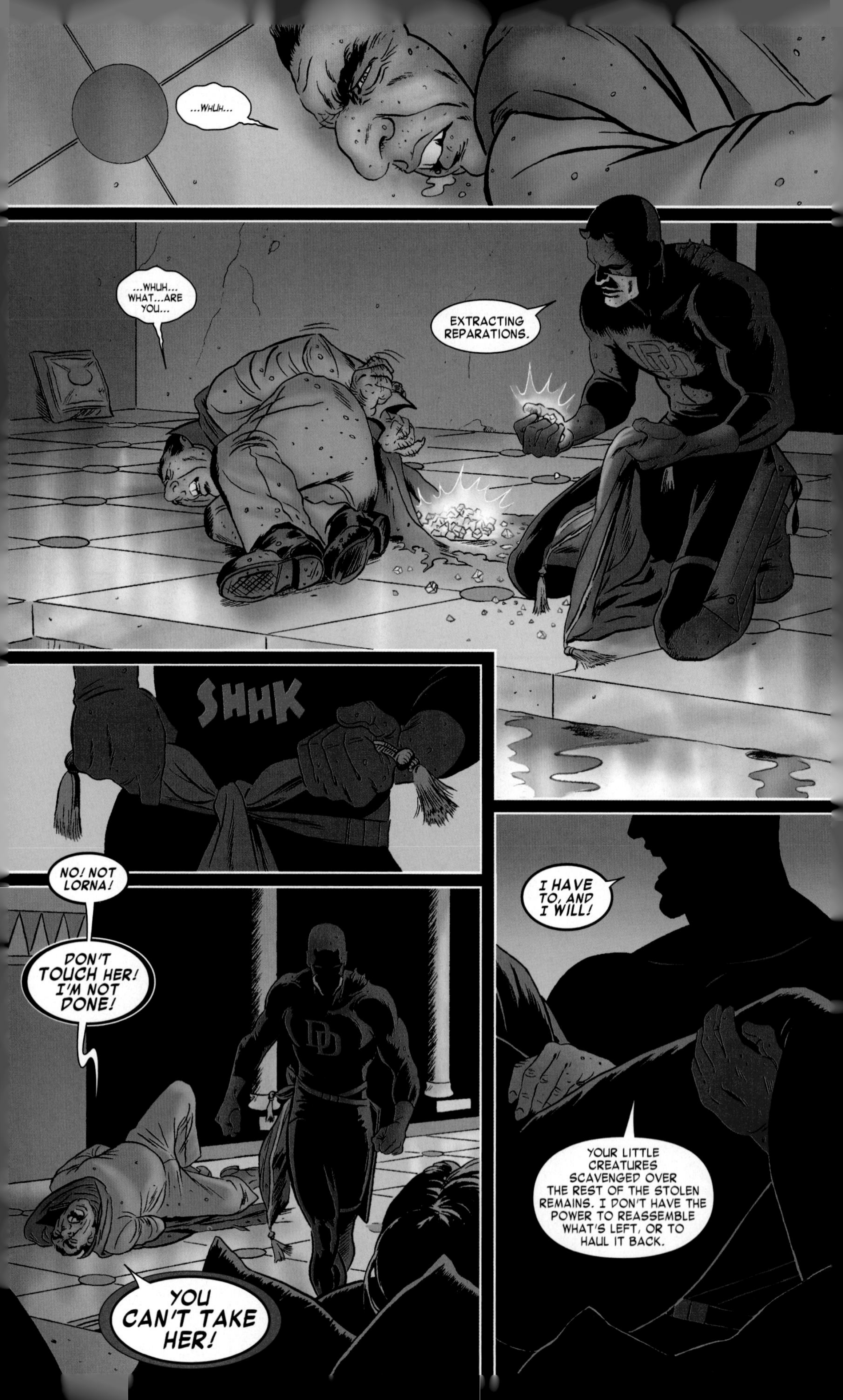
...WHUH...
...WHUH... WHAT...ARE YOU...
EXTRACTING REPARATIONS.
SHHK
NO! NOT LORNA!
DON'T TOUCH HER! I'M NOT DONE!
YOU CAN'T TAKE HER!
I HAVE TO, AND I WILL!
YOUR LITTLE CREATURES SCAVENGED OVER THE REST OF THE STOLEN REMAINS. I DON'T HAVE THE POWER TO REASSEMBLE WHAT'S LEFT, OR TO HAUL IT BACK.

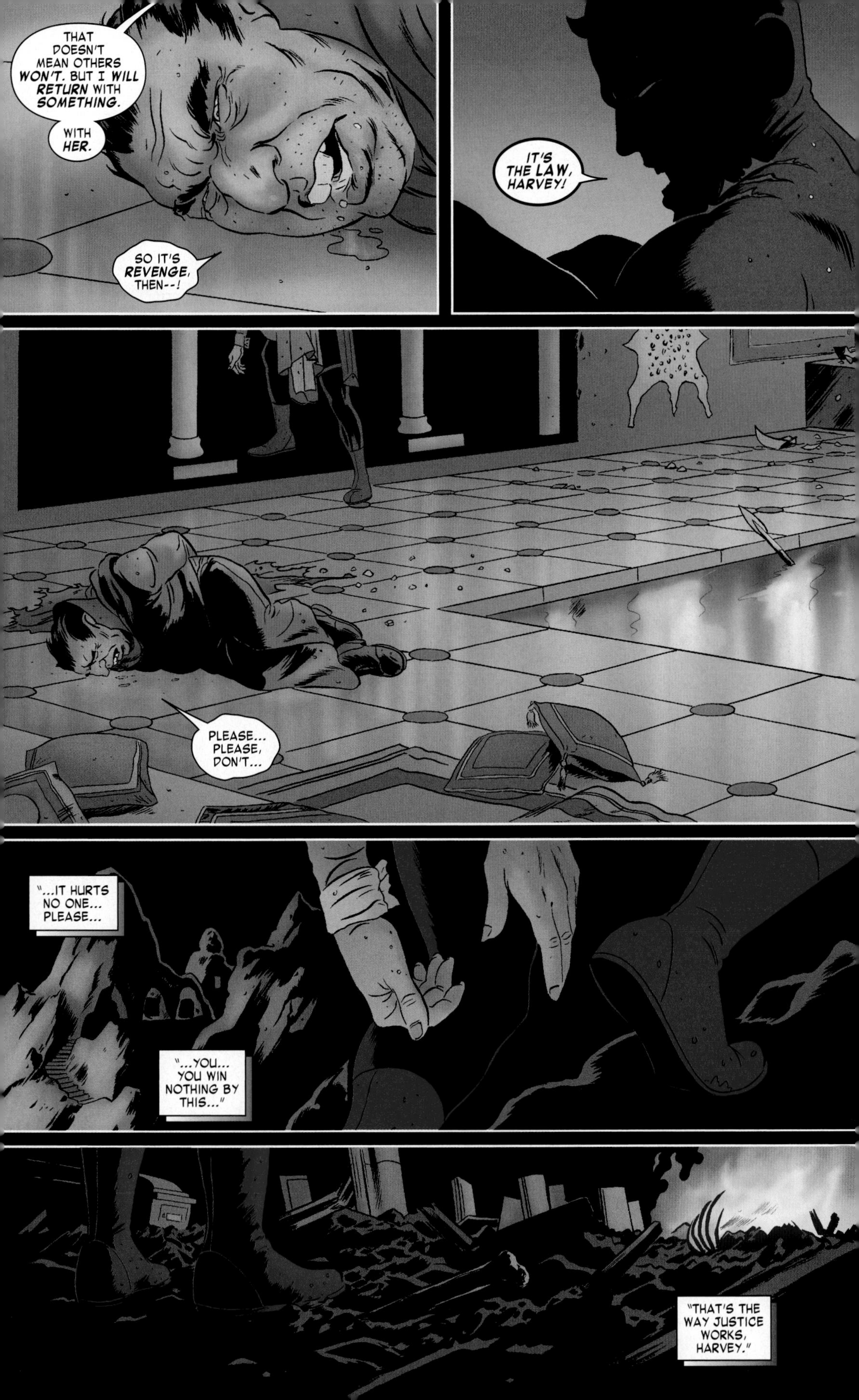
THAT DOESN'T MEAN OTHERS WON'T. BUT I WILL RETURN WITH SOMETHING.
WITH HER.
SO IT'S REVENGE, THEN--!
IT'S THE LAW, HARVEY!
PLEASE... PLEASE, DON'T...
"...IT HURTS NO ONE... PLEASE...
"...YOU... YOU WIN NOTHING BY THIS..."
"THAT'S THE WAY JUSTICE WORKS, HARVEY."

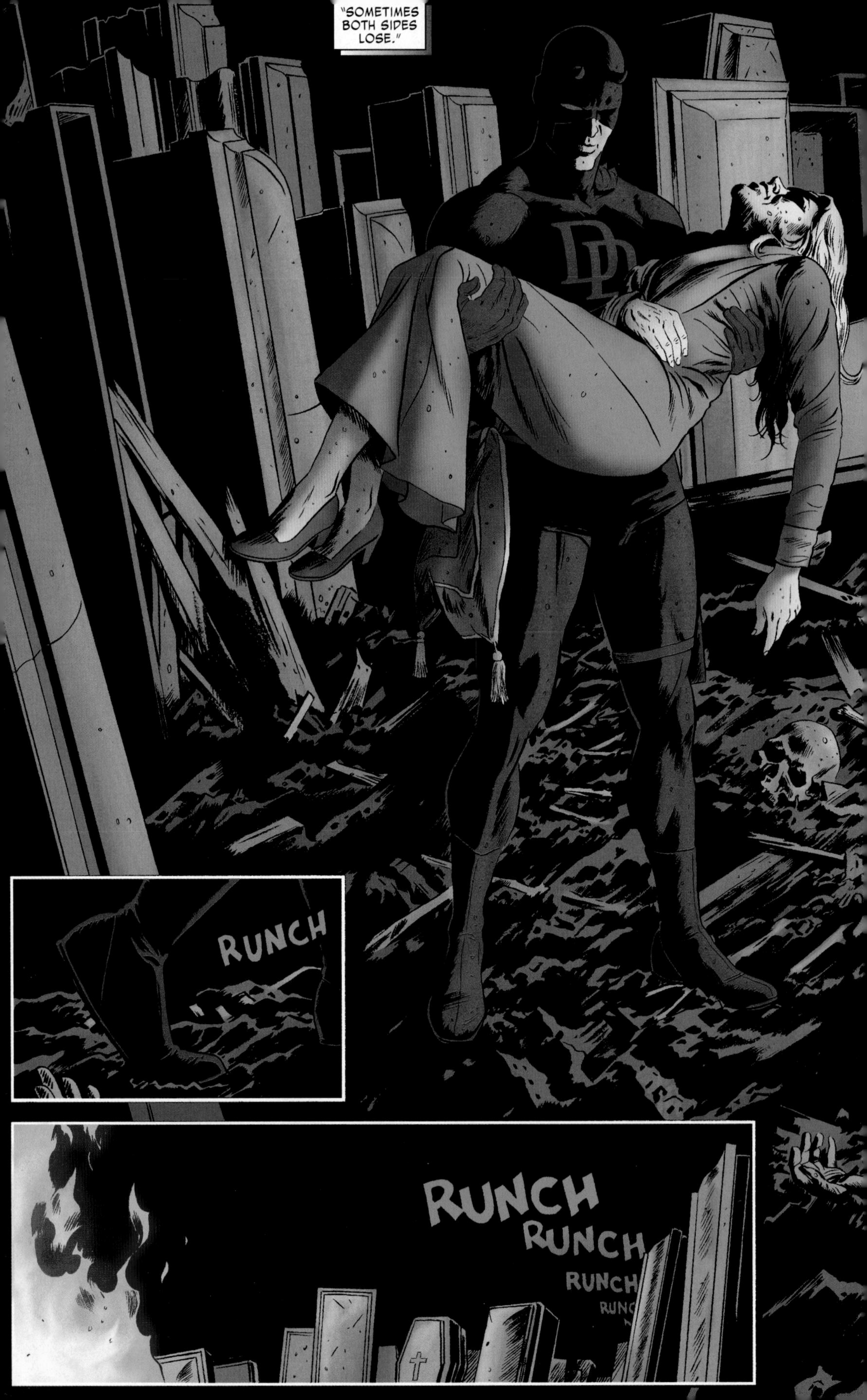
"SOMETIMES BOTH SIDES LOSE."
RUNCH
RUNCH
RUNCH
RUNCH

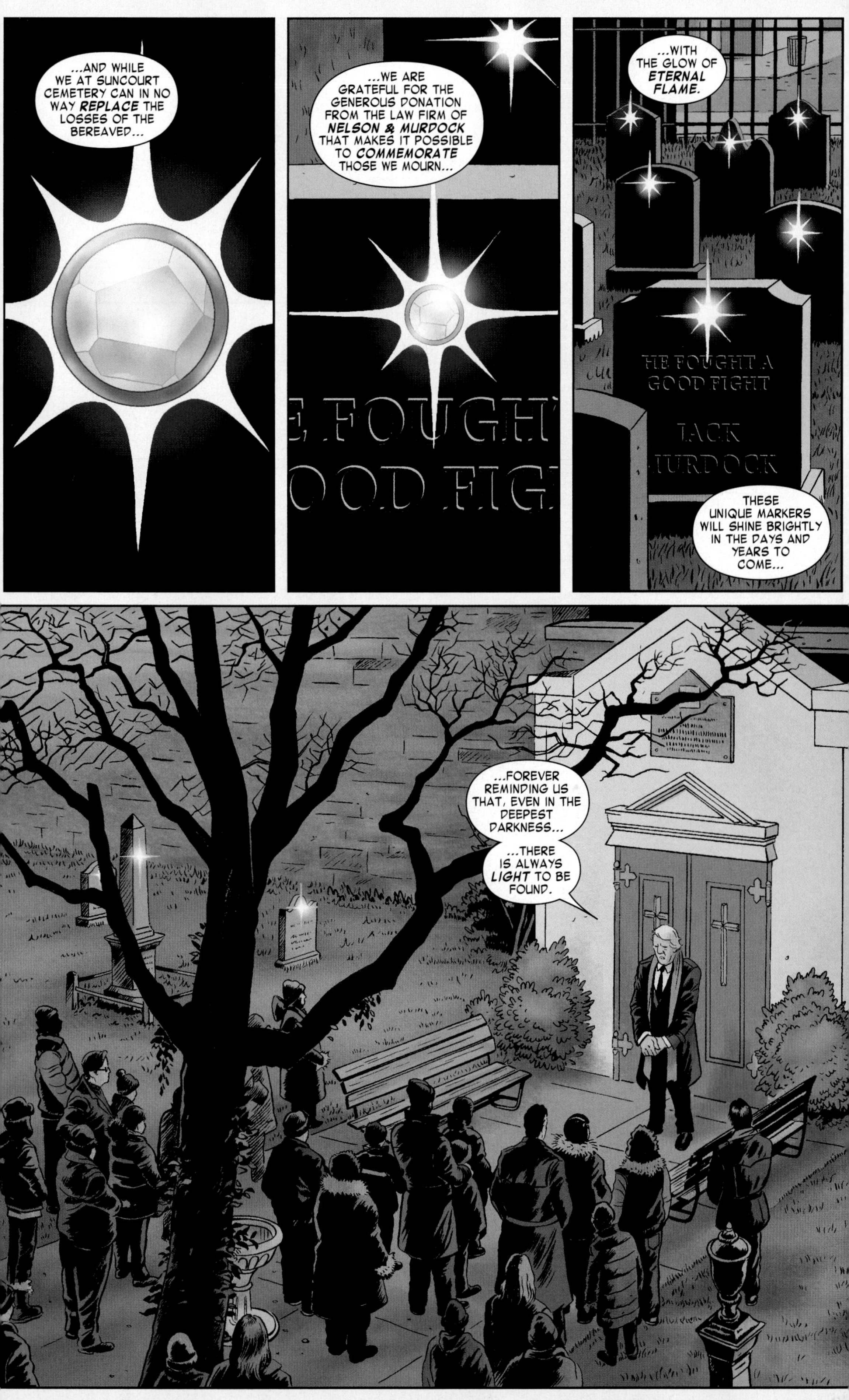
...AND WHILE WE AT SUNCOURT CEMETERY CAN IN NO WAY REPLACE THE LOSSES OF THE BEREAVED...
...WE ARE GRATEFUL FOR THE GENEROUS DONATION FROM THE LAW FIRM OF NELSON & MURDOCK THAT MAKES IT POSSIBLE TO COMMEMORATE THOSE WE MOURN...
...WITH THE GLOW OF ETERNAL FLAME.
HE FOUGHT A GOOD FIGHT
JACK MURDOCK
THESE UNIQUE MARKERS WILL SHINE BRIGHTLY IN THE DAYS AND YEARS TO COME...
...FOREVER REMINDING US THAT, EVEN IN THE DEEPEST DARKNESS...
...THERE IS ALWAYS LIGHT TO BE FOUND.

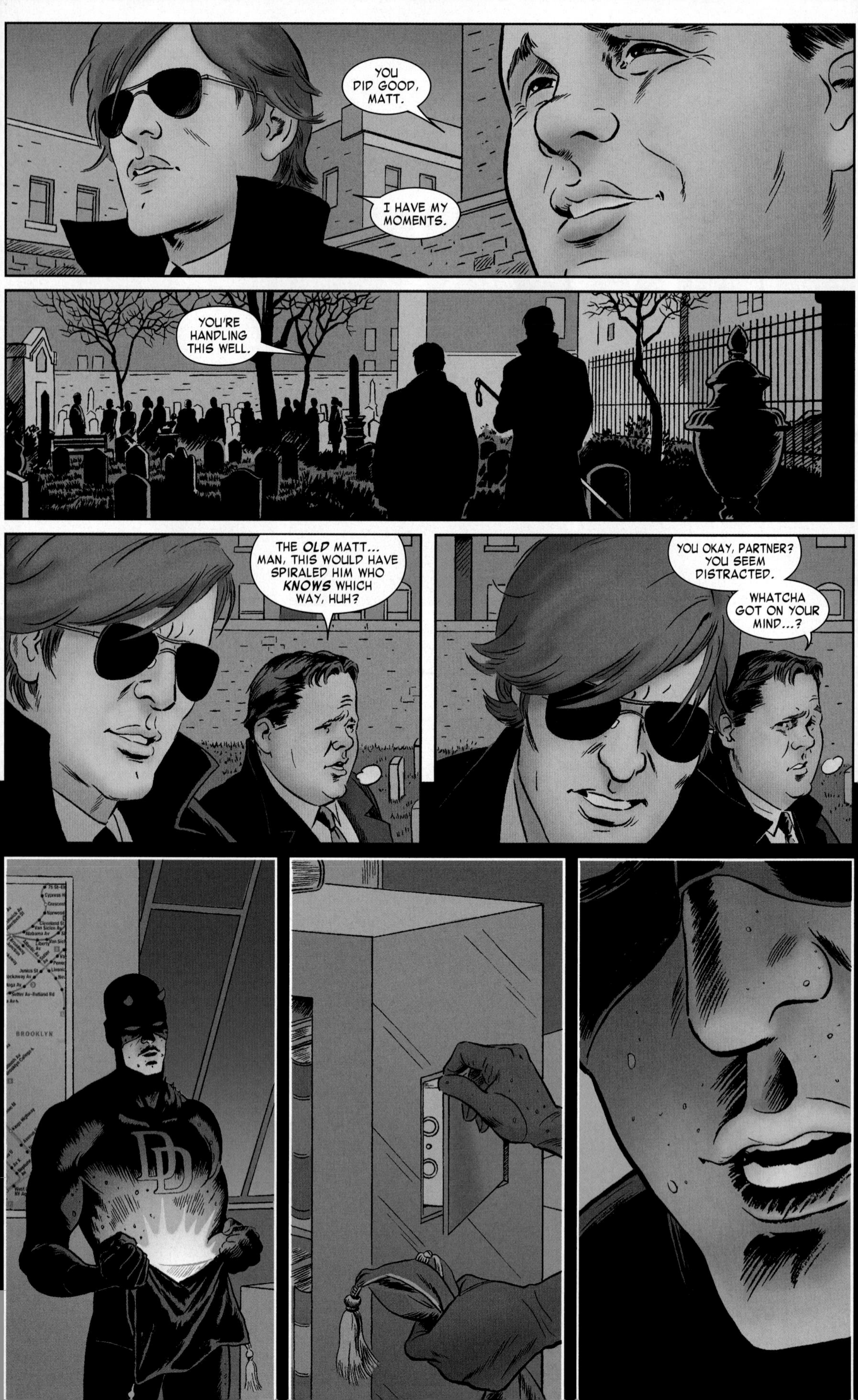
YOU DID GOOD, MATT.
I HAVE MY MOMENTS.
YOU'RE HANDLING THIS WELL.
THE OLD MATT... MAN, THIS WOULD HAVE SPIRALED HIM WHO KNOWS WHICH WAY, HUH?
YOU OKAY, PARTNER? YOU SEEM DISTRACTED.
WHATCHA GOT ON YOUR MIND...?
BROOKLYN

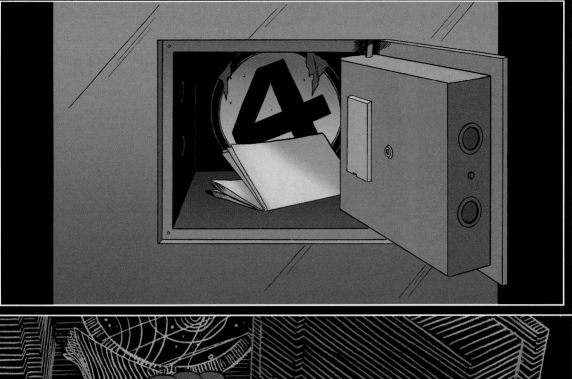

Sorry for the intrusion, love, but I had to be sure this device was what they said it was--

--before I took a drastic but necessary step.

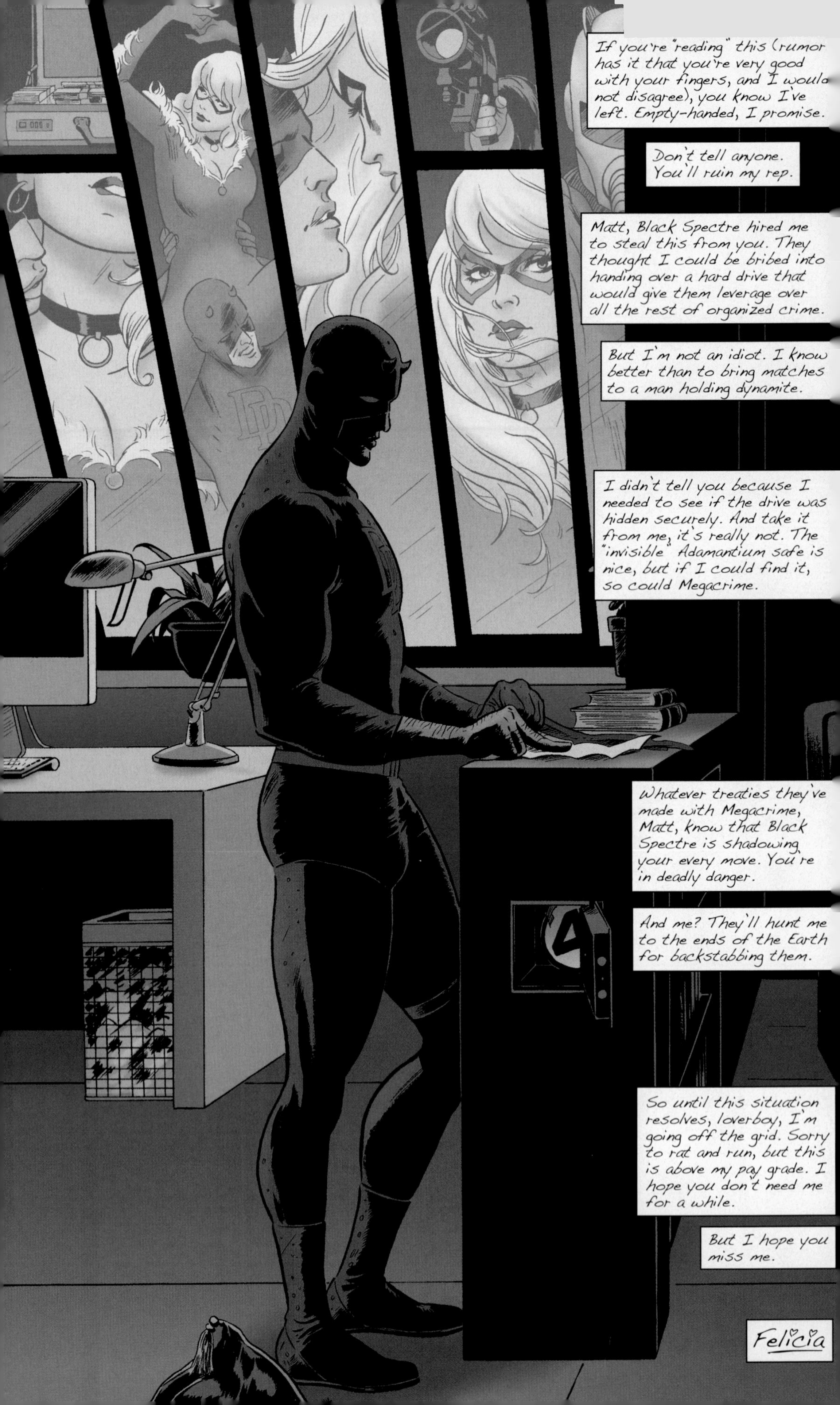
If you're "reading" this (rumor has it that you're very good with your fingers, and I would not disagree), you know I've left. Empty-handed, I promise.
Don't tell anyone. You'll ruin my rep.
Matt, Black Spectre hired me to steal this from you. They thought I could be bribed into handing over a hard drive that would give them leverage over all the rest of organized crime.
But I'm not an idiot. I know better than to bring matches to a man holding dynamite.
I didn't tell you because I needed to see if the drive was hidden securely. And take it from me, it's really not. The "invisible" Adamantium safe is nice, but if I could find it, so could Megacrime.
Whatever treaties they've made with Megacrime, Matt, know that Black Spectre is shadowing your every move. You're in deadly danger.
And me? They'll hunt me to the ends of the Earth for backstabbing them.
So until this situation resolves, loverboy, I'm going off the grid. Sorry to rat and run, but this is above my pay grade. I hope you don't need me for a while.
But I hope you miss me.
Felicia

MATT, WHERE ARE YOU--?

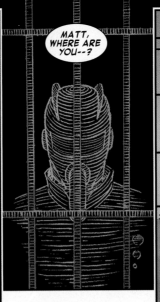

YOU'RE FOLLOWING ME *HERE*, YOU BASTARD?

WHAT DID I *WARN* YOU ABOUT COMING--

MATT?

--AFTER--

--ME?

MATTY, WHAT'S ⸮HFF⸮ WHAT'S *WRONG*?

A *BLACK SPECTRE* AGENT! YOU *SAW* HIM, RIGHT? HE WAS *JUST HERE*!

HE WAS *FOLLOWING* ME! HE WAS *RIGHT HERE*!

MATT--

DON'T *USE* THAT TONE, FOGGY! I'M *NOT* CRAZY!

I'M *NOT*!

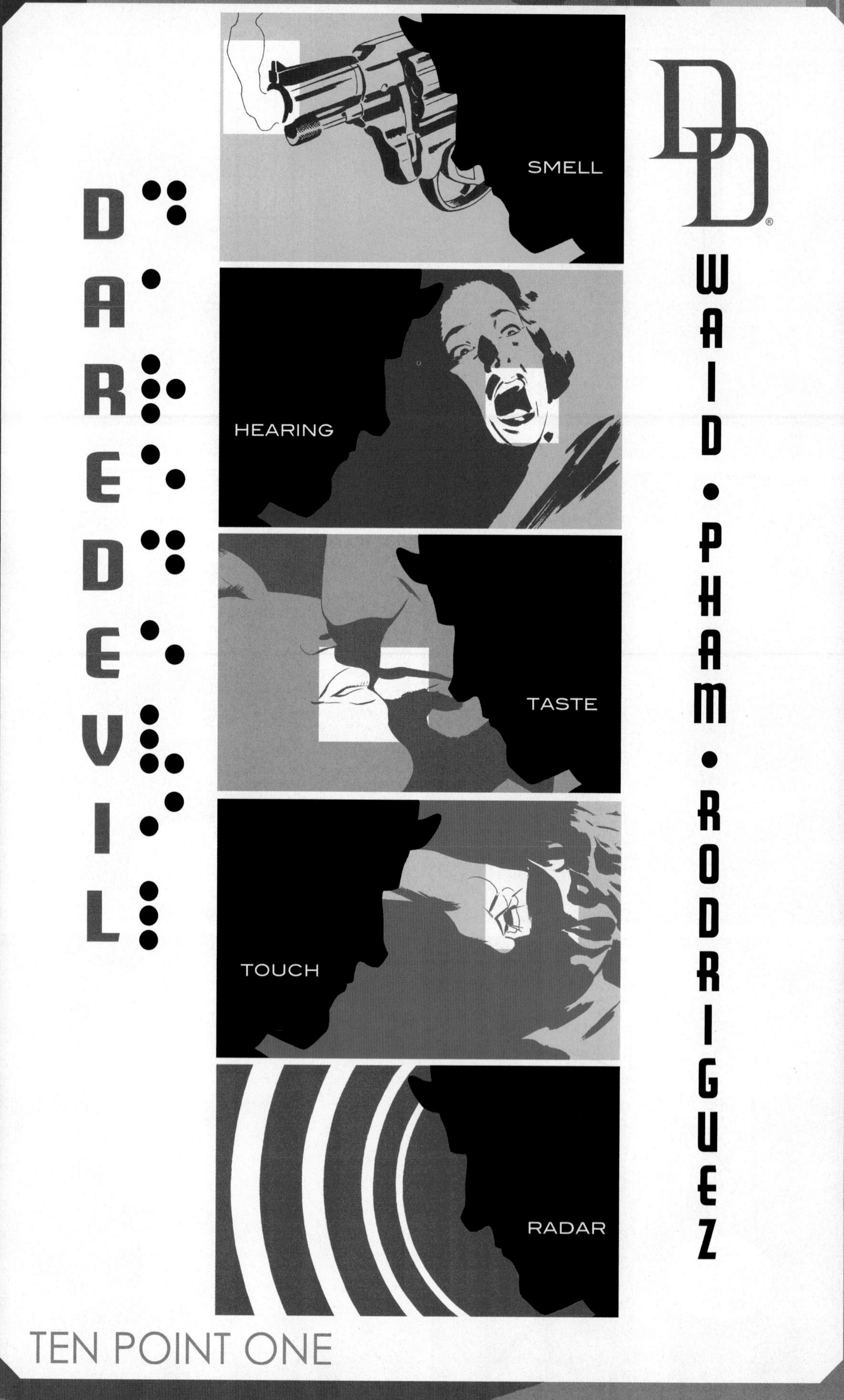

DAREDEVIL
SMELL
HEARING
TASTE
TOUCH
RADAR
DD
WAID • PHAM • RODRIGUEZ
TEN POINT ONE

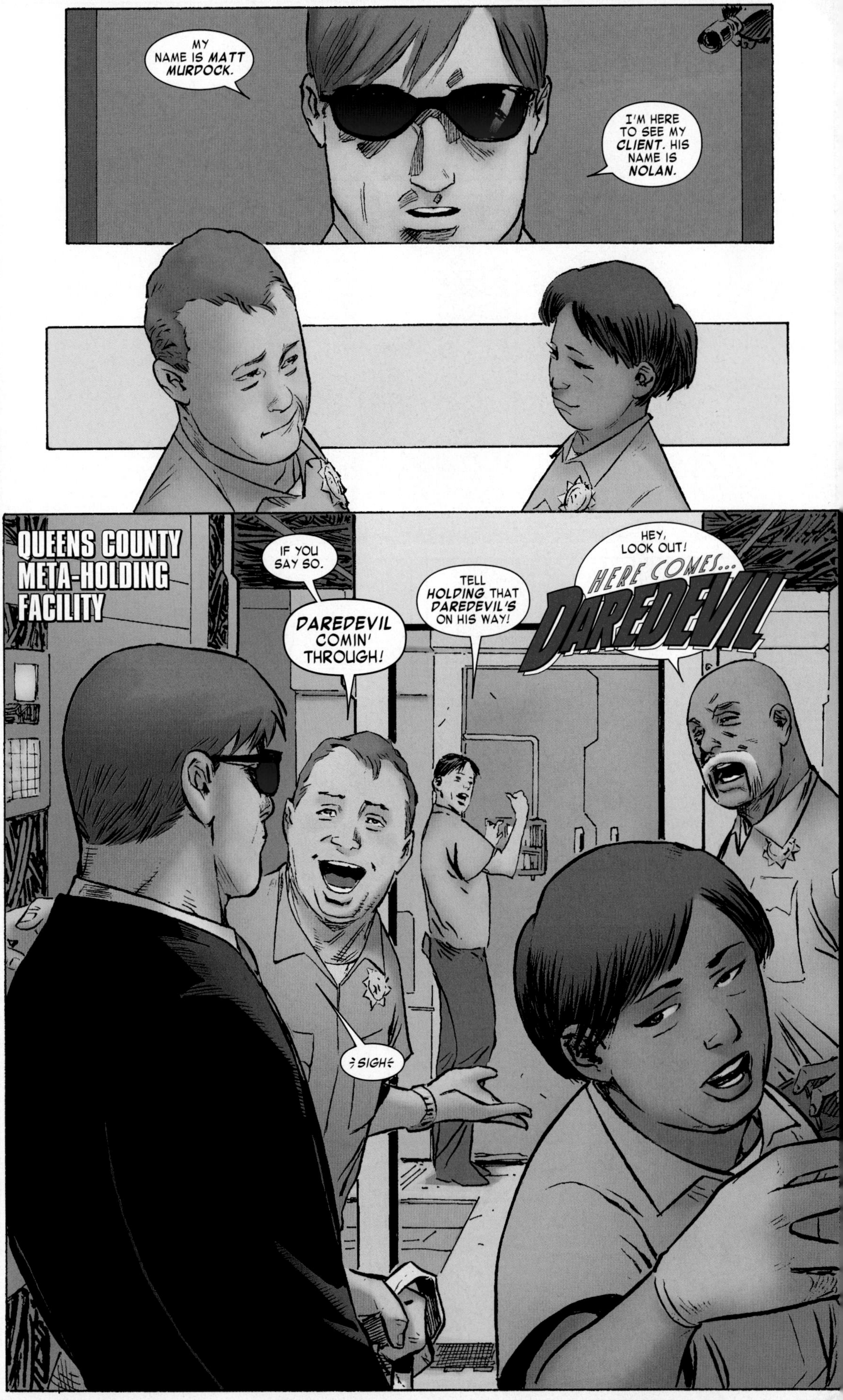
MY NAME IS MATT MURDOCK.
I'M HERE TO SEE MY CLIENT. HIS NAME IS NOLAN.
QUEENS COUNTY META-HOLDING FACILITY
IF YOU SAY SO.
DAREDEVIL COMIN' THROUGH!
TELL HOLDING THAT DAREDEVIL'S ON HIS WAY!
HEY, LOOK OUT!
HERE COMES... DAREDEVIL
SIGH

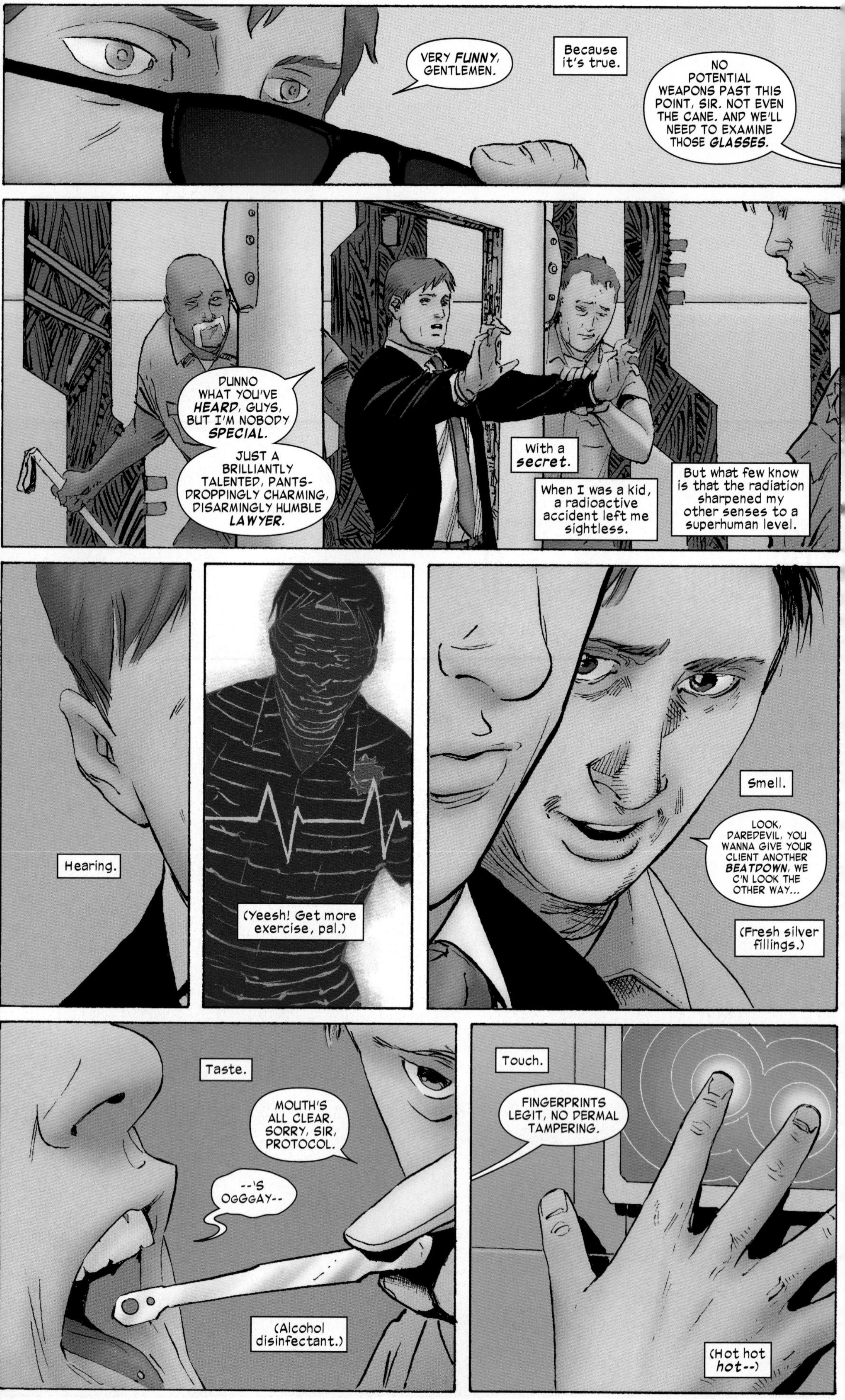

VERY FUNNY, GENTLEMEN.
Because it's true.
NO POTENTIAL WEAPONS PAST THIS POINT, SIR. NOT EVEN THE CANE. AND WE'LL NEED TO EXAMINE THOSE GLASSES.
DUNNO WHAT YOU'VE HEARD, GUYS, BUT I'M NOBODY SPECIAL.
JUST A BRILLIANTLY TALENTED, PANTS-DROPPINGLY CHARMING, DISARMINGLY HUMBLE LAWYER.
With a secret.
When I was a kid, a radioactive accident left me sightless.
But what few know is that the radiation sharpened my other senses to a superhuman level.
Hearing.
(Yeesh! Get more exercise, pal.)
Smell.
LOOK, DAREDEVIL, YOU WANNA GIVE YOUR CLIENT ANOTHER BEATDOWN, WE C'N LOOK THE OTHER WAY...
(Fresh silver fillings.)
Taste.
MOUTH'S ALL CLEAR. SORRY, SIR, PROTOCOL.
--'S OGGGAY--
(Alcohol disinfectant.)
Touch.
FINGERPRINTS LEGIT, NO DERMAL TAMPERING.
(Hot hot hot--)

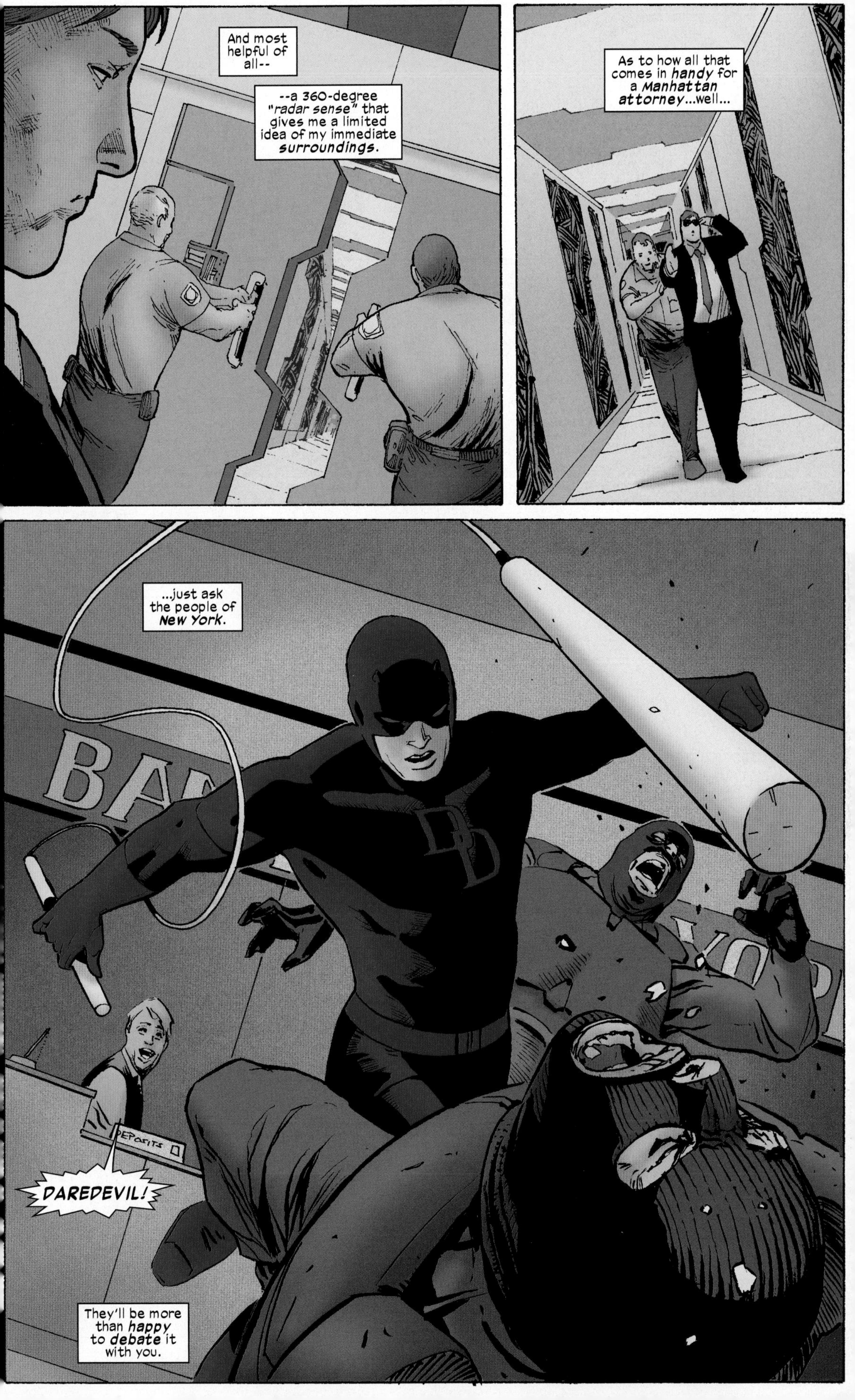
And most helpful of all--
--a 360-degree "radar sense" that gives me a limited idea of my immediate surroundings.
As to how all that comes in handy for a Manhattan attorney...well...
...just ask the people of New York.
DEPOSITS
DAREDEVIL!
They'll be more than happy to debate it with you.

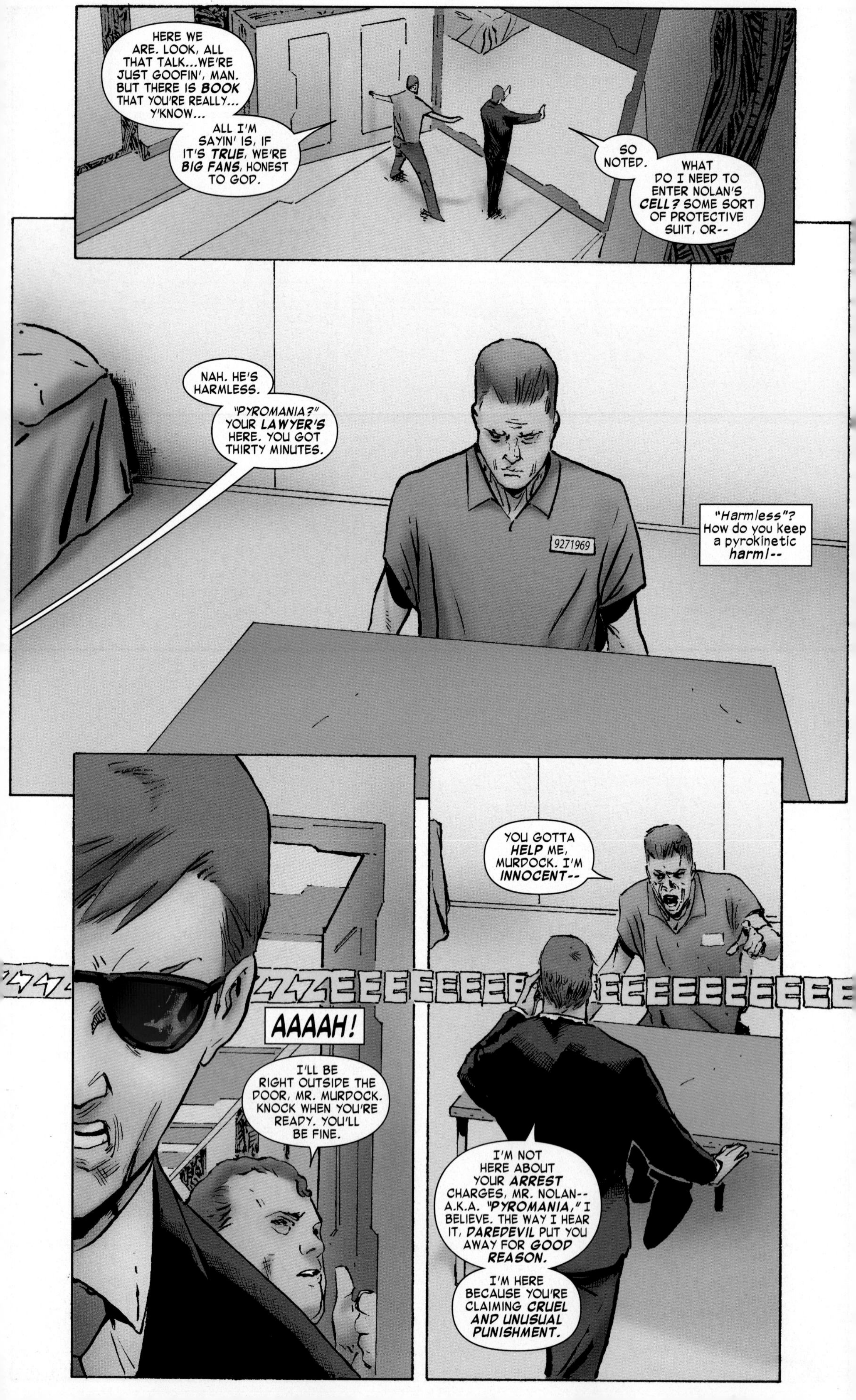
HERE WE ARE. LOOK, ALL THAT TALK...WE'RE JUST GOOFIN', MAN. BUT THERE IS BOOK THAT YOU'RE REALLY... Y'KNOW...
ALL I'M SAYIN' IS, IF IT'S TRUE, WE'RE BIG FANS, HONEST TO GOD.
SO NOTED.
WHAT DO I NEED TO ENTER NOLAN'S CELL? SOME SORT OF PROTECTIVE SUIT, OR--
NAH. HE'S HARMLESS.
"PYROMANIA?" YOUR LAWYER'S HERE. YOU GOT THIRTY MINUTES.
9271969
"Harmless"? How do you keep a pyrokinetic harml--
ZZZZZEEEEEEEEEEEEEEEEEEEEEE
AAAAH!
I'LL BE RIGHT OUTSIDE THE DOOR, MR. MURDOCK. KNOCK WHEN YOU'RE READY. YOU'LL BE FINE.
YOU GOTTA HELP ME, MURDOCK. I'M INNOCENT--
I'M NOT HERE ABOUT YOUR ARREST CHARGES, MR. NOLAN-- A.K.A. "PYROMANIA," I BELIEVE. THE WAY I HEAR IT, DAREDEVIL PUT YOU AWAY FOR GOOD REASON.
I'M HERE BECAUSE YOU'RE CLAIMING CRUEL AND UNUSUAL PUNISHMENT.

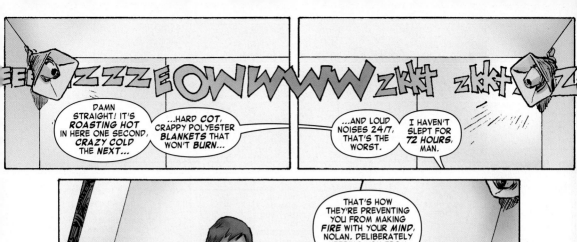

FEE ZZZEE OWWWW ZKKT ZKKT ZZ

DAMN STRAIGHT! IT'S *ROASTING HOT* IN HERE ONE SECOND, *CRAZY COLD* THE *NEXT...*

...HARD *COT,* CRAPPY POLYESTER *BLANKETS* THAT WON'T *BURN...*

...AND LOUD NOISES 24/7, THAT'S THE *WORST.*

I HAVEN'T SLEPT FOR *72 HOURS,* MAN.

THAT'S HOW THEY'RE PREVENTING YOU FROM MAKING *FIRE* WITH YOUR *MIND,* NOLAN. DELIBERATELY KEEPING YOU FROM *CONCENTRATING.*

IT'S *HELL* IN HERE!

No kidding. I can't decide if I'm standing in an *oven* or a *meat locker.*

TAKE IT FROM THE TOP. TELL ME IN *YOUR* OWN WORDS HOW AND WHY YOU ENDED UP BEHIND BARS.

NOLAN?

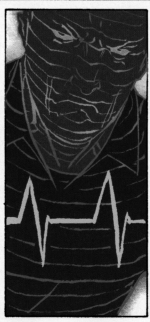

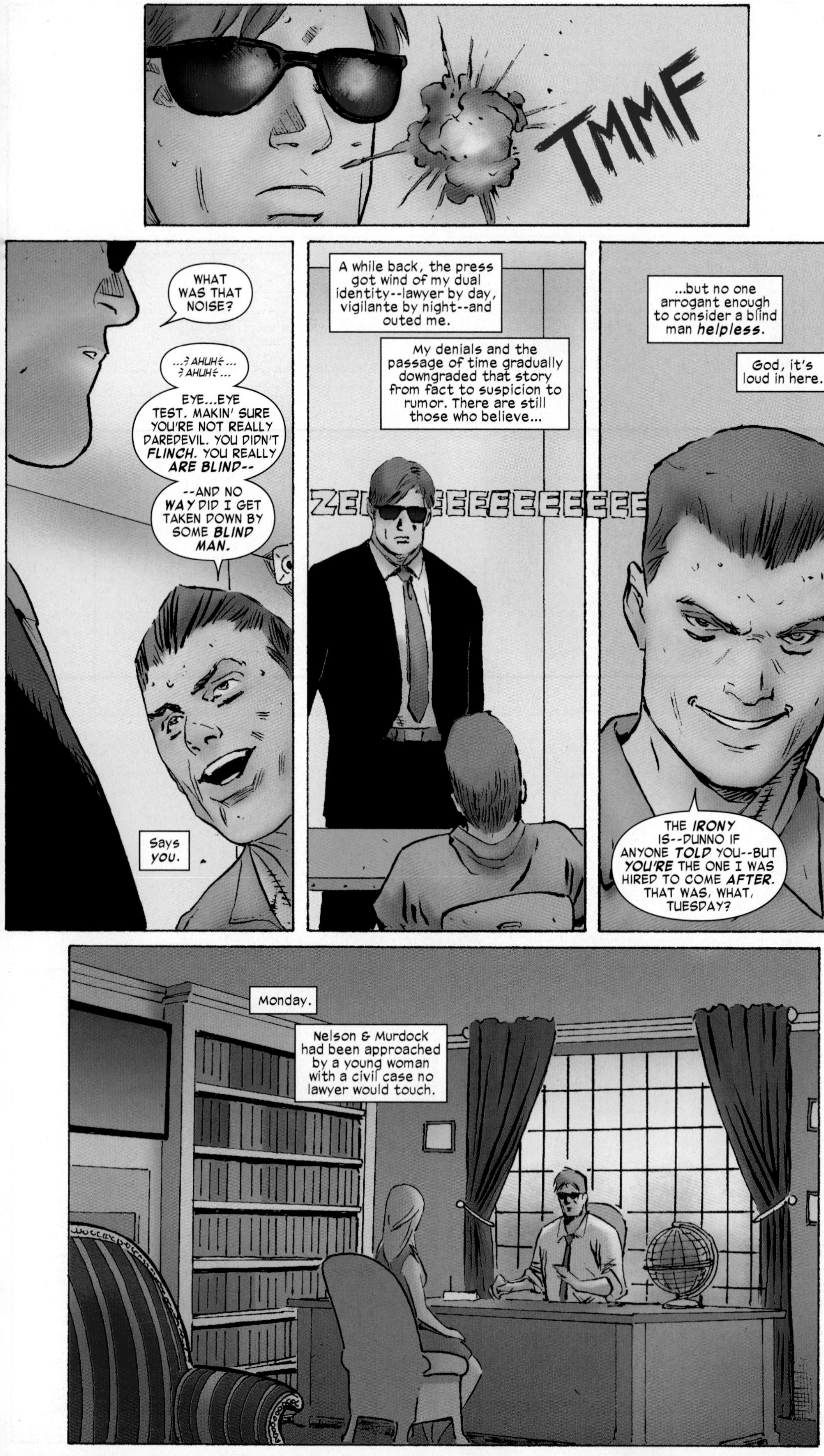
TMMF
WHAT WAS THAT NOISE?
...AHUH... AHUH...
EYE...EYE TEST. MAKIN' SURE YOU'RE NOT REALLY DAREDEVIL. YOU DIDN'T FLINCH. YOU REALLY ARE BLIND--
--AND NO WAY DID I GET TAKEN DOWN BY SOME BLIND MAN.
Says you.
A while back, the press got wind of my dual identity--lawyer by day, vigilante by night--and outed me.
My denials and the passage of time gradually downgraded that story from fact to suspicion to rumor. There are still those who believe...
ZEEEEEEEEEEEEE
...but no one arrogant enough to consider a blind man helpless.
God, it's loud in here.
THE IRONY IS--DUNNO IF ANYONE TOLD YOU--BUT YOU'RE THE ONE I WAS HIRED TO COME AFTER. THAT WAS, WHAT, TUESDAY?
Monday.
Nelson & Murdock had been approached by a young woman with a civil case no lawyer would touch.

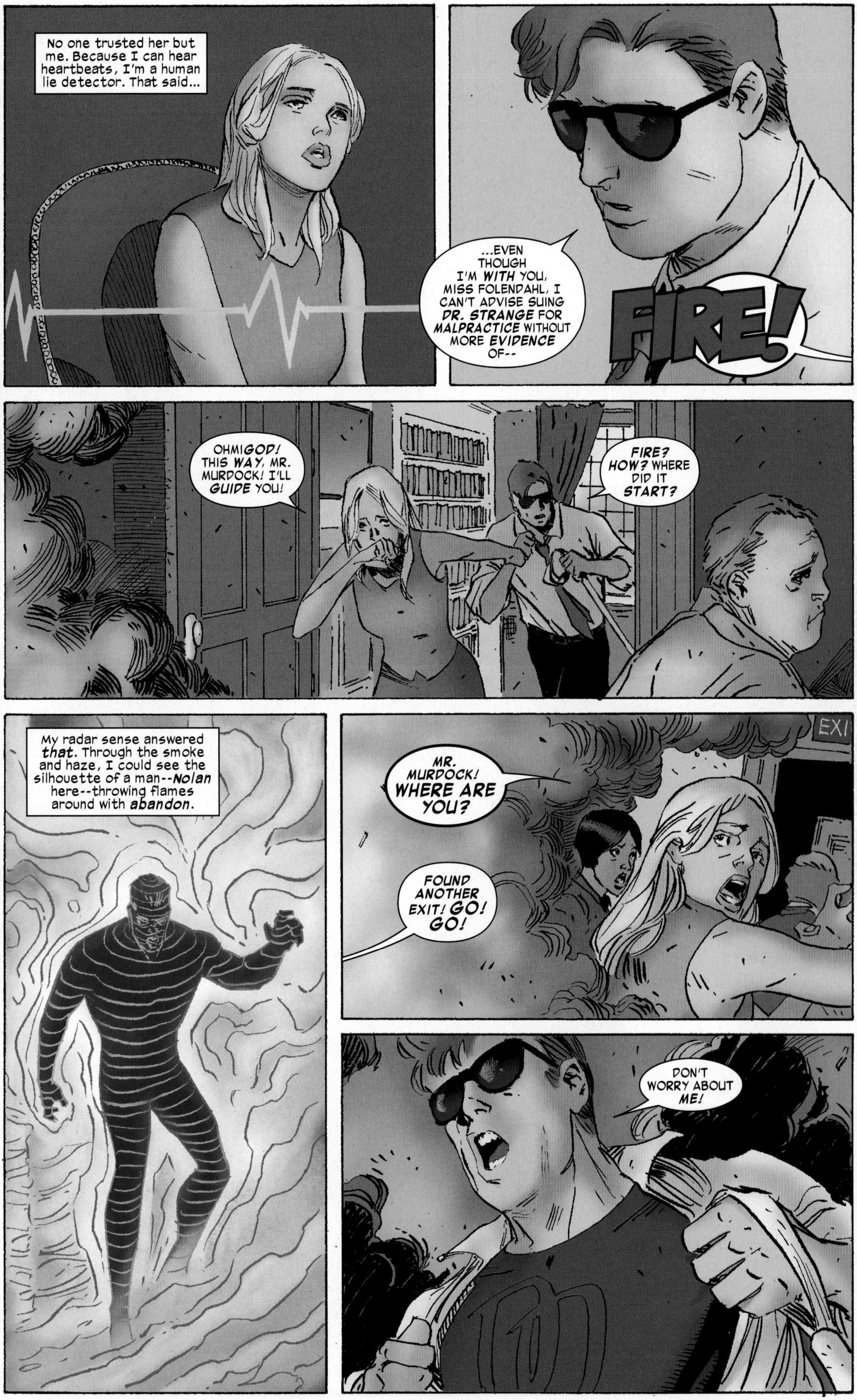
No one trusted her but me. Because I can hear heartbeats, I'm a human lie detector. That said...
...EVEN THOUGH I'M WITH YOU, MISS FOLENDAHL, I CAN'T ADVISE SUING DR. STRANGE FOR MALPRACTICE WITHOUT MORE EVIDENCE OF--
FIRE!
OHMIGOD! THIS WAY, MR. MURDOCK! I'LL GUIDE YOU!
FIRE? HOW? WHERE DID IT START?
My radar sense answered that. Through the smoke and haze, I could see the silhouette of a man--Nolan here--throwing flames around with abandon.
EXI
MR. MURDOCK! WHERE ARE YOU?
FOUND ANOTHER EXIT! GO! GO!
DON'T WORRY ABOUT ME!

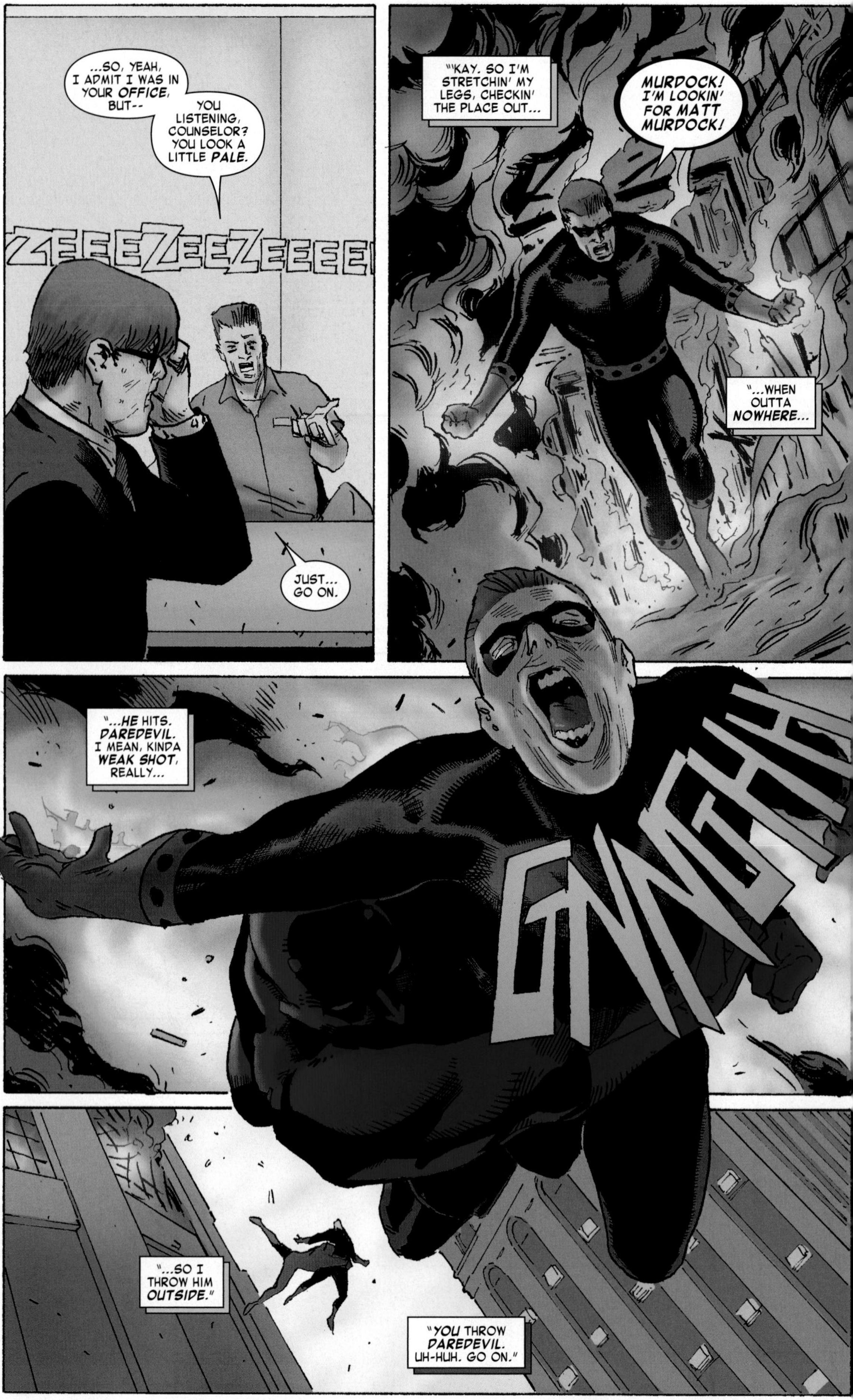
...SO, YEAH, I ADMIT I WAS IN YOUR OFFICE, BUT--
YOU LISTENING, COUNSELOR? YOU LOOK A LITTLE PALE.
ZEEEZEEZEEEEE
JUST... GO ON.
"'KAY. SO I'M STRETCHIN' MY LEGS, CHECKIN' THE PLACE OUT...
MURDOCK! I'M LOOKIN' FOR MATT MURDOCK!
"...WHEN OUTTA NOWHERE...
"...HE HITS. DAREDEVIL. I MEAN, KINDA WEAK SHOT, REALLY...
GNNGH
"...SO I THROW HIM OUTSIDE."
"YOU THROW DAREDEVIL. UH-HUH. GO ON."

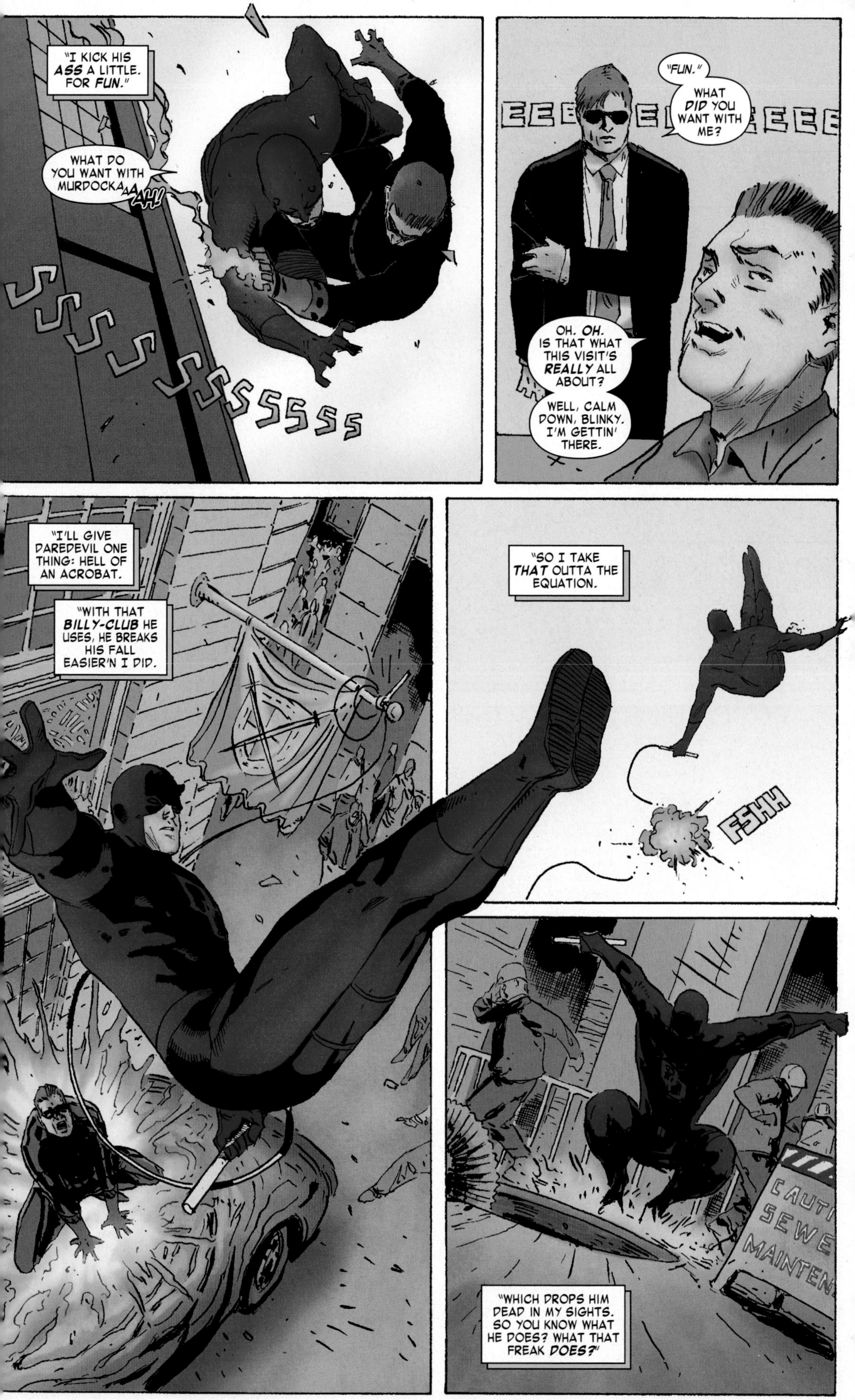

"I KICK HIS ASS A LITTLE. FOR FUN."
WHAT DO YOU WANT WITH MURDOCKAAAAH!
SSSSSSSSSSSS
"FUN." WHAT DID YOU WANT WITH ME?
EEEEEEEEEE
OH. OH. IS THAT WHAT THIS VISIT'S REALLY ALL ABOUT?
WELL, CALM DOWN, BLINKY. I'M GETTIN' THERE.
"I'LL GIVE DAREDEVIL ONE THING: HELL OF AN ACROBAT.
"WITH THAT BILLY-CLUB HE USES, HE BREAKS HIS FALL EASIER'N I DID.
"SO I TAKE THAT OUTTA THE EQUATION.
FSHH
CAUTI SEWE MAINTEN
"WHICH DROPS HIM DEAD IN MY SIGHTS. SO YOU KNOW WHAT HE DOES? WHAT THAT FREAK DOES?"

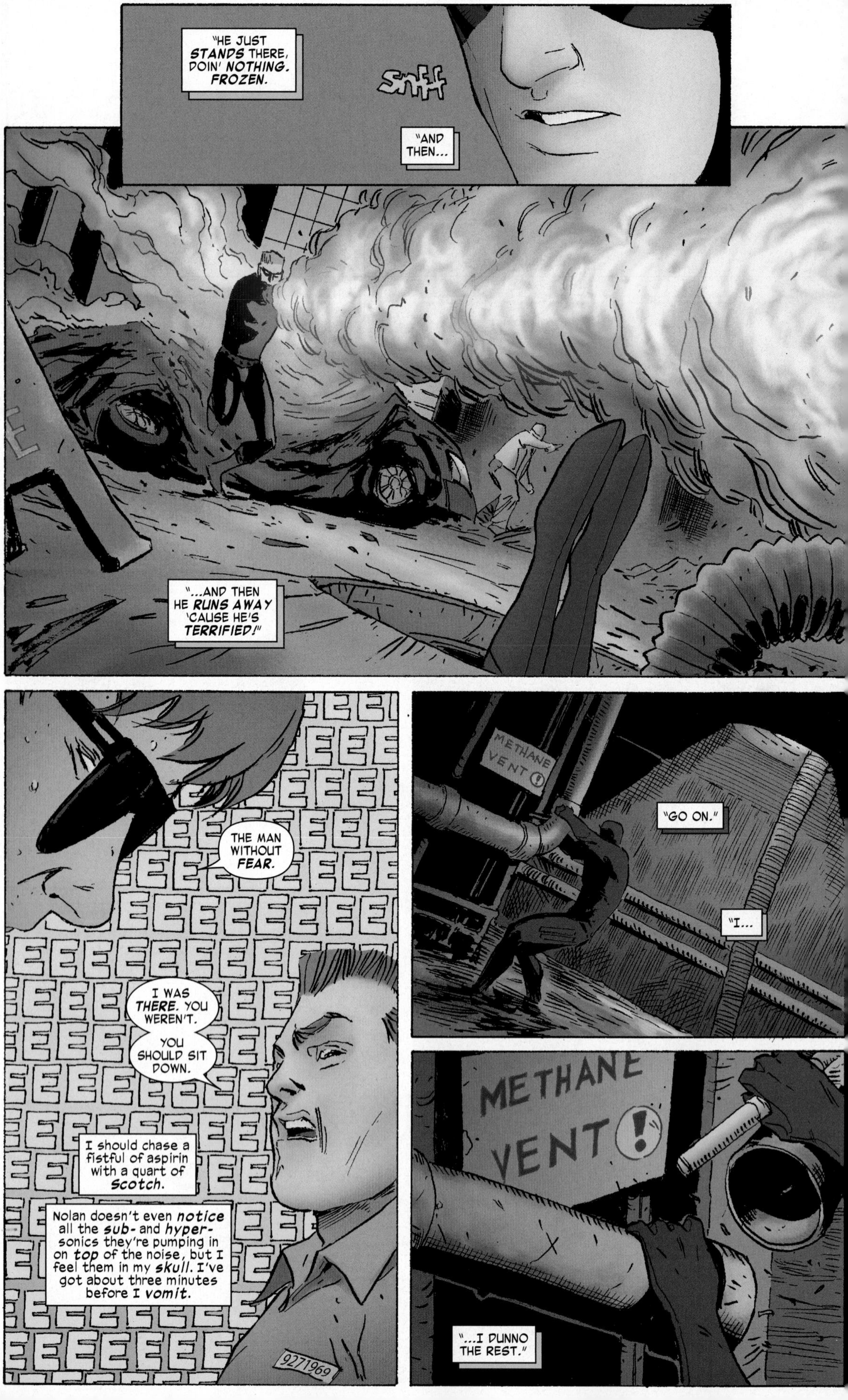
"HE JUST STANDS THERE, DOIN' NOTHING. FROZEN.
SNFF
"AND THEN...
"...AND THEN HE RUNS AWAY 'CAUSE HE'S TERRIFIED!"
THE MAN WITHOUT FEAR.
I WAS THERE. YOU WEREN'T.
YOU SHOULD SIT DOWN.
I should chase a fistful of aspirin with a quart of Scotch.
Nolan doesn't even notice all the sub- and hyper-sonics they're pumping in on top of the noise, but I feel them in my skull. I've got about three minutes before I vomit.
9271969
METHANE VENT !
"GO ON."
"I...
METHANE VENT !
"...I DUNNO THE REST."

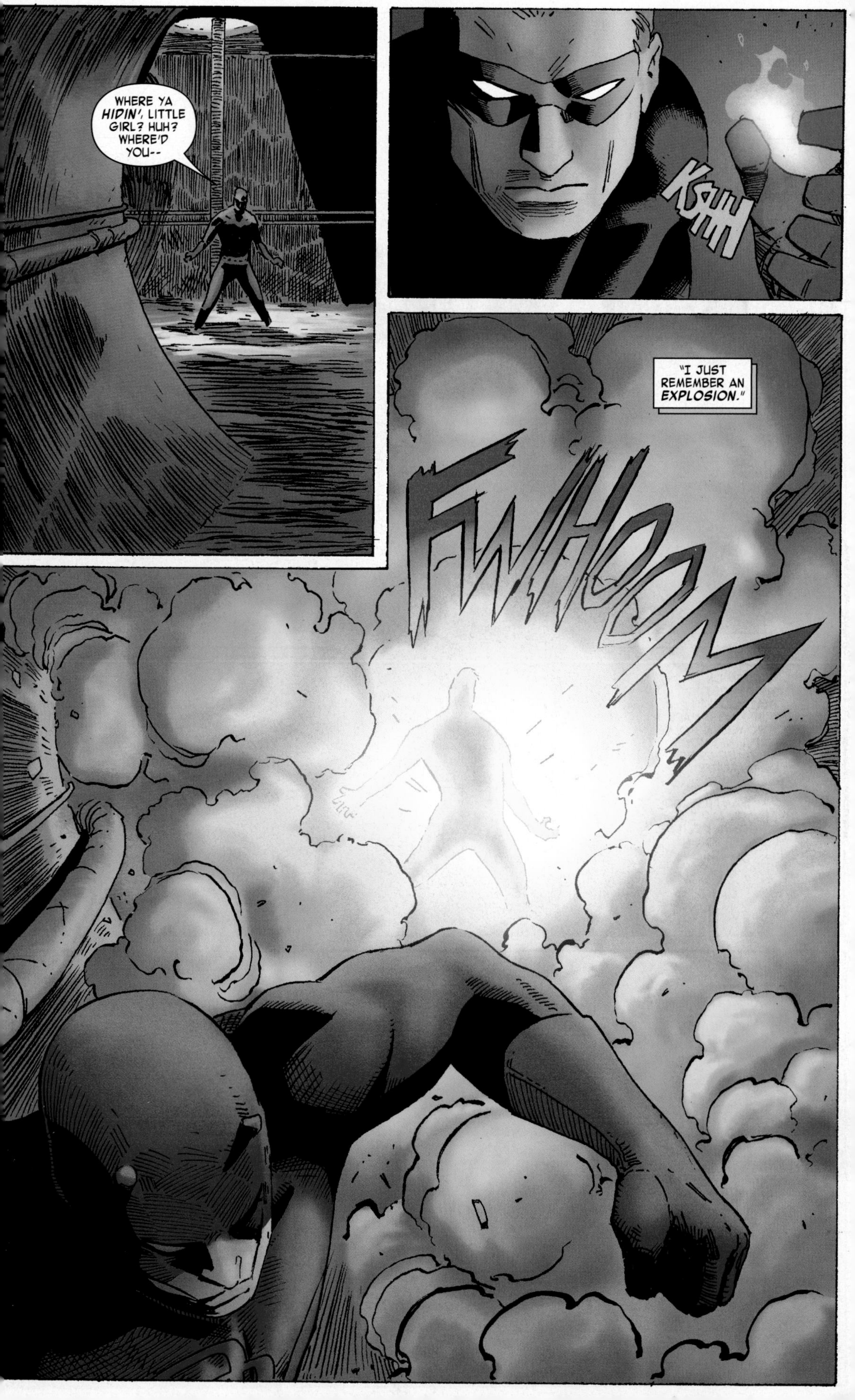

WHERE YA HIDIN', LITTLE GIRL? HUH? WHERE'D YOU--
KSHH
"I JUST REMEMBER AN EXPLOSION."
FWHOOM

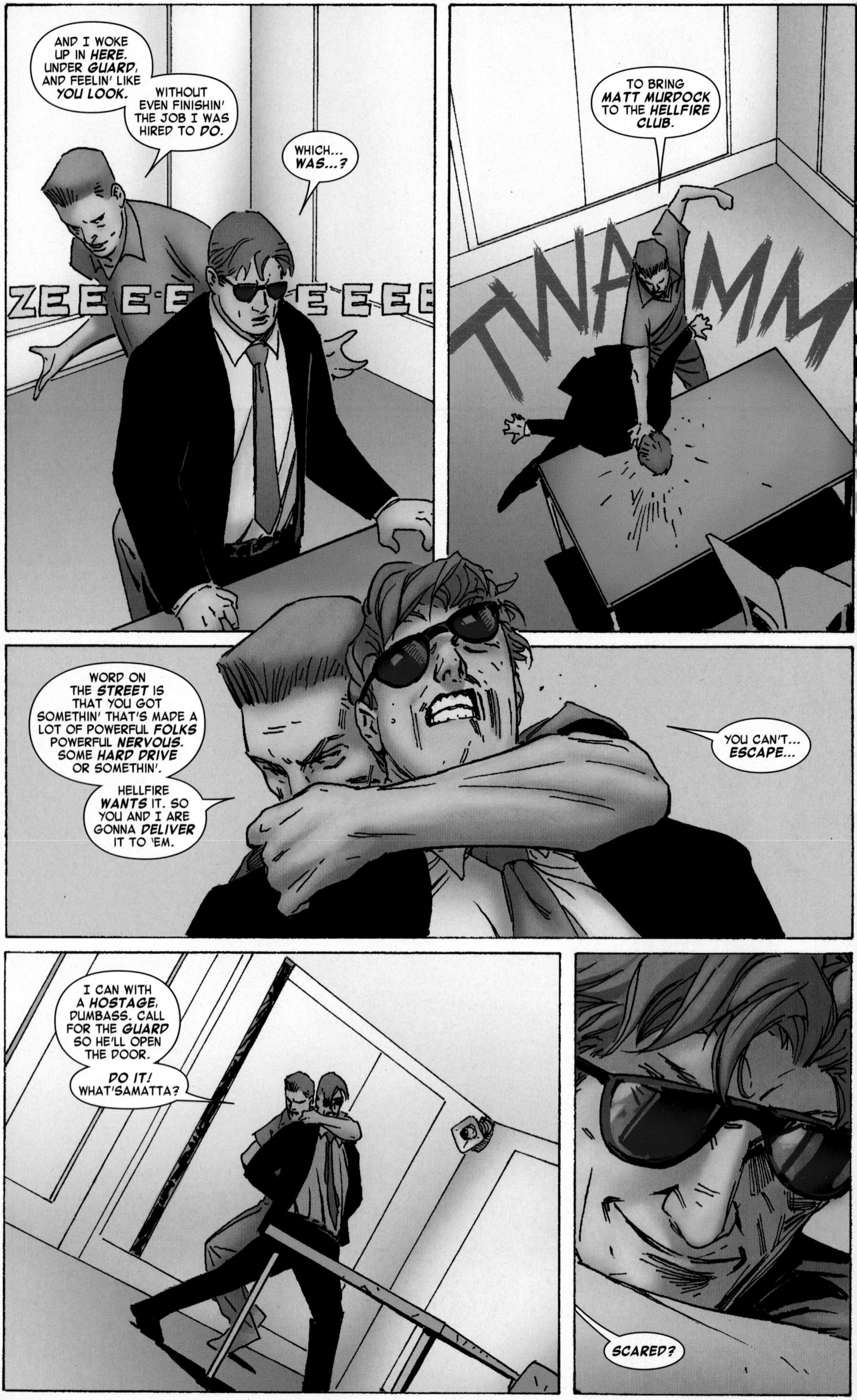
AND I WOKE UP IN HERE. UNDER GUARD, AND FEELIN' LIKE YOU LOOK.
WITHOUT EVEN FINISHIN' THE JOB I WAS HIRED TO DO.
WHICH... WAS...?
ZEEEEEEEEE
TO BRING MATT MURDOCK TO THE HELLFIRE CLUB.
TWAMM
WORD ON THE STREET IS THAT YOU GOT SOMETHIN' THAT'S MADE A LOT OF POWERFUL FOLKS POWERFUL NERVOUS. SOME HARD DRIVE OR SOMETHIN'.
HELLFIRE WANTS IT. SO YOU AND I ARE GONNA DELIVER IT TO 'EM.
YOU CAN'T... ESCAPE...
I CAN WITH A HOSTAGE, DUMBASS. CALL FOR THE GUARD SO HE'LL OPEN THE DOOR.
DO IT! WHAT'SAMATTA?
SCARED?

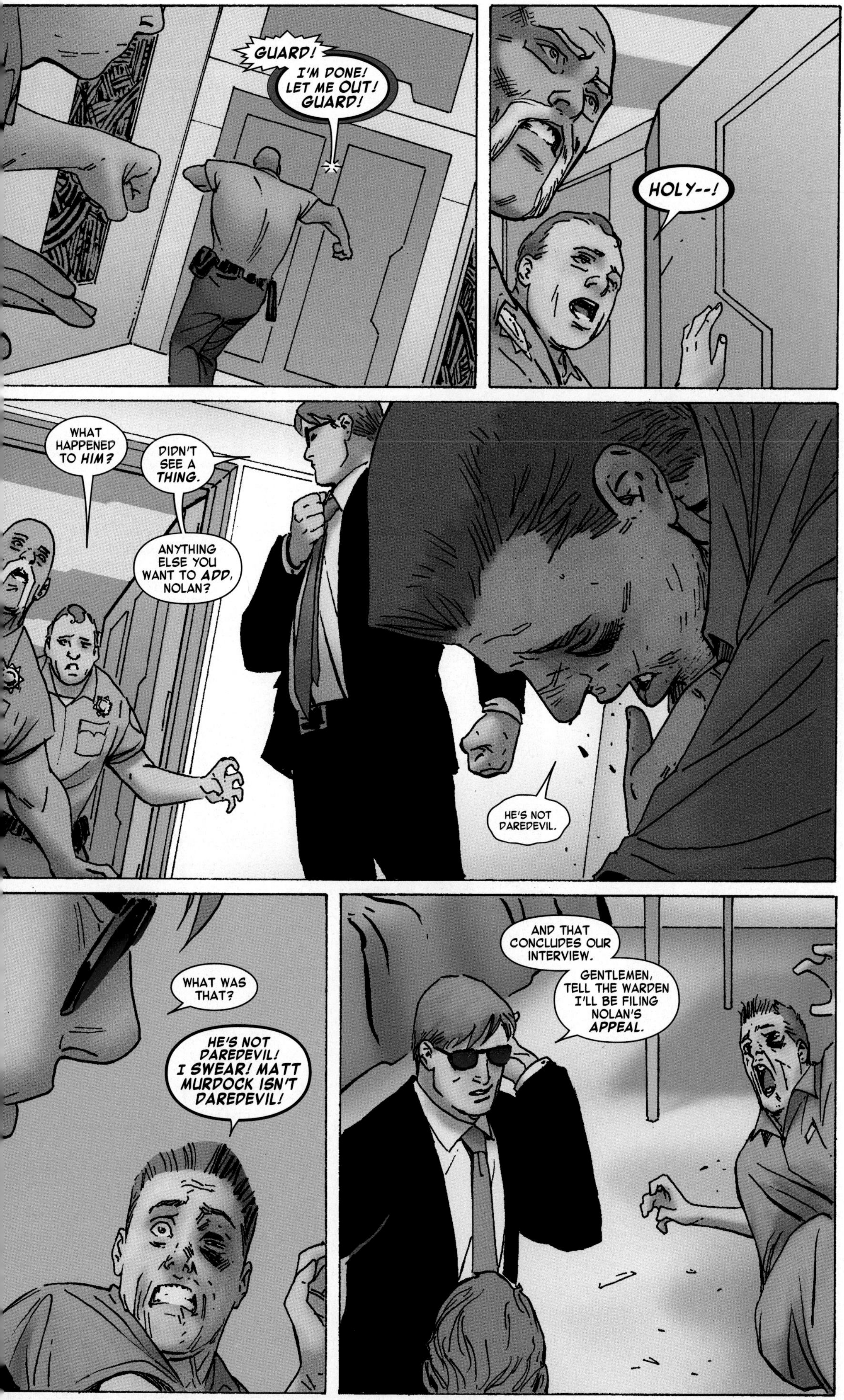
GUARD!
I'M DONE! LET ME OUT! GUARD!
HOLY--!
WHAT HAPPENED TO HIM?
DIDN'T SEE A THING.
ANYTHING ELSE YOU WANT TO ADD, NOLAN?
HE'S NOT DAREDEVIL.
WHAT WAS THAT?
HE'S NOT DAREDEVIL! I SWEAR! MATT MURDOCK ISN'T DAREDEVIL!
AND THAT CONCLUDES OUR INTERVIEW.
GENTLEMEN, TELL THE WARDEN I'LL BE FILING NOLAN'S APPEAL.

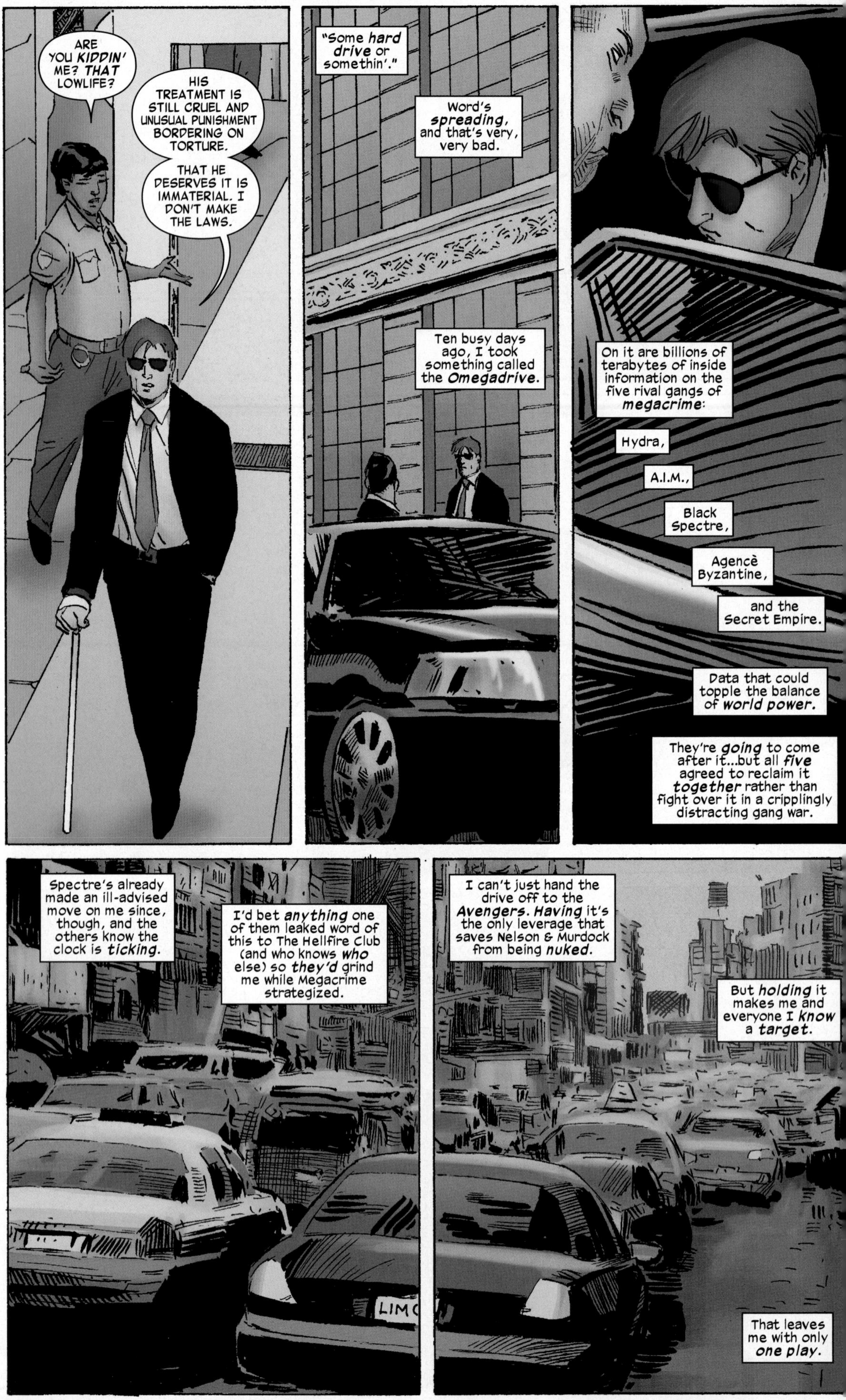

ARE YOU *KIDDIN'* ME? *THAT* LOWLIFE?
HIS TREATMENT IS STILL CRUEL AND UNUSUAL PUNISHMENT BORDERING ON TORTURE.
THAT HE DESERVES IT IS IMMATERIAL. I DON'T MAKE THE LAWS.
"Some *hard drive* or somethin'."
Word's *spreading*, and that's very, very bad.
Ten busy days ago, I took something called the *Omegadrive*.
On it are billions of terabytes of inside information on the five rival gangs of *megacrime*:
Hydra,
A.I.M.,
Black Spectre,
Agencè Byzantine,
and the Secret Empire.
Data that could topple the balance of *world power*.
They're *going* to come after it...but all *five* agreed to reclaim it *together* rather than fight over it in a cripplingly distracting gang war.
Spectre's already made an ill-advised move on me since, though, and the others know the clock is *ticking*.
I'd bet *anything* one of them leaked word of this to The Hellfire Club (and who knows *who* else) so *they'd* grind me while Megacrime strategized.
LIMO
I can't just hand the drive off to the *Avengers*. *Having* it's the only leverage that saves Nelson & Murdock from being *nuked*.
But *holding* it makes me and everyone I *know* a *target*.
That leaves me with only *one play*.

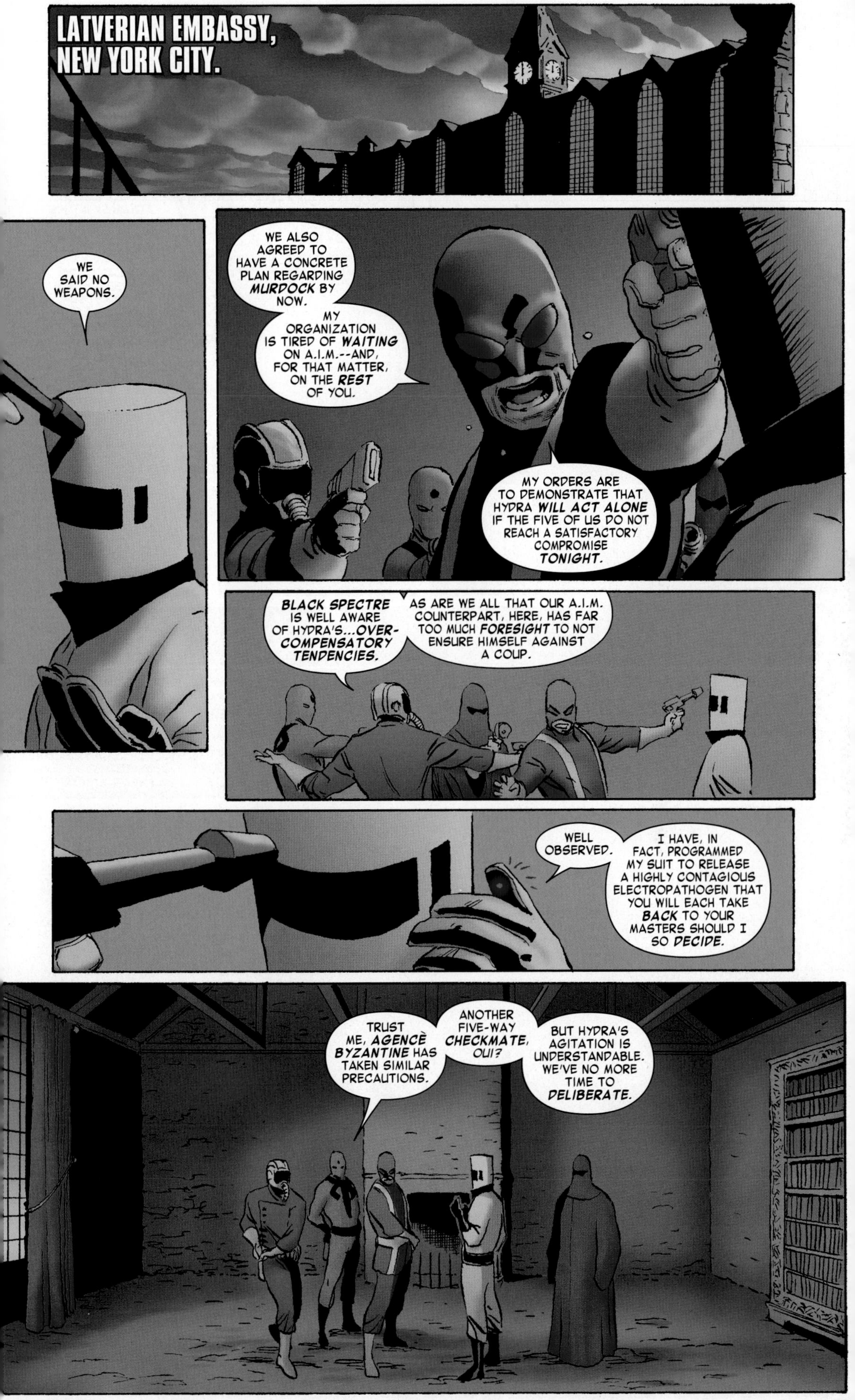
LATVERIAN EMBASSY, NEW YORK CITY.
WE SAID NO WEAPONS.
WE ALSO AGREED TO HAVE A CONCRETE PLAN REGARDING MURDOCK BY NOW.
MY ORGANIZATION IS TIRED OF WAITING ON A.I.M.--AND, FOR THAT MATTER, ON THE REST OF YOU.
MY ORDERS ARE TO DEMONSTRATE THAT HYDRA WILL ACT ALONE IF THE FIVE OF US DO NOT REACH A SATISFACTORY COMPROMISE TONIGHT.
BLACK SPECTRE IS WELL AWARE OF HYDRA'S...OVER-COMPENSATORY TENDENCIES.
AS ARE WE ALL THAT OUR A.I.M. COUNTERPART, HERE, HAS FAR TOO MUCH FORESIGHT TO NOT ENSURE HIMSELF AGAINST A COUP.
WELL OBSERVED.
I HAVE, IN FACT, PROGRAMMED MY SUIT TO RELEASE A HIGHLY CONTAGIOUS ELECTROPATHOGEN THAT YOU WILL EACH TAKE BACK TO YOUR MASTERS SHOULD I SO DECIDE.
TRUST ME, AGENCÈ BYZANTINE HAS TAKEN SIMILAR PRECAUTIONS.
ANOTHER FIVE-WAY CHECKMATE, OUI?
BUT HYDRA'S AGITATION IS UNDERSTANDABLE. WE'VE NO MORE TIME TO DELIBERATE.

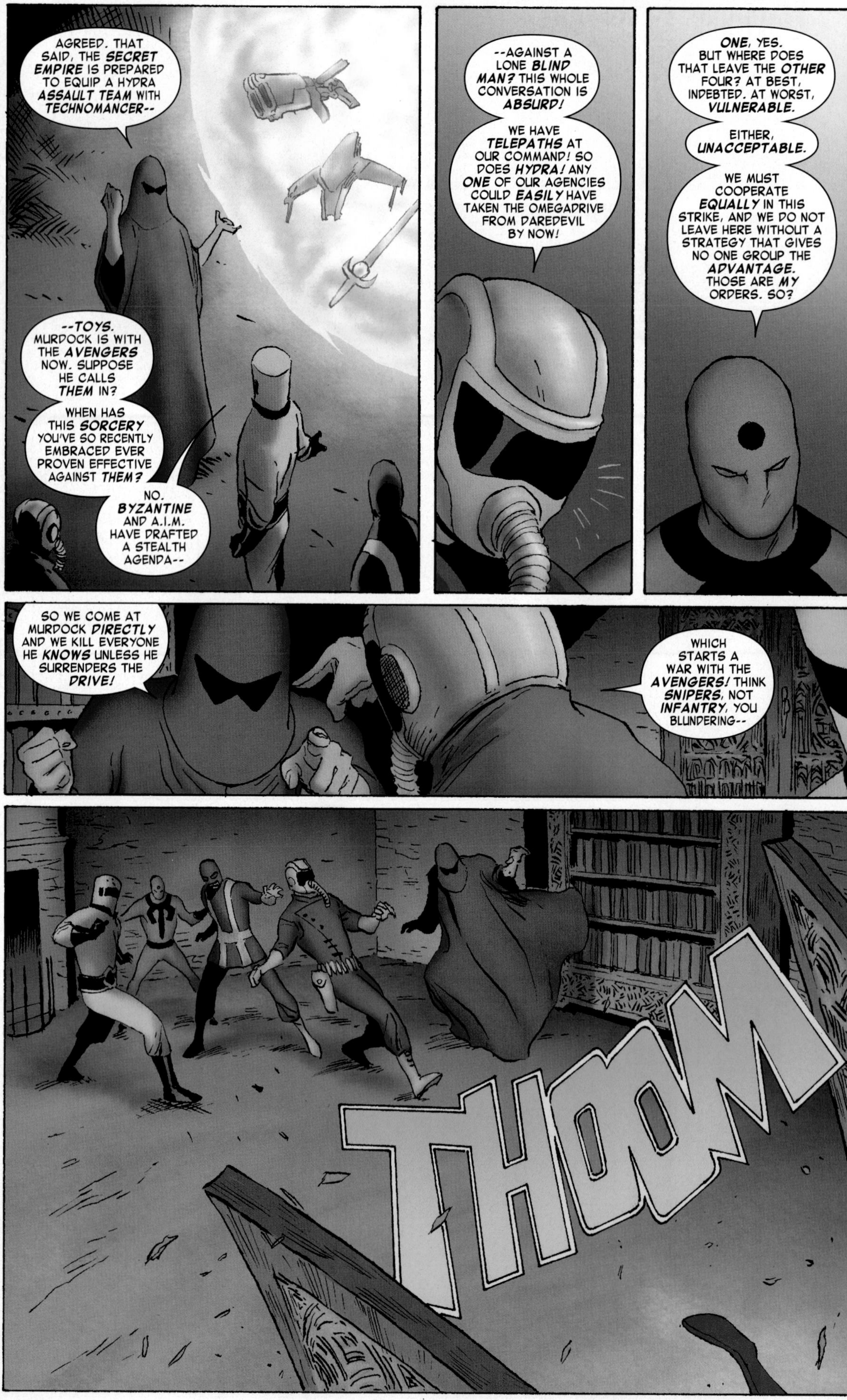
AGREED. THAT SAID, THE SECRET EMPIRE IS PREPARED TO EQUIP A HYDRA ASSAULT TEAM WITH TECHNOMANCER--
--TOYS. MURDOCK IS WITH THE AVENGERS NOW. SUPPOSE HE CALLS THEM IN?
WHEN HAS THIS SORCERY YOU'VE SO RECENTLY EMBRACED EVER PROVEN EFFECTIVE AGAINST THEM?
NO. BYZANTINE AND A.I.M. HAVE DRAFTED A STEALTH AGENDA--
--AGAINST A LONE BLIND MAN? THIS WHOLE CONVERSATION IS ABSURD!
WE HAVE TELEPATHS AT OUR COMMAND! SO DOES HYDRA! ANY ONE OF OUR AGENCIES COULD EASILY HAVE TAKEN THE OMEGADRIVE FROM DAREDEVIL BY NOW!
ONE, YES. BUT WHERE DOES THAT LEAVE THE OTHER FOUR? AT BEST, INDEBTED. AT WORST, VULNERABLE.
EITHER, UNACCEPTABLE.
WE MUST COOPERATE EQUALLY IN THIS STRIKE, AND WE DO NOT LEAVE HERE WITHOUT A STRATEGY THAT GIVES NO ONE GROUP THE ADVANTAGE. THOSE ARE MY ORDERS. SO?
SO WE COME AT MURDOCK DIRECTLY AND WE KILL EVERYONE HE KNOWS UNLESS HE SURRENDERS THE DRIVE!
WHICH STARTS A WAR WITH THE AVENGERS! THINK SNIPERS, NOT INFANTRY, YOU BLUNDERING--
THOOM

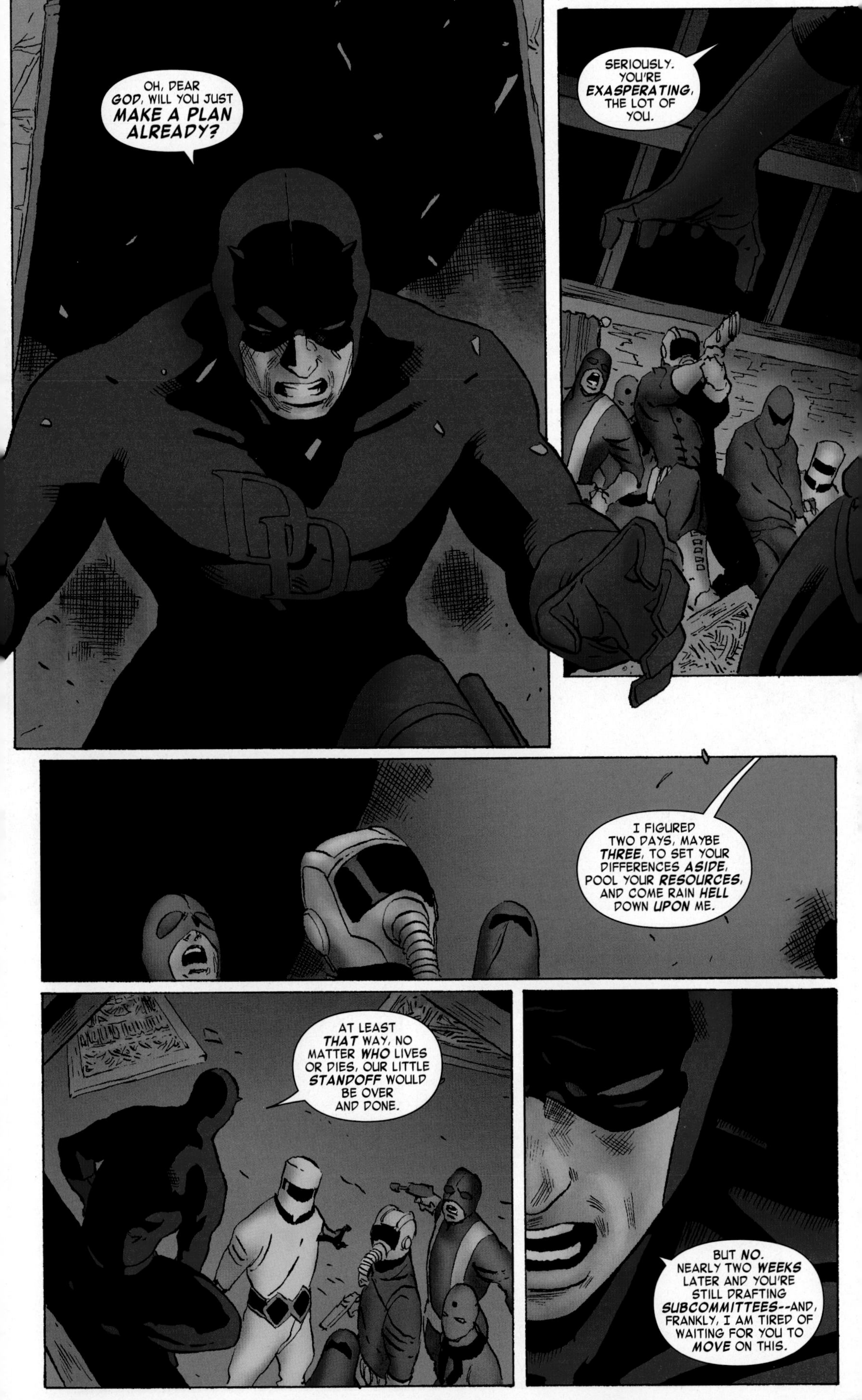

OH, DEAR GOD, WILL YOU JUST MAKE A PLAN ALREADY?
SERIOUSLY. YOU'RE EXASPERATING, THE LOT OF YOU.
I FIGURED TWO DAYS, MAYBE THREE, TO SET YOUR DIFFERENCES ASIDE, POOL YOUR RESOURCES, AND COME RAIN HELL DOWN UPON ME.
AT LEAST THAT WAY, NO MATTER WHO LIVES OR DIES, OUR LITTLE STANDOFF WOULD BE OVER AND DONE.
BUT NO. NEARLY TWO WEEKS LATER AND YOU'RE STILL DRAFTING SUBCOMMITTEES--AND, FRANKLY, I AM TIRED OF WAITING FOR YOU TO MOVE ON THIS.

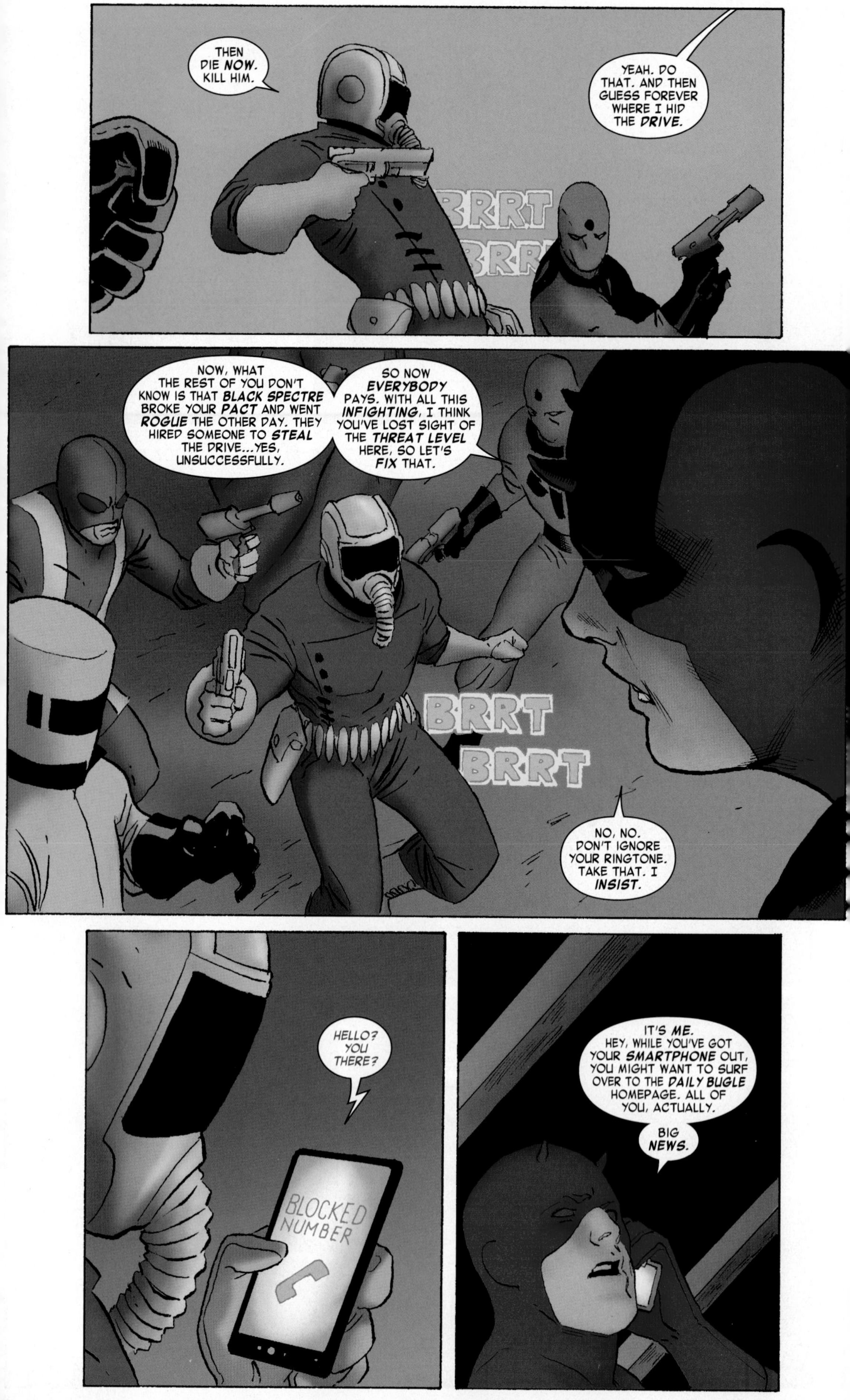
THEN DIE NOW. KILL HIM.
YEAH. DO THAT. AND THEN GUESS FOREVER WHERE I HID THE DRIVE.
BRRT BRRT
NOW, WHAT THE REST OF YOU DON'T KNOW IS THAT BLACK SPECTRE BROKE YOUR PACT AND WENT ROGUE THE OTHER DAY. THEY HIRED SOMEONE TO STEAL THE DRIVE...YES, UNSUCCESSFULLY.
SO NOW EVERYBODY PAYS. WITH ALL THIS INFIGHTING, I THINK YOU'VE LOST SIGHT OF THE THREAT LEVEL HERE, SO LET'S FIX THAT.
BRRT BRRT
NO, NO. DON'T IGNORE YOUR RINGTONE. TAKE THAT. I INSIST.
HELLO? YOU THERE?
BLOCKED NUMBER
IT'S ME. HEY, WHILE YOU'VE GOT YOUR SMARTPHONE OUT, YOU MIGHT WANT TO SURF OVER TO THE DAILY BUGLE HOMEPAGE. ALL OF YOU, ACTUALLY.
BIG NEWS.

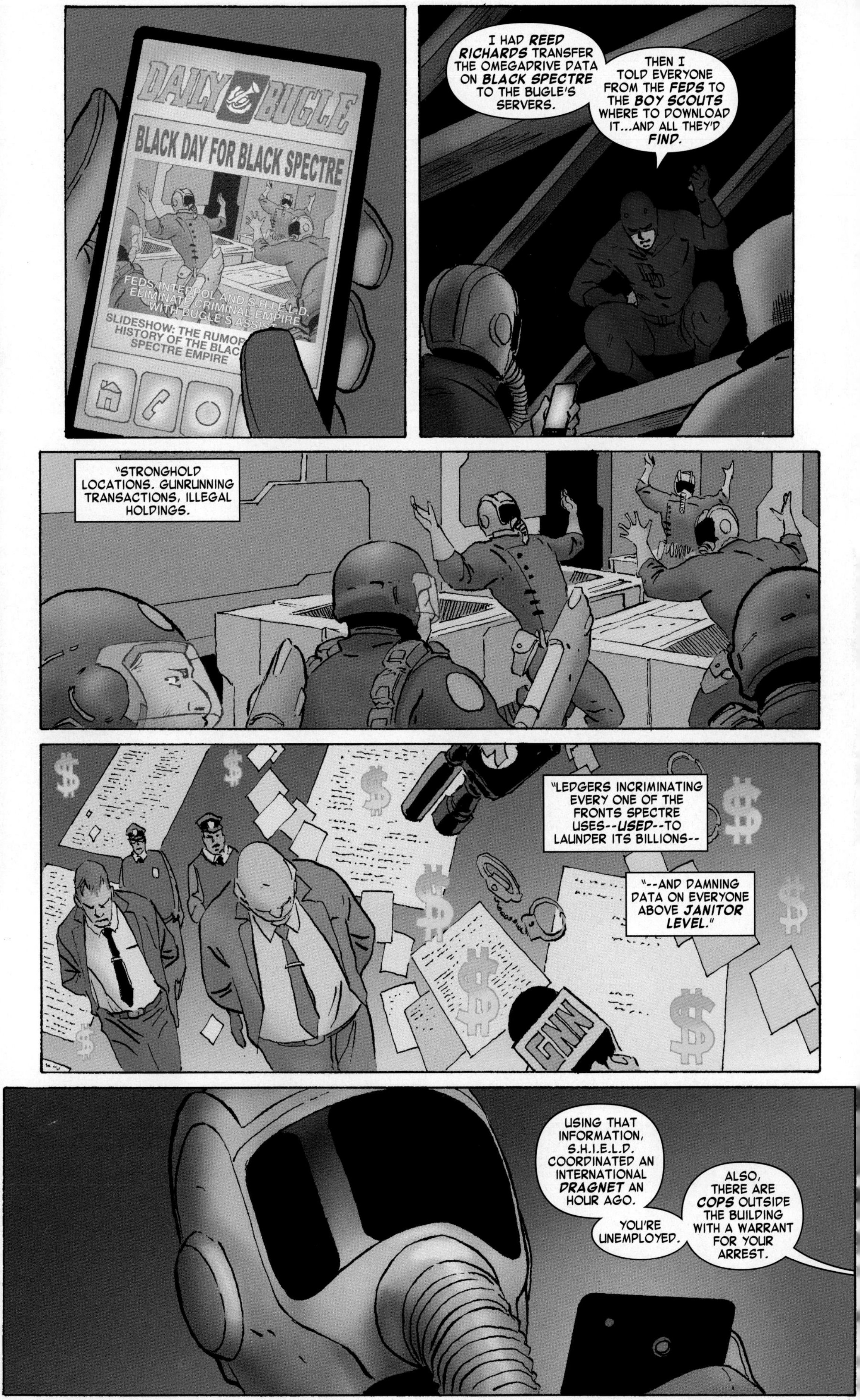
DAILY BUGLE
BLACK DAY FOR BLACK SPECTRE
FEDS/INTERPOL AND S.H.I.E.L.D. ELIMINATE CRIMINAL EMPIRE WITH BUGLE'S ASSIST
SLIDESHOW: THE RUMOR HISTORY OF THE BLACK SPECTRE EMPIRE
I HAD REED RICHARDS TRANSFER THE OMEGADRIVE DATA ON BLACK SPECTRE TO THE BUGLE'S SERVERS.
THEN I TOLD EVERYONE FROM THE FEDS TO THE BOY SCOUTS WHERE TO DOWNLOAD IT...AND ALL THEY'D FIND.
"STRONGHOLD LOCATIONS. GUNRUNNING TRANSACTIONS, ILLEGAL HOLDINGS.
"LEDGERS INCRIMINATING EVERY ONE OF THE FRONTS SPECTRE USES--USED--TO LAUNDER ITS BILLIONS--
"--AND DAMNING DATA ON EVERYONE ABOVE JANITOR LEVEL."
GNN
USING THAT INFORMATION, S.H.I.E.L.D. COORDINATED AN INTERNATIONAL DRAGNET AN HOUR AGO.
YOU'RE UNEMPLOYED.
ALSO, THERE ARE COPS OUTSIDE THE BUILDING WITH A WARRANT FOR YOUR ARREST.

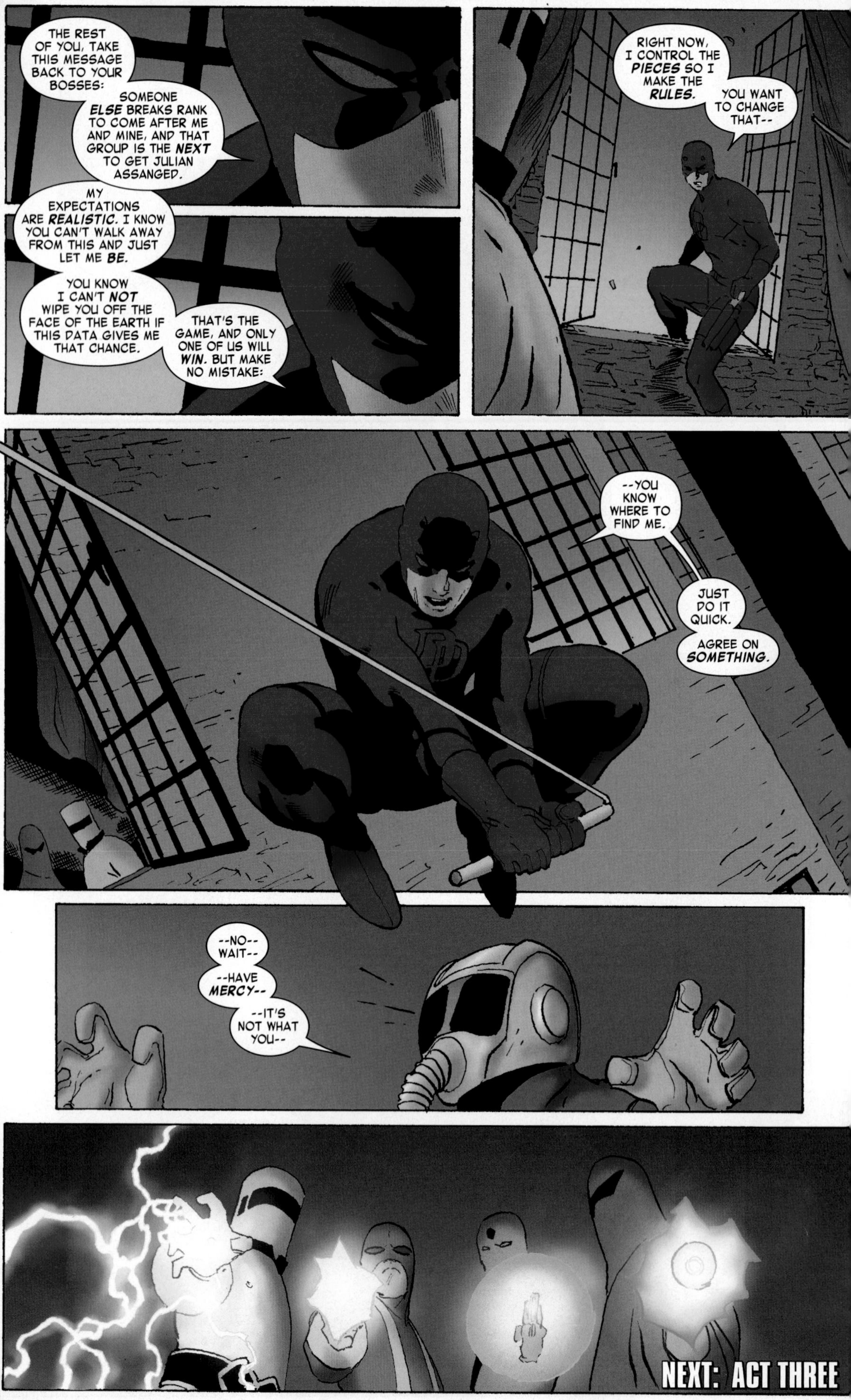
THE REST OF YOU, TAKE THIS MESSAGE BACK TO YOUR BOSSES:
SOMEONE ELSE BREAKS RANK TO COME AFTER ME AND MINE, AND THAT GROUP IS THE NEXT TO GET JULIAN ASSANGED.
MY EXPECTATIONS ARE REALISTIC. I KNOW YOU CAN'T WALK AWAY FROM THIS AND JUST LET ME BE.
YOU KNOW I CAN'T NOT WIPE YOU OFF THE FACE OF THE EARTH IF THIS DATA GIVES ME THAT CHANCE.
THAT'S THE GAME, AND ONLY ONE OF US WILL WIN. BUT MAKE NO MISTAKE:
RIGHT NOW, I CONTROL THE PIECES SO I MAKE THE RULES.
YOU WANT TO CHANGE THAT--
--YOU KNOW WHERE TO FIND ME.
JUST DO IT QUICK.
AGREE ON SOMETHING.
--NO-- WAIT--
--HAVE MERCY--
--IT'S NOT WHAT YOU--
NEXT: ACT THREE

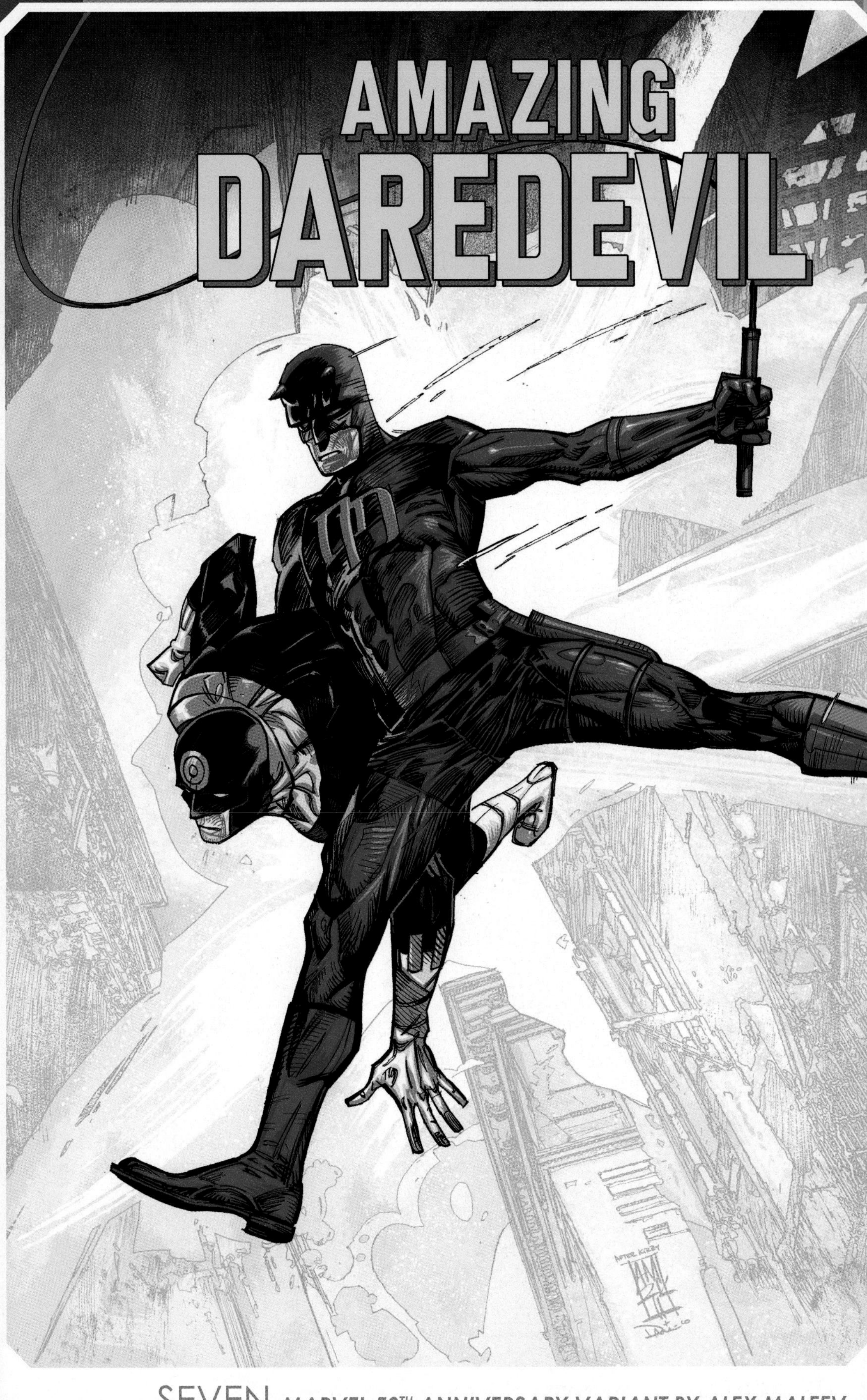
AMAZING
DAREDEVIL

SEVEN *MARVEL 50TH ANNIVERSARY VARIANT BY ALEX MALEEV*

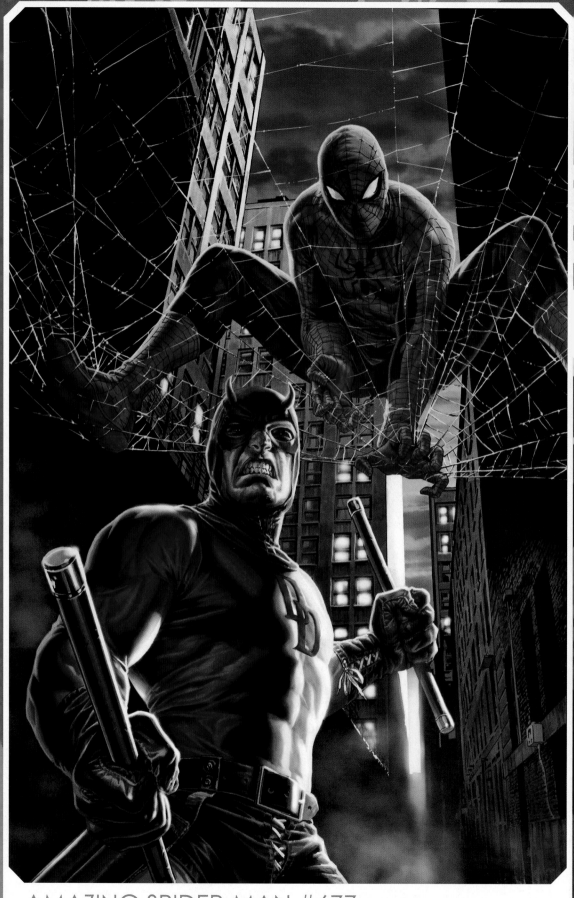

AMAZING SPIDER-MAN #677 *VARIANT BY LEE BERMEJO*

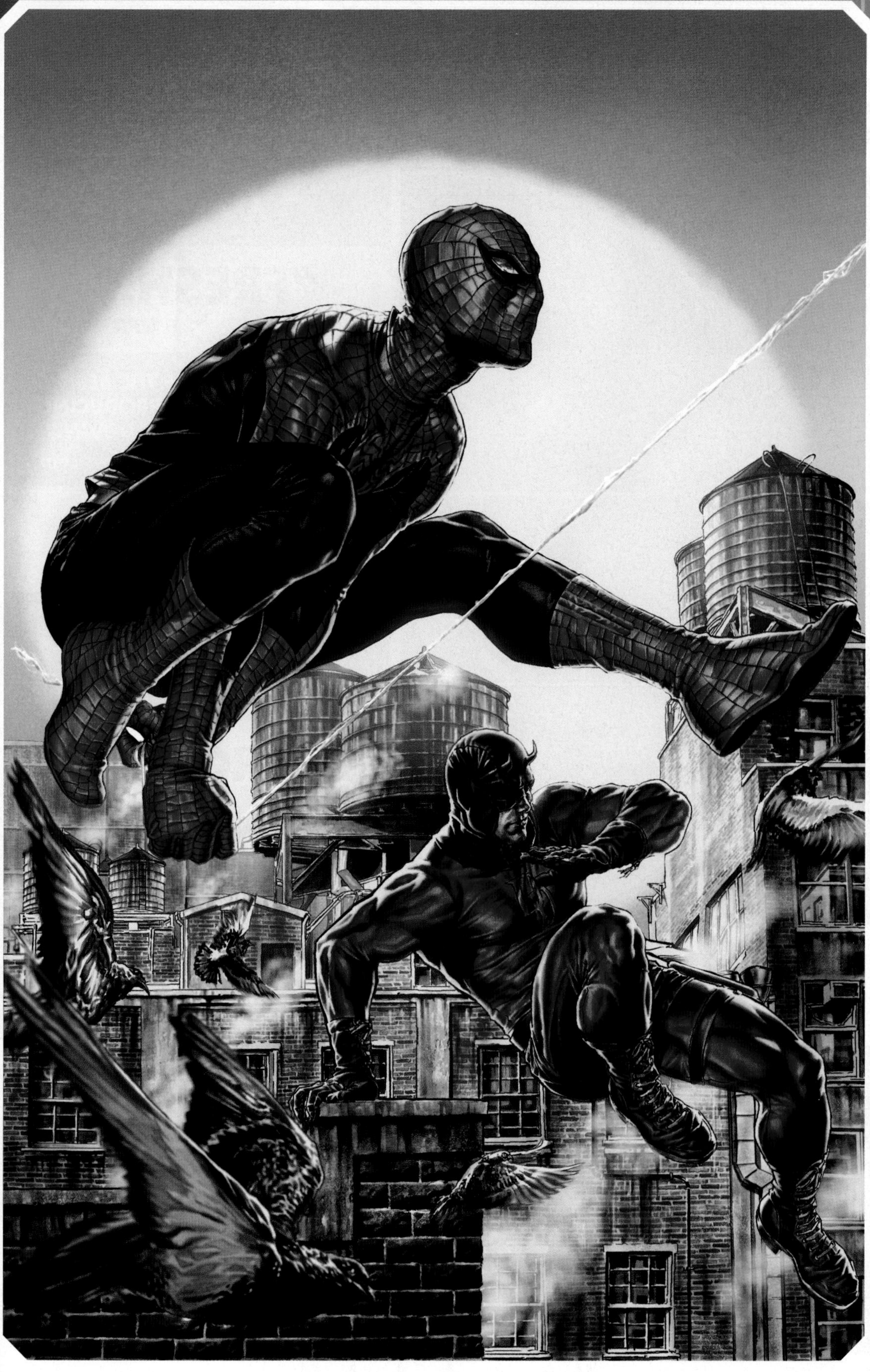

EIGHT **VARIANT BY LEE BERMEJO**

BEST NEW SERIES OF 2011

- IGN.COM

MARVEL
HERE COMES...
DAREDEVIL

"FRESH."
– NPR

"THIS IS ONE OF THE *BEST* COMICS MARVEL IS PRODUCING RIGHT NOW, HANDS DOWN."
– *AintItCoolNews.com*

"PERFECT."
– *Newsarama.com*

"#1 COMIC OF 2011 IT'S SIMPLY THE BEST COMIC ON STANDS TODAY"
– *COMPLEX*

"PHENOMENAL"
– *ComicsAlliance.com*

"...EASILY AMONG THE BEST NEW SERIES TO COME OUT IN 2011"
– *CNN.COM*

"SIMPLY A BEAUTIFUL, BEAUTIFUL BOOK BOTH THEMATICALLY AND VISUALLY."
– *MTV.COM*

"#1 NEW BOOK OF 2011...TRULY A NEW DAREDEVIL FOR A NEW GENERATION."
– *iFANBOY.COM*

"BEST RELAUNCH...MARK WAID'S BROUGHT HIM BACK WITH A NEW FRESHNESS AND MARCOS MARTIN AND PAOLO RIVERA HAVE CHIPPED IN EXQUISITE ARTWORK"
– *USA TODAY*

"*DAREDEVIL* IS THE BEST TITLE MARVEL IS PUTTING OUT TODAY."
– *ComicsBulletin.com*

"★★★★★"
– *Comicvine.com*

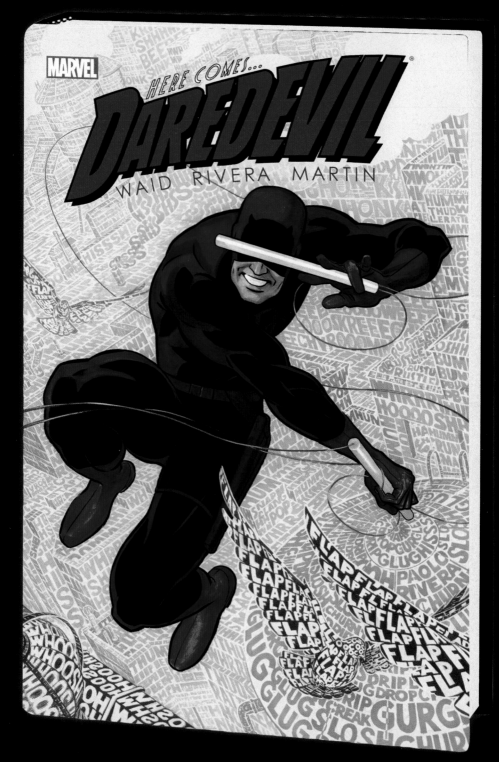

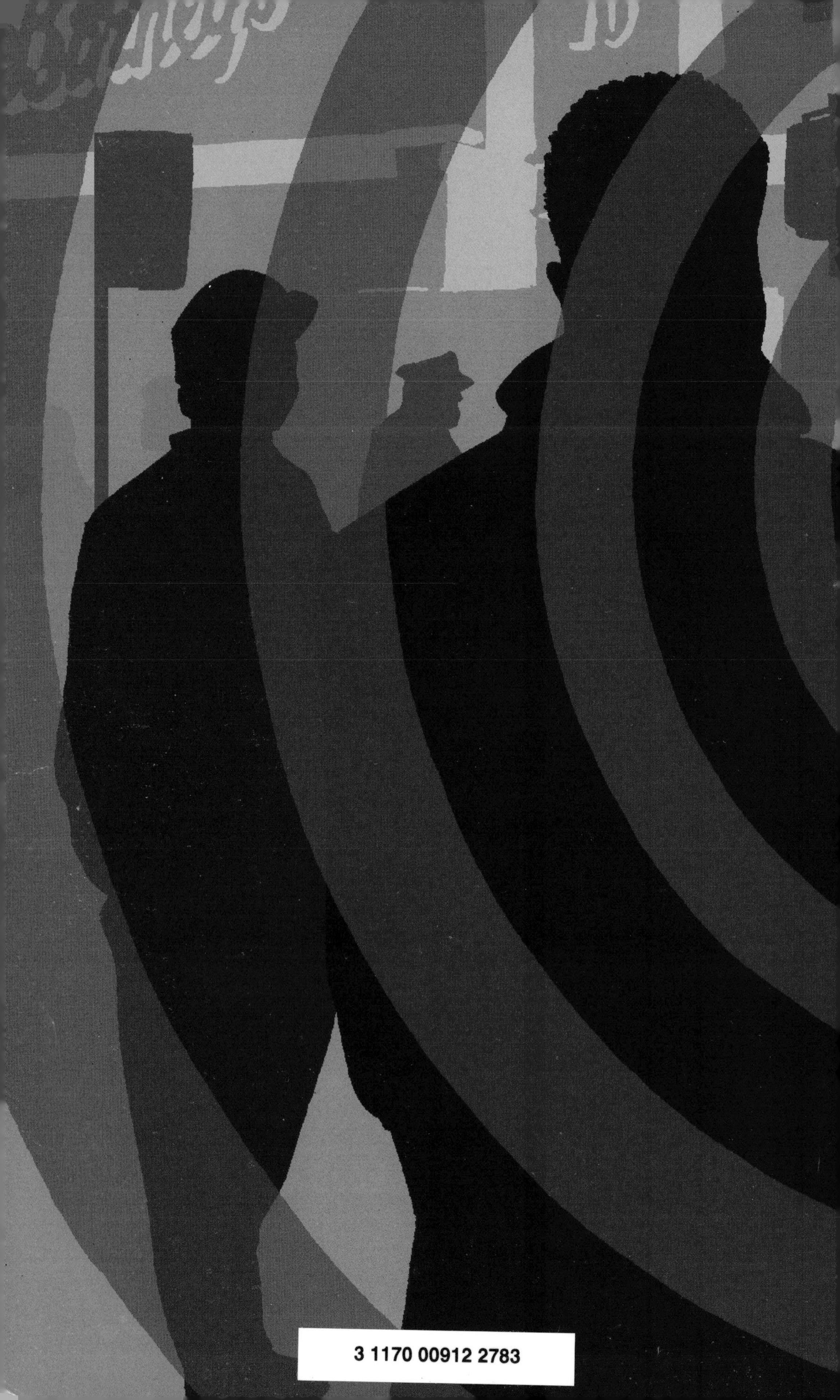